HOW TO GET THE MOST FROM FAMILY PICTURES

by Jayne Shrimpton

SOCIETY OF GENEALOGISTS ENTERPRISES LTD

Published by
Society of Genealogists Enterprises Limited
14 Charterhouse Buildings, Goswell Road
London EC1M 7BA

© The Society of Genealogists Enterprises 2011.

ISBN: 978-1-907199-04-2

British Library Cataloguing in Publication Data
A CIP Catalogue record for this book is available from the British Library.

The Society of Genealogists Enterprises Limited is a wholly owned
subsidiary of the Society of Genealogists, a registered charity, no 233701.

About the Author

Jayne Shrimpton is a professional dress historian and picture specialist. Attaining a MA degree in the History of Dress (Courtauld Institute of Art, University of London), she gained curatorial experience as an Archive Assistant at the National Portrait Gallery, London before becoming a freelance consultant, writer and lecturer. She holds regular workshops at the Society of Genealogists and speaks at regional family history society meetings, also running a photograph dating stand for *Family Tree* magazine at the *Who Do You Think You Are? Live* annual show at Olympia. The author of *Family Photographs and how to Date Them* (Countryside Books, 2008), she also dates photographs and writes columns and articles for several UK family history magazines. For private picture inquiries visit: www.jayneshrimpton.co.uk

Dedication

To my sister Jude

Cover Image

Central portrait: Drs Barbara and Gerald Hargreaves. *Outer pictures,* clockwise from top right:
Claire Dulanty, Geoff Hallett, Jayne Shrimpton, Private Collection, Jayne Shrimpton, David Vesey,
Fiona Adams, Katharine Williams, Chris Cobb.

CONTENTS

CONTENTS

Acknowledgements

Although the author's name is on the cover of this book, valuable contributions have been made by many other people, above all the dedicated family historians whose artworks and photographs are reproduced inside. Special thanks are due to Pat Brady, Chris Cobb, Patrick Davison, Claire Dulanty, Jon Easter, Alan Fraser, Julian Hargreaves, Simon Martin and Katharine Williams, whose information, technical assistance and unwavering interest in this project are much appreciated. In addition I am grateful to my colleague, Ron Cosens, who has provided specialist help, and to my sister, Jude Shrimpton. I am also indebted to Else Churchill, Graham Collett and the team at the Society of Genealogists for their advice and support.

PREFACE

During the 19th century many public art galleries and museums were established in cities and towns throughout Britain for the exhibition of portraits and other works deemed to be of national or local significance. Further pictures are on display in our castles, stately homes and historic houses - dynastic images portraying successive generations of illustrious families. The nation's principal portrait collections are well documented in catalogues and on databases, important artworks by eminent artists have been covered in monographs and exhibition catalogues and likenesses of influential individuals from history have been published in many popular books. Occasionally previously unseen portraits of interest are unearthed or sold at auction, making the news headlines. Research is ongoing within the art establishment - museum and gallery curators and archivists, university departments, art dealers, collectors and specialists, ensuring that our knowledge about historical portraiture is continually evolving.

While depictions of distinguished sitters by acclaimed artists continue to arouse public, academic and commercial interest, there exist numerous unseen privately-owned portraits - personal heirlooms passed down the generations and treasured by the families to whom they belong, but which have never been published, may never have been viewed outside the home and in most cases have not been scrutinised by an 'expert'. It was when handling inquiries from members of the public as a curatorial assistant at the National Portrait Gallery, London during the 1990s, that I first realised how little is known of the many provincial artists who worked at a local level during the 18th and 19th centuries, about the portraits they created and about the 'ordinary' people who were their customers. There remains much work to be carried out in this arena, despite the growing interest in family history - hence the decision to include a selection of original artworks in this guide to family pictures. The custodians of the paintings, drawings and many photographic portraits that feature in this book have generously allowed me access to their private collections, sharing the painstaking research which underlies these fascinating images, and permitting further analysis. Every one is a genuine family artwork or photograph, each unique and personal, yet representative of the kinds of pictures to be found in many households. Collectively they add to our understanding of the portrait tradition, enlighten our perceptions of the past and form part of our wider cultural heritage.

Jayne Shrimpton, Brighton 2010.

INTRODUCTION

ow to get the most from Family Pictures is essentially about interpreting, understanding and enjoying inherited portraits - surviving likenesses of real people who were ancestors and more recent relatives. The emphasis is on British images and subjects (sitters), although a few of the pictures reproduced here originated overseas, being connected with forebears who lived, worked and travelled abroad. The time period covered by this guide has been determined partly by the natural range of the material and also by what experience suggests is most appropriate: the earliest paintings submitted were late 18th century in date, reflecting the significant growth in British portraiture at that time, while 1950 seemed a suitable end date since many family historians will remember the 1950s and following decades, or may at least feel on more familiar territory with the later 20th century. Privately-owned portraits can take various forms so in these pages are included original, hand-crafted artworks, as well as the photographs that crop up in all family collections. Preserved in the home as a rule, pictures are personal keepsakes and in this respect are akin to the private documents and other memorabilia often hoarded by families - old passports, diaries, letters, wedding invitations, school reports, landmark birthday cards and so on. Like those mementoes from bygone eras, pictures are objects that past family members viewed and touched and therefore provide a very intimate link with earlier generations. They are also extraordinarily diverse, as demonstrated in the pictures featured here which depict individuals from all occupational and social backgrounds - miners, milliners, butchers, plumbers, clerks, engineers, domestic servants, soldiers, farmers and landowners, to name but a few.

Historical portraits provide unique and fascinating information about the past - a visualisation of a family member captured at a moment in time, offering a glimpse of an earlier age. Frustratingly, however, inherited artworks and, especially photographs are often random images that have survived with no supporting details and without a firm historical context: unlike the documentary sources used by genealogists, which are generally a straightforward registration of a dated fact or event and provide a finite amount of information, pictures are imprecise records, can be perceived on various levels, may show different things to different observers and rarely offer up all their evidence at first glance. Portraits benefit from repeated viewing and further investigation into the visual clues contained within them as they may embody layers of truth and meaning that need to be deciphered, unravelled and considered in the light of other findings and knowledge of family circumstances, before they are fully understood. The elusive nature of visual images, their ability to conceal as much as they reveal, can present a challenge when researching family pictures, but at their centre there are always facts to be discovered.

Determining an accurate date range for family artworks and photographs is essential when attempting to assign them to their rightful place in history and so the various dating methods that can be used to establish the correct time frame are given due attention in the following pages. Additionally this book aims to take the picture research process further by guiding readers in analysing their portraits at a more advanced level. It hopes to encourage questions about what is on view, inspiring deeper probing into those images whose subject matter may already seem obvious and offering suggestions as to how to discover more about unidentified 'mystery' portraits. In some cases investigations may overturn long-held theories, or they may provide the key to the whole picture - or a collection of pictures. Only when every aspect of an image has been fully explored can an effective assessment be made of the evidence that it provides and its relevance evaluated within the context of wider research into the family's history. Rarely does research material offer the chance for such enthralling detective work and the potential for further revelations.

Pictures are the focus of this guide and around 220 firmly- or closely-dated images are reproduced here, offering plentiful visual material for comparison with readers' own portraits. Some examples are imperfect, showing fractured glass, folds in the card, fading and discolouration, reflecting the reality that not all surviving images are in immaculate condition. The media, format and subject matter of the pictures, which are typical of those to be found in many family collections, has dictated the basic organisation of the book, which firstly examines different types of pictures and discusses how to research, date and analyse them, before moving on to look more precisely at what they can tell us about the past. While detailed explanatory text has been necessary at the beginning of each chapter to address the many issues that can arise when looking at this topic, the intention has always been to let the pictures themselves do much of the talking. Numbered references to the illustrations are to be found throughout the text, linking them to the main points under discussion, while individual picture captions highlight the key visual elements of each image, explaining how they have been analysed and connecting the findings with their subjects. Personal names have been deliberately omitted, chiefly for reasons of privacy, but the research techniques are carefully explained - methods that can be successfully employed by anyone with an inquiring mind, an eye for detail and, ideally, access to the internet.

Today's family historians are very fortunate in possessing or having access to pictures that have been passed down the generations. More immediate and engaging than any official documents or registers, old portraits are unique genealogical records - enigmatic and thought-provoking images that bring us literally face to face with our own history. Replicating and standing in for the individuals they represent, they offer a visual impression of past family members, convey a sense of their appearance and identity and powerfully evoke their human presence in the mind of the viewer, perpetuating their existence long beyond their natural lives.

ONE

CHAPTER ONE
Family Artworks

This first chapter of the book aims to help researchers discover more about original artworks surviving within the family - paintings, drawings or silhouettes of ancestors passed down the generations as precious heirlooms. Understanding these pictures, which often pre-date the photographic era, means looking at the portrait tradition and the growing demand for portraits in the late 18th and early 19th centuries, as well as considering the circumstances in which family pictures were produced: for example, what kinds of ancestors were likely to have commissioned a professional artist to capture their likeness (or were they, perhaps, portrayed by members of their own family?); what types of portraits were available, and at what prices? It may be difficult to find out very much about the artist, particularly if their work is not signed, but there are ways of making further investigations. Establishing when pictures were painted or sketched is essential for further research and for working out who their subject may be, if identity is uncertain; an accurate date range may even suggest what particular event prompted the portrait - perhaps a wedding or landmark birthday or anniversary. The fashionable clothing worn by ancestors for a portrait sitting is important, being a demonstration of their wealth and status and the best indication of when they were portrayed.

Few families possess original artworks amongst their picture collections, compared with the majority, whose ancestral portraits are mainly photographs, but they are an important survival from the past which deserve special attention. Relatively little has been written to date about portraits by lesser known, local or 'provincial' artists but hopefully in the future more information will become available to family history researchers. Meanwhile this survey, illustrated by reproductions of previously unpublished family artworks from different private collections, offers a basic framework for analysing these kinds of heirlooms. Hand crafted portraits paved the way for more popular photographs in the mid-19th century, so this chapter should be of interest to all readers wanting to discover more about family pictures.

History of the portrait

The first portrait images were made as long ago as the Neolithic era and over thousands of years various types of portrait have circulated in different areas of the globe, fulfilling many functions. During the Middle Ages in Europe, *votive portraits* or *donor portraits* began to appear in religious works of art such as manuscripts and altar pieces - depictions of the person who commissioned the piece, and who was usually shown kneeling in the foreground of the picture. Following this trend, portraiture as we know it in the western world developed rapidly. European Renaissance thinking embraced a growing sense of self-awareness, encouraging the expression of ideas about personal identity, and this cultural environment, which elevated the concept of the individual, was ideal for the production of visual images depicting specific likenesses of 'real' people. By the 1430s Flemish artists such as Jan van Eyck (c.1395-1441) were producing free-standing paintings of named individuals - desirable material objects of a purely secular nature. By the 16th century portraits were becoming more detailed in composition and more diverse; portraiture as an art form was inspiring greater interest and some professional artists started to specialise as portrait painters. With the arrival of Hans Holbein the Younger (1497-1543) at the court of Henry VIII in 1526, the new artistic genre was introduced into Tudor England.

Initially portraiture was confined mainly to the monarch and those moving in royal and aristocratic circles, but gradually it percolated down through society to embrace not only the propertied and titled elite but also military and naval commanders, scientists, artists, writers and other pioneering individuals whose endeavours helped to shape the rapidly-expanding world of the late 16th and 17th centuries. By the middle of the 18th century the fashion for having a likeness committed to canvas for posterity had extended further down the social scale to minor landed gentry and prominent members of the emerging professional, industrial and commercial sectors - lawyers, clergymen, physicians, bankers, merchants and new industrialists eager to confirm and proclaim their success and status in a picture. The founding of the Royal Academy in 1768 and its programme of annual exhibitions fuelled public demand for professional art works and portraiture enjoyed a prime position. London was the hub of artistic activity and home to some of Britain's greatest painters including Sir Joshua Reynolds (1723-92) and George Romney (1734-1802). Prosperous customers sat for their portraits while visiting town, or they could employ the services of itinerant painters who travelled between different locations, staying in each for as long as business demanded before moving on. Other 18th century portrait artists were based in fashionable towns like Bath, notably Thomas Gainsborough (1727-88) who had moved there in 1759, or in burgeoning industrial cities like Edinburgh, where Sir Henry Raeburn (1756-1823) operated a successful portrait business from 1787. Until the end of the century, however, few British towns could boast more than one or two resident artists, at most.

During the early 19th century, as public appreciation of the fine arts developed, the popularity of portraiture reached new heights, especially in the provinces, which were becoming increasingly independent of London. After 1800, art institutions were founded and public art exhibitions became more commonplace outside the capital, while rising numbers of professional artists, confident of their ability to attract local commissions, established themselves in provincial centres such as Norwich, Manchester, Birmingham, Bristol, Plymouth, Exeter, Southampton and Brighton - cities and towns which, significantly, were later amongst the first to open daguerreotype photography studios (see Chapter 2). To a large extent supply created demand: often, following the arrival in town of a portrait artist, local citizens would discover a desire to have their likenesses taken - the minor gentry of the neighbourhood, members of the learned professions and middle-class *nouveaux riches,* who might be heirs to an earlier generation of merchants and industrialists, or successful businessmen in their own right. The coming together of these various forces determined that from the late 18th century until the 1840s, that is, until commercial photography began to rival traditional forms of portraiture, there was a flourishing market for hand-crafted family pictures. This economic, social and cultural setting provides the historical background to the majority of inherited family artworks.

Oil paintings

Demand for portraits was basically determined by their price. We know how much some well-known portrait painters charged for their work from surviving documents, especially their studio 'sitter books' and financial ledgers. The National Portrait Gallery holds a collection of original artists' papers (see the NPG website under 'Collected Archives: Research'), and this sort of information is often published in artists' monographs or catalogues of their work. The formal portrait painted in oils onto canvas by a competent professional artist always remained a luxury product aimed at the higher end of the market (Figs. 2, 7, 9, 10, 13(a) & (b) and 15). This ensured the enduring appeal of oil portraits, even after photography had superseded cheaper artworks. In theory the cost of a portrait depended upon the time it took the artist to paint: bust-length (head and shoulders) views were cheapest, followed by half-lengths and three-quarter lengths, full-length compositions being most expensive. Some artists personally painted only the head of their subjects, leaving their workshop assistants to complete the hands, drapery and any background details. Painters at the outset of their career generally earned considerably less than they did once they were established: for example in the 1740s the young Joshua Reynolds charged three and a half guineas for his early paintings, but by the early-1780s was commanding 200 guineas or more for a full-length portrait. Few artists, however, charged such high prices and the cost of portraiture outside London was also generally much cheaper than in the capital. The few published sources covering provincial art suggest that recently-trained artists in the provinces or new arrivals in town might charge as little as one guinea for a modest portrait, although fees could be expected to rise rapidly to around three guineas or more.

Portrait copies and engravings

Many professional artists also offered copy pictures - popular images of royalty, politicians and other well-known personages for people to collect, as well as duplicate family portraits for wealthy customers to display in their various residences. These could either be replicated to the same dimensions as the original picture or copied in miniature, and this was such a profitable line of work that some artists became specialist copyists. The vogue for copies led to a demand during the 18th century for mezzotint engravings - cheaper, printed reproductions of oil portraits. The circulation and sale of engravings of the royal family, military heroes and popular theatrical and literary figures, through specialist printsellers, booksellers, stationers and other retail outlets, helped to publicise an artist's services, introducing his or her work to potential customers in the provinces. By the 19th century demand had also extended to pictures of local dignitaries such as MPs, mayors and councillors, the original painting often being displayed beforehand to promote sales of the engraved copies. Mezzotint engravings sometimes crop up in family archives and may in some cases depict ancestors who played an important role in their area, although prints of royalty or famous historical or national figures are unlikely to relate directly to the family (Fig. 1); like the 'celebrity' *carte de visites* that became popular in the 1860s, they show the sort of pictures that forebears collected, but usually have no genealogical significance.

Another type of reproduction that may occasionally occur in a collection is the painting or drawing copied from a photograph (Figs. 20(a) & (b)). Necessarily dating from at least the mid-19th century, these realistic portraits are works of art in their own right and are not to be confused with photographic images that have been re-touched by hand using watercolour paint (see Chapter 2). Nonetheless the artist who produced the copy portrait and the photographer who took the original photograph may in some cases have been the same person, since many painters switched to photography in the mid-Victorian era, embracing the new medium in order to remain in business.

Painted miniatures and small portraits

From the earliest days of portraiture in Britain, the demand for substantial oil portraits co-existed alongside that for much smaller pictures and for miniatures - small-scale likenesses typically measuring from around 1cm to 10cms in height (Figs. 3, 5(a-c), 6, 8(a) & (b), 11(a) & (b) and 20(a)). Framed miniatures, like larger portraits, could be displayed at home and were sometimes arranged in viewing cabinets; however being easily packaged and portable, miniature portraits had a wider function and played an important role in defining and maintaining personal relations. In the 16th century they were sometimes used in long-distance marriage negotiations, as a way of introducing potential marriage candidates to interested suitors. Miniatures were also popular throughout their history as tokens of love and affection: held in the hand or carried in ornamental boxes (like today's snapshots, slipped into a wallet), they effectively stood in for absent loved ones. The smallest miniature paintings provided even more intimate images when concealed in lockets, hung on pendants, or set into bracelets, brooches and other personal jewellery, as did tiny photographic portraits later, in the Victorian and Edwardian eras. By the end of the 18th century there was a huge demand for miniatures, the standard medium by then being watercolour on ivory, although paper and card were also used as support materials. Many artists earned a successful living as miniature painters, in London or in the provinces, some establishing themselves in flourishing centres while others travelled between smaller towns as itinerants. The prices which they charged ranged widely and again depended upon the scale of the picture and the artist's reputation and skill. Published works on miniature painting note that masters of the genre like London-based Richard Cosway (1742-1821) commanded between 25 and 30 guineas for a miniature portrait at the turn of the 18th and 19th centuries, whereas lesser provincial miniaturists often charged between one and five guineas for a portrait.

Escalating demand and growing competition also encouraged portrait artists to offer new lines, for example pencil portraits on paper; sometimes quick and unrefined drawings were a preliminary sketch for working up into a more detailed picture, as was perhaps the case with Fig. 4(a) although other pencil drawings were highly detailed, finished pictures, as demonstrated by Figs. 8(a) & (b). Watercolour painting also advanced during the 18th century: amateur artistic activity was increasing significantly, inspired by the teaching of painting and drawing as part of a genteel education, and a growing market for middle-class domestic art and for collectible, hand-illustrated books raised the profile of watercolour painting. By the late 18th century it was developing into a respected, independent art form in the hands of professional artists. Watercolour worked well as a portrait medium when used independently or in combination with other media, for example as a wash or highlight for pencil, chalk or crayon drawings. From the 18th century onwards, pastel and crayon also became fashionable methods of capturing an engaging likeness, their soft tones reproducing well the effect of the flesh and producing a lifelike and seemingly touchable human image (Figs. 16 and 17).

Silhouettes

During this period, portraiture also embraced the likenesses known as 'profile shades' or silhouettes. Demand for these small profile portraits soared during the late 18th century, their greatest period of popularity extending from the 1770s until the 1850s, when the market declined in the face of cheaper photographic portraits. Silhouette studios operated in major cities including London, Edinburgh and Dublin and in fashionable resorts like Bath, Cheltenham and later Brighton, while other profile artists travelled between smaller towns, announcing their arrival in the local press. The shades themselves were created in various ways, the basic format being the portrait cut from black paper (or paper which was blackened after cutting) and mounted onto card. Artists either worked freehand with a pair of scissors, or using a silhouette machine which, like a camera, aided those with little natural artistic ability. Paper silhouettes were quick to execute: sittings usually took between one and five minutes, and an infinite number of duplicate shades could easily be produced from the original, a convenient feature which was to pre-empt the possibilities of photography.

By the 1790s many shades or silhouettes were being painted in black watercolour directly onto paper, card, plaster, ivory, even glass, and these became increasingly popular during the early 19th century (Figs. 4(b) and 12). Details of the sitter's features, hair and dress could, if required, be delineated afterwards in pen or pencil or in paint, a common practise being 'bronzing' whereby the black picture was highlighted with gold or bronze paint (Fig. 12). Painted profiles were more expensive than cut-outs, the materials being more costly, but they were still much cheaper than conventional miniatures; therefore silhouettes were the most affordable type of portrait likeness available to the public before the advent of the *carte de visite* photograph. Prices, as ever, varied according to the artist's skill and the amount of work involved, busts being more economical than a full-length figure, although bronzing added to the cost. A well-known silhouette artist employed by royalty might command 10 - 12 shillings for a bronzed bust, whereas newspaper advertisements show that by the 19th century basic black cut-outs might cost as little as 6d, or one shilling for a complete picture, including glass and frame.

Ancestral artworks

In the past commissioning a substantial oil portrait was a luxury available only to those with the motivation, leisure time and usually the financial means to employ a professional artist to capture their likeness. Typically subjects - or 'sitters' - made several visits to the artist's studio before their picture was finished, or they might receive him or her at their own home on consecutive days, even offering them board and lodging for the duration of the work if they lived some distance from town (Fig. 15). Miniature portraits were a more convenient and economical portrait option, although even the cheapest miniature painting priced at one guinea in 1800 was roughly equivalent to six days' wages for a craftsman in the building trade, or five days' wages by 1840 (statistics obtained from The National Archives Currency Converter - www.nationalarchives.gov.uk/currency/). Silhouettes were cheaper still, and took only minutes to complete, but even a shilling or two was more than many labouring families could afford to spend on a non-essential item around 200 years ago. The fundamentally elitist nature of the hand-made picture largely explains why relatively few of today's researchers possess original artworks portraying their forebears. If an ancestor is represented in a painting or drawing, this generally reveals something of their social status, financial position or aspirations at that time. Usually the survival of artworks accords well with what is known about a family's past, especially if they were socially well-connected, owned property, entered a lucrative profession or succeeded in business. Judging from larger private collections of artworks, some families commissioned several portraits over a period of time - a visual demonstration of the continuing good fortune of successive generations. However, as researchers sometimes discover, an expensive picture of an ancestor may not reflect the progress of their entire lives: reckless ancestors are known to have splashed out portraits that they could probably ill afford (Fig. 13(a) & (b)), while others were portrayed at what eventually turned out to be a brief period of prosperity before family fortunes took a downward turn (Fig. 14).

Ancestors sometimes personally commissioned their own portraits, although the subject of a painting or drawing was not always the person who paid for it: for example a father might employ an artist to paint his daughter and, since fewer women than men in the past had control over large sums of money, many female portraits would have been commissioned by a male relative. When researching any family picture it is interesting to speculate who may have ordered it to be made and for what purpose. From the earliest times, a common reason for commissioning a portrait was to mark a special event, to serve as a lasting visual record and a reminder of the occasion. The sort of human experiences which were commemorated in a painting, drawing or silhouette included coming of age or 21st birthday (possibly Figs. 6, 9, 10 & 20(a) & (b)), betrothal and marriage (Figs. 11-

14), wedding anniversary (possibly Figs. 19(a) & (b)), departure overseas (Fig. 18) and high points in a successful career (Figs. 7 and 8(a) & (b)) - significant rites of passage and landmarks in the lives of our ancestors. Similar occasions were celebrated later on, in photographic portraits, and these are explored more fully in Chapters 4 and 5. Following artistic convention, the details of the event itself were seldom depicted, so the theme or subject of a picture may not be immediately obvious at first glance, but accurate dating and further investigations can often reveal more of the story. A portrayal of an ancestor or a family group in a stylised studio setting, or posed against a blank background may be of limited documentary value in itself, but its very existence - and survival - symbolise the importance of the subject(s) and any connected occasion within the family.

Some portraits may have had a more personal function, for example being given to a friend, lover or close relative. As mentioned earlier, miniatures offered a way of keeping in contact, especially if the subject and the recipient were physically distanced from one another through work, war or travel. Other pictures had a commemorative purpose; a portrait of a deceased relative reminded the bereaved of whom they had lost, their enduring image offering a sense of immortality. Remaining relatives might also be portrayed after the event so that their likenesses could be displayed alongside an earlier portrait of the departed, thus bringing together the living and the dead to provide a semblance of family unity (Figs. 5(a)-(c)). Some artworks demonstrate a very close connection between the artist and the sitter that adds an extra dimension to a family picture. If ancestors were artistically inclined, it is very likely that at some stage they sketched or painted members of their own family. In prosperous and upper middle-class households, girls especially might learn to paint and sketch - accomplishments which formed part of a wider education and aimed to equip them for genteel society; women with some artistic training often practised their skills on relatives, creating informal yet attractive and intimate portraits of parents, siblings, husbands and children (Fig. 18). Painting portraits could also secure a reasonable living in the late 18th and 19th centuries when demand was high, and some of our ancestors worked professionally in this arena, like the artist who portrayed his own brother in the Title picture, which dates from the early 1860s.

Identifying the ancestor

Many family artworks survive as pictures without a name, label or any kind of original inscription identifying the person in the picture. Occasionally someone has helpfully written a name on the back, as in Fig. 3; if the writer revealed their own identity and is known to have been a contemporary of the sitter, then their record may well be reliable; conversely, an elderly relative or a later descendant may have identified a portrait from memory, or from information given to them, and such sources may be misleading or incorrect, potentially leading to confusion over who is who in family pictures. In many cases special paintings and drawings are accompanied by an unwritten yet confident family tradition identifying the subject, a verbal account passed down the generations, along with the picture itself. As with any other historical 'facts' surrounding family history, it is important to double-check any inherited information about a portrait, or at least to establish whether oral tradition may be accurate. There are various ways of attempting verification - tracing the history and origins of the portrait within the family, seeking out other sources confirming its existence, comparing physical likeness between different pictures and establishing when the picture was created.

Inherited artworks as material possessions and domestic objects are fundamentally different to family photographs, especially photographic prints, which have often been filed away in albums or piled into boxes or envelopes and stored out of sight. Original paintings and drawings are generally more visible, difficult to mix up or misplace, and at some stage will probably have hung on the walls of a family home, perhaps being recognised and discussed over many years as a portrayal of a certain ancestor. Whether or not they have been displayed within living memory, special pictures typically have a strong provenance (ownership history), having been safeguarded and passed down amongst close relatives. Even if a portrait has been geographically relocated, it may not have strayed too far from its place within the family: by working backwards from its current owner, researchers can often trace a picture's history right back to its origins, linking it closely to a particular branch of the family and the relevant generation; its present guardian may even claim direct descent from the ancestor depicted in the picture, the unbroken line offering a good chance of accurate identification.

Since commissioning an artwork was a notable event, there may be a separate, written reference to a picture somewhere in the family archive. For example, it is conceivable that a portrait was mentioned by the person who sat for it - or by someone close to them - around the time it was made. Fig. 15 is an unmarked oil painting that may have remained unidentified, but fortunately it was meticulously recorded in the subject's personal journal: the diary entry confirms her identity, the exact dates of the sittings, the name of the artist and also relates something of the portrait experience, including her choice of clothes - useful and interesting details which helped with accurate identification of the painting itself. Alternatively the commissioning of a family portrait may have been noted for financial purposes, its details and cost entered in a household account book recording domestic expenses, or described and listed amongst other furniture and fittings if an inventory was made of the house contents. As a treasured possession, a special picture may also have formed part of a bequest, itemised in an ancestor's will, along with other personal belongings. Sources of information can present themselves in various ways, so researchers may be successful in finding separate written details about their pictures and notes about their subjects in private journals, diaries, letters, wills, inventories or other documents surviving amongst family papers.

Perhaps a record of an ancestral picture is proving difficult to find, yet it may still be possible to identify a portrait with some success through face recognition, that is, by comparing an image with other known representations of the suspected person, if any exist - either a different painting or drawing, or a photograph (see Figs. 20(a) & (b)). Remember that artworks can vary widely in their visual effect and there is usually an even greater contrast between hand-crafted portraits and photographic images, so it may be necessary to exercise a degree of imagination when assessing different kinds of pictures, particularly if they show an ancestor at different stages of life. Whereas photographs offer accurate likenesses, captured for better or worse by the lens of the camera, paintings or sketches were naturally subject to artistic license and convey only the artist's *impression* of the sitter's physical appearance - or a prescribed version of what they saw, as approved by the person who commissioned the picture. Professional artists were expected to represent their subjects favourably, portraying them to their best advantage, and certainly the most sought-after, fashionable painters often flattered their sitters, awarding them physical attributes according to contemporary ideals of good looks and beauty but which may not have been altogether present in reality. Clearly artists trod a delicate path in this respect, for generally clients also wanted a convincing likeness: that this was an important requirement, in theory at least, is demonstrated by the fact that provincial painters vying for business often stressed in newspaper advertisements their ability to catch a 'correct likeness'. Ultimately it is difficult to know for sure how honest or realistic a depiction of an ancestor may be, but we must trust that most artists managed to capture something of their sitters' true appearance.

Dating family artworks

There is one more essential tool that can aid identification of a family member in a portrait - establishing an accurate date range for the picture. It is difficult to over emphasise the importance of dating any kind of historical portrait, as this provides the most effective starting point for further investigations into both the identity of the subject and the circumstances surrounding their portrayal. Even where a date is already suspected, or has been communicated by word of mouth, confirming its reliability at an early stage can save confusion, potential disappointment and ultimately a great deal of effort. A firm date range will in most cases either help to support oral history - a long-held theory concerning identity, or may, in the event, firmly disprove it, as transpired with Fig. 2, a portrait that was reassessed following accurate dating of the boy's appearance. A realistic time frame opens up a range of likely possibilities from the outset and where there are no ideas about the name of the subject, this will certainly suggest some potential candidates. As with any unmarked portrait, it is never possible to establish an exact year for an undated artwork, but a close date *range* can make all the difference to understanding a picture. This is demonstrated well by Fig. 18, whose subjects were already known, but where a revision of the date revealed the underlying purpose of the painting and, in the process, also the identity of the artist.

Before explaining more about dating portraits, a brief mention of picture frames seems appropriate. If an artwork has been displayed or transported at any time, it will have been framed, a frame being necessary for its protection and also having an important aesthetic function, as a good or poor choice of mounting can enhance or diminish the overall appearance of a picture. Solid frames can be loosely dated from their style, material and manufacture and theoretically a frame may be contemporary with the image it contains; however artworks may have been re-framed at any point in their existence, perhaps several times, for example for restoration purposes, or to suit a new room scheme. Consequently the frame surrounding a picture today may well date from a different era to the image so, unless an expert opinion has been sought, the frame is best ignored for the purposes of working out when the picture originated.

Looking more closely at the visual image, often a portrait of an ancestor is just that - a human figure portrayed against a blank or painted background. There may be a glimpse of a chair, or perhaps a more extensive studio or contrived room setting involving draped curtains, flowers, a window, bookcase or other architectural features, as seen in Figs. 2, 10, 14 and 17; such features are often 'props', artistic elements added to give depth, interest and a sense of reality to the picture, although in some cases painted accessories may have reflected or symbolised the sitter's profession or interests. Portraits were intended to express their subjects' social standing, success, wealth and good taste yet in many cases, especially in miniatures, only their head and shoulders, or part of their body is visible. A pleasing countenance was desirable, but equally important was the way in the subject presented himself or herself. Ancestors took care to dress in fine clothing when attending a portrait sitting, wearing their best quality garments, as well as a fashionable hairstyle and complementary accessories. Subjects who were young when they were portrayed probably followed fashion closely, and their images will exhibit some of the most up to date styles of clothing, hair and jewellery for their time. Older family members would also have been concerned to dress appropriately for their portrait in a mature and modest or dignified manner, in keeping with their advanced years and prevailing etiquette. The general appearance of ancestors in a picture can, then, reveal personal taste and age and also demonstrates that they dressed well and correctly in relation to their position in life.

Unless the date of a portrait has been recorded elsewhere, the visual appearance of the subject - their clothing, hairstyle and jewellery - is of the greatest importance when dating the image, as these features offer accurate evidence of when the portrait sitting took place. In the 1950s the study of dress history became recognised as a serious and respectable academic subject, that is, when the art establishment first acknowledged that the costume seen in paintings provided a valuable research tool; since then art historians have commonly used fashion clues to accurately date and analyse historical pictures. Meanwhile recent generations of trained dress historians have continued to research and publish their findings about past styles of dress, using portraits as well as surviving clothing and a wide variety of historical written and documentary sources, and there is now, as it were, a detailed time line of fashion which can aid art professionals and researchers with identifying, dating and understanding the fashions of the past. Some recommended costume surveys covering the 18th and 19th centuries are listed in the Bibliography at the end of the book. Meanwhile for present readers the following section charts the main developments in fashionable dress, suggesting clues to look out for in family artworks dating from the late 18th century to the 1860s.

Fashion clues, 1780-1870

(A) Men's dress

1780-1800
By the late 18th century, the principal male garment was the frock coat made in sober-coloured cloth, slender in cut, with a collar and narrow sleeves. Since many family portraits are bust-length or half-length, coats, waistcoats, neckwear and hairstyles are often the only fashion features on show, so subtle shifts in style may offer important dating clues. During the 1780s coats for men and boys had very large buttons, often made of metal, and the waistcoat was cut straight across at the waist (Fig. 2). Older and conservative men might still wear a wig in the 1780s, but younger men preferred their own hair, although fashion dictated a rather 'coiffured' look, hair being frizzed at the sides and sometimes dusted lightly with hair powder. By the late-1780s the coat was usually black or dark blue and its collar was beginning to rise noticeably at the neck - another dating clue. A fashion was also developing for a version of country or sporting dress: dark, cutaway coat, buff-coloured breeches and leather riding boots or top boots, instead of white stockings

and buckled shoes. These features were refined during the 1790s, coats usually worn double-breasted with smaller buttons again, their collars continuing to rise. This was mirrored in the neckline of spotless white shirts, a white cravat being swathed around the collar and tied under the chin. By the turn of the century hair was being cut shorter, closer to the head, was often curled and sideburns began to appear (Fig. 3).

1800-1825

By 1800 fashionable male clothing closely followed the outline of the body, emulating ancient Greek or Roman statuary, the neo-classical vogue being fully established. Skin-tight, pale-coloured pantaloons extending to the ankle were an alternative to knee breeches and were worn with flat pumps or leather boots. Men's appearance in the early 1800s remained fairly static, until at least 1825, so male clothing of this era can be difficult to date closely, especially from short portraits (Figs. 4(a) & (b) and 5(a) & (c)). Trousers were introduced c.1807 and worn increasingly during the 1810s and 1820s, but this dating feature is not visible when the legs are omitted from paintings. High-collared coats were plain and usually dark in colour, the emphasis on quality of cloth and an immaculate fit. Tailoring techniques were improved: for example the M-notch lapel was introduced in 1800 - an M-shaped opening at the join of the collar and lapel - and where this is visible it can help to assign a 19th century date to portraits, although it does not offer a close date as the M-notch was used in tailoring until c.1855 (Figs. 5(a) & (c) and 8(a)). Shirt collars were worn very high, often resting on the cheek (Figs. 4(a) & (b), 7 and 8(a) and were kept in place with white cravats, which could be tied in various ways. Hair was cropped short, often fashionably waved and brought forward around the forehead and temples 'a la Titus', and worn with sideburns (Figs. 4(a) and 5(c)).

1825-1850s

By the 1820s, new 'Romantic' aesthetic tastes were developing, favouring bolder shape and colour. This was reflected in the style of men's coats after c.1825, sleeves becoming puffed at the shoulders and coat bodies attaining an hour-glass silhouette, echoing female fashion. The gathering of sleeve heads from the late 1820s until the late 1830s is a useful dating clue for pictures of this era (Figs. 7, 10 and 11(a)). Between the 1830s and 1850s men's clothing could also be quite varied and flamboyant, depending on personal taste (Figs. 10, 14 and 18), although male garments were narrowing in cut again by 1840 and remained slim fitting until the end of the 1850s (Figs. 14, 18 and 19(a)). By the 1830s the fashion for white cravats was giving way to black silk stocks or cravats (Figs. 10 and 11(a)), black remaining usual for men's neckwear throughout the 1840s and 1850s (Figs. 13(b), 16 & 18), although coloured versions were not uncommon (Figs. 14 & 19(a)). During the 1830s and early 1840s there was a vogue for tousled and windswept or fuller curled hair (Figs.

10 & 11(a)) and long sideburns or bushy side whiskers were fashionable from the 1830s through to the 1850s (Figs. 10, 13(b), 14, 16, 18 and 19(a)), after which time beards became more common. See Chapter 3 for a summary of men's fashions 1860s-1940s.

(B) Women's dress

1780-1800

By the 1780s women's dress was characterised by two main styles. One strand of fashion, using lightweight fabrics like silk gauze and cotton muslin that created a fluttering, floating effect, was the informal *chemise* dress, first popularised by Queen Marie Antoinette of France and revolutionary in its simplicity. The chemise was usually caught at the waist with a sash, but its details varied, being either low necked or having a frilled collar, and sleeves could be either short and puffed, or long to the wrists. The other main fashion of the 1780s was a tailored walking costume based on women's riding habits or on the male greatcoat, with a caped collar and reveres. Styles included a fitted jacket and skirt combination, or a 'greatcoat dress' which was usually worn closed to the waist, the overskirt falling away on either side, revealing an underskirt beneath. Women's hair during the 1780s was worn full around the face, often frizzed and powdered, like men's hair, with loose curls around the neck. These fashions continued into the 1790s, the waistline gradually rising from the mid-1790s onwards, as neo-classical tastes developed. The positioning of the waistline is one of the main dating tools for late 18th and 19th century female dress and usually this feature is visible in portraits. As waistlines rose, women's hairstyles changed, becoming more natural looking, arranged with loose curls, an antique-style bandeau often being worn around the head. Hair powder was more or less obsolete by 1800.

1800-1825

In Britain the neo-classical styles did not reach the same extremes as they did in post-Revolutionary and Napoleonic-era France, but by the early 1800s British women were wearing trained white or pale muslin dresses secured well above natural waist level, their clinging, draped style evoking a sense of antique statuary. Classical bandeaux and turban-style headdresses were much in vogue, the hair spilling out in loose curls.

By the mid-1810s the simple styles were beginning to break up and new decorative features were becoming influential: waistlines were set higher than ever, directly under the bust, but fabrics became heavier and clothing was more detailed and structured. By the late 1810s and early 1820s, the bodices of high-waisted dresses were often pleated or ruched, sometimes worn over a *chemisette* (a short, sleeveless bodice) and might include historical revival features from the past such as a ruff-like neckline (Fig. 5(b)), while sleeves gained stiff puffs at the top of the arm (Fig. 6). Hair in the late 1810s and early 1820s was centrally-parted, short curls framing the face around the temples and cheeks (Figs. 5(b) & 6). During the early 1820s waistlines finally began to drop noticeably, year by year, reaching their natural level in around 1827.

1825-60s

Some elements of female dress were fashionable over long periods of time, so offer less precise dating tools: for example narrow, gauzy stoles or *tippets* were popular in the early decades of the century, but continued in use right up until the 1840s, often completing a plain outfit (Figs. 6, 9, 11(b) and 13(a)). However stole and shawl-like garments can indicate more about the wearer's age: mature or elderly women often favoured a kerchief (a square scarf) or capacious shawl about the shoulders instead of a flimsy stole, modest, substantial accessories often seen in pictures (Figs. 5(b) 8(b) and 19(b)). Following long established tradition, married women generally wore a white day cap of a fine fabric such as muslin, perhaps pleated or trimmed with frills and ribbons: in the 1820s and early 1830s these caps were tall in shape - a useful dating clue (Figs. 5(b) and 8(b), but their styles changed over time and from the mid-1830s through to the 1850s and beyond, neat round caps fitted the head more closely, any flowers and frills concentrated around the ears (Figs. 12, 13(a) and 19(b)). Elaborate wedding caps are common in marriage portraits (Figs. 12 and 13(a)) but even by the 1840s some younger married women were choosing not to wear traditional caps for portrait sittings (Fig. 15); from mid-century onwards this rather matronly custom continued to decline in popularity amongst younger married women, later 19th century paintings and photographs usually showing only older ladies wearing frilled caps.

By the late 1820s, bodices had acquired a natural waistline again, often being belted, and as 'Romantic' aesthetic tastes influenced dress, clothing became more dramatic and fabrics bolder in colour (Fig. 9). The earlier, neat puffed sleeves began to balloon out on the upper arm into the 'leg o' mutton' or *gigot* shape, the padded puffs growing steadily larger during the late 1820s and early 1830s (Figs. 8(b) and 9). Striking jewellery was also fashionable in the late 1820s and early 1830s and hairstyles became very inventive, twisted on top into elaborate chignons, one version of which was the distinctive 'Apollo knot' (Figs. 9 and 11(b)). Combs and hair ornaments also accompanied these styles. From the mid 1830s, the shape of dress and women's general appearance was loosing its bouncy exuberance and beginning to droop: huge sleeves deflated, first becoming full and floppy in the upper arm, and hairstyles lowered, the upper hair no longer curled and knotted but being drawn down smoothly over the crown. By 1840 sleeves had narrowed and the dress bodice, ruched or gathered over the bust, grew rigid in the body and lengthened, reflecting the new fashionable 'Gothic' line (Fig. 12).

During the 1840s formal dresses as seen in portraits featured a very low décolletage, revealing an expanse of delicate white neck and breast, sleeves either exceedingly narrow or gathered into neat puffs along the arm (Figs. 13(a), 14 and 15). Vertical boning is usually evident in figure-hugging bodices of this decade, which narrowed to a point in front, accentuating the full, gathered skirt (Figs. 14 and 15). Centrally parted hair was worn smooth on top then curled or dressed into longer ringlets at the sides, the back hair drawn into a chignon behind (Figs. 14 and 15). The main dress feature of the 1840s through to the early 1860s was the widening, bell-shaped skirt, created initially by many layers of petticoats, then supported by the vast crinoline frame from 1856 onwards. By the mid 1860s the crinoline was flattening noticeably in front, the fullness becoming increasingly focused on the back of the skirt. By the end of the 1860s, the bustle was being worn to support the skirt behind the waist and bodices could be very decorative (Figs. 20(a) & (b)). See Chapter 3 for further information about women's dress.

(C) Children's dress

Boys 1780s-1850s
By the late 18th century new influences were affecting the dress of the young. Enlightenment philosophy encouraged progressive views about education, fostering an understanding that children had their own social and physical needs, quite separate to those of adults, and these included clothing. Infants of both sexes were dressed alike in dresses and petticoats, so it is often difficult to tell very small girls and boys apart. At around 4 or 5 boys donned more grown-up clothing and had traditionally worn a miniature version of adult male dress, but as pictures show, by the 1780s fashions were changing: boys were now keeping their hair in a natural, casual style, with a fringe and long locks, and wore knee-breeches with broad-collared, open-necked shirts - far more comfortable than the high collars and cravats worn by men (Fig. 2). The development of longer, looser leg wear in the form of trousers during the early 1800s was perfect for children and boys wore ankle-length trousers with open-necked shirts and short jackets, the 'skeleton suit', in which the trousers buttoned onto the jacket, being a popular outfit for small boys from the 1780s until the 1820s. Another early 19th style was the tunic suit and during the 1830s this became very fashionable: based on women's gowns, this comprised a full-skirted tunic or dress reaching to the knees and worn with trousers. Although minor details changed over the years, skirted, knee-length tunics were still being worn by boys in the 1850s (Fig. 18).

Girls 1780s-1850s
Comfortable clothing for girls followed women's styles in the late 18th and early 19th centuries, the fashionable lightweight cotton chemise gown being a natural

choice. Usually these simple dresses were secured at the waist with a sash of coloured ribbon and as women's waistlines rose in the later 1790s, so did those of girls' dresses, again providing an important dating clue. Girls' garments were often made shorter, above the ankle, and by the early 19th century simple, high-waisted, calf-length dresses revealed the cotton drawers worn underneath. By the late 1820s and 1830s, following changing adult fashions, girls' dresses featured a longer bodice and were becoming fuller in the skirt, again displaying loose drawers or *pantalettes*, decorated with lace or tucks at the hems. Fitted bodices with low necklines and very full, knee length skirts shaped girls' dresses of the 1840s, through to the 1870s (Figs. 17 and 18).

Tracing the artist

Dating and positively identifying representations of ancestors are of most concern to family historians, yet one final aspect of researching pictures should also be mentioned. Discovering who painted or sketched a painting or drawing is unlikely on its own to provide a very close date range for the image, but finding out more about the artist is something that may well interest the owners of original artworks; after all craftsmanship is another significant feature of a hand-made artefact. Some portraits seem to justify special investigation because they are so well executed or perhaps resemble the work of a familiar artist from the past. Popular TV programmes like *Antiques Roadshow* and *Cash in the Attic* raise hopes that one day an unexpected treasure will turn up amongst the family heirlooms; however, as most genealogists will already know, priceless objects do not lurk in every corner of the average family house, and even fine oil paintings like Figs. 2 and 7 are unlikely to be undiscovered masterpieces by a 'famous' artist. It is conceivable that a painting may be connected with a recognised artist, as in the case of Fig. 6, although many surviving family pictures are the work of minor or provincial artists, whose techniques varied enormously, ranging from distinctly naïve to highly skilled. Some artists consciously adopted the style of the great painters of their day, working 'in the manner of...', or merely followed the fashionable artistic conventions of their times; the most skilled practitioners were capable of producing accomplished portraits that captured something of the grandeur and beauty of a great work of art.

At present there is only limited published information available about the kinds of artists who painted or sketched many of today's surviving family portraits. Although a few general publications touch on the work of Britain's provincial artists (see Bibliography), comparatively little detailed research has been conducted into the thousands of professional portraitists who operated mainly at a local level during the later 18th and 19th centuries. One reason for this is that traditionally most art historians have eschewed the notion of art as a commercial venture and have tended to concentrate their attentions on significant artworks by esteemed and well-known artists, while many artworks surviving in private hands - family pictures - have not been viewed, analysed or recorded by experts, so they remain a largely unexplored resource. It is also true that past artists have themselves done little to promote understanding of their work, since many omitted to sign their name, or even their initials on the portraits that they created, so in many cases their works remain unattributed. Useful information, although not plentiful, may crop up in a variety of places. For example, the Society of Genealogists Library contains a considerable amount of reference material relating to what ancestors did in their working lives - see www.sog.org.uk. A search in the Society's free online library catalogue under 'Artists' reveals many sources listing artists, portraitists etc. that may potentially be of use, while the Society's collections pertaining to apprenticeship in this period might also be of interest. Local museums and art galleries will also probably know about artists who operated in their respective areas. Certain regional studies have been published about painters working in various cities and counties, some of which are also listed in the Bibliography: copies of these may possibly be found in the relevant local public libraries, or at major reference libraries such as the Society of Genealogists, the National Portrait Gallery and the National Art Library at the Victorian & Albert Museum - all situated in London.

Sometimes it is possible to pursue original research into named artists who have not been recorded in any art history publications, especially if it is known or suspected where the picture in question originated. Artists may have left contemporary evidence of their existence, for example by advertising their business in local newspapers, in trade directories, or in both; if their name can be located in any of these publications, it may be possible to establish approximately when they were in business, the type of portrait work they carried out and the prices they charged. The British Library holds all UK daily, UK national daily and Sunday newspapers from 1801 to the present, as well as most UK and Irish regional and local newspapers, some dating from the early 18th century. These can be viewed in the reading rooms at Colindale, North London, while selected titles are now available online: check the website to see if your area is covered - http://newspapers.bl.uk/blcs. Additionally the Irish Newspaper Archives is a project involving the complete digitisation of Ireland's national and many leading regional newspapers, ranging from the 18th century to the present - www.irishnewsarchive.com. Trade directories, the historical equivalent of our Yellow Pages, first became common in the 1780s and were being produced regularly by the early 19th century: the local library for the area in question should hold a good selection of local directories, while the Guildhall Library and Society of Genealogists in London both have impressive collections covering the entire United Kingdom. It is also possible to view some directories for free online at www.historicaldirectories.org or copies of directories on CD-ROM can be bought from some genealogy publishers. Some portraitists may even have exhibited examples of their work in local art exhibitions during their lifetimes: catalogues were usually published in conjunction with these public events and most catalogues featured an index of exhibitors, often giving their name and address, or at least town of residence. Surviving art exhibition catalogues are usually held in the principal public library for the respective city or town, or may be amongst the art reference material held by the National Art Library at the Victoria & Albert Museum.

Requesting professional help

If a blank has been drawn, or if it seems advisable to show the portrait to a trained art historian for a specialist opinion, a good starting point is to contact the city museum or art gallery covering the area in which the picture originated - or if this is not known, a local public art institution close to home. Any public art gallery or museum holding artworks will have a designated curator, keeper or other professional member of staff responsible for the pictures in the collection. Their role includes helping members of the public, although be aware that they do not usually offer artwork valuations (for appraisals and valuations it is necessary to contact a reputable auction house). Academic research inquiries are generally welcomed, but it is recommended to check arrangements and find out the appropriate person to approach - information that is usually to be found on the institution's official website. For example, the National Portrait Gallery, London handles portrait inquiries on a national level and staff in the Heinz Archive & Library can research a limited number of artist or sitter names by telephone or by post, fax or email - see www.npg.org.uk . An experienced gallery or museum curator or keeper should be able to suggest an approximate date range for a historical picture if this is an aspect that still needs to be established. They may even be able to explain more about a named artist, especially if he or she was well-known locally. Occasionally an expert may recognise the artist responsible for painting an unsigned portrait from its style, if his or her technique was distinctive and is familiar from other, signed examples of their work: three of the portraits featured here (two being a pair) bearing partial artists' details were analysed by regional museum staff who were able to comment on the artistic style and to suggest some possible artists' names (Figs. 6 and 19(a) & (b)). Alternatively, it may be possible to find a professional, trained picture specialist who is not linked to any public institution or commercial organisation, but who is proficient in dating and interpreting portraits. There is no official association of experts, but a few independent specialists are listed under 'Links' on www.portraits.specialistnetwork.org.uk - and it is always worth trying a simple internet search. Whatever kind of professional help is sought, researchers should, though, be prepared for the possibility that even experienced specialists may not necessarily be able to firmly identify the artist who painted an unsigned picture.

Using archives and research facilities

Besides offering expert advice and a professional opinion, the remit of the principal art galleries and museums in Britain also includes facilitating outside research, by making the material in their libraries, archives and print rooms available to members of the public, by appointment. Resources usually include not only information about their main collections, but also further primary and published sources relating to the study of art and, in the case of galleries with strong portrait collections, to portraiture. The Heinz Archive & Library, National Portrait Gallery, London holds the most comprehensive information about British portraiture, its collection of British portraits records comprising over 1 million visual and written portrait records arranged alphabetically by both artists' and sitters' names, so it is worth checking these to see whether ancestors appear in any pictures known to the gallery, or whether your named artist is known to have painted other sitters. These records are not at present held in a database so cannot be consulted online (although in 2010 the gallery was beginning to explore ways of automating some of its recording activities and developing an online Portrait Finder). However they are kept on open access in the Archive & Library's Public Study Room, along with other research material, and can be viewed by members of the public by appointment. The research facilities of the Scottish National Portrait Gallery, Edinburgh (www.nationalgalleries.org) are currently closed to the public due to work on its 'Portrait of the Nation' project, but they aim to re-open in autumn 2011; meanwhile inquiries concerning the resources can still be submitted (see website). The National Gallery of Ireland in Dublin (www.nationalgallery.ie), which incorporates an Irish portrait collection, also offers various research facilities to the public, by appointment. For details about study arrangements at other museums and galleries, see the individual websites.

Fig. 1 Mezzotint engraving of Lady Arabella Stuart, by James Basire, 1791

The vogue for portrait copies in the 18th and 19th centuries included reproductions of family pictures for different homes and also mezzotint engravings of famous people. This engraving, based on an early 17th century miniature painting by Isaac Oliver, was produced in 1791 by James Basire, a London engraver specialising in antiquarian prints. Lady Arabella Stuart (1575-1617) was a romantic historical figure who was for some time considered a possible successor to Elizabeth I on the English throne and ended her days in the Tower of London. Images of such popular characters are usually examples of the pictures that ancestors collected, rather than genuine family portraits.

Fig. 2 Oil on canvas (81cms x 94cms), c.1784-8

This fine unsigned and undated oil painting depicts a young boy who looks to be aged somewhere between 7 and 11 years old. Previously the family researcher believed him to be an ancestor born in 1812, but accurate dating of his appearance established a firm 1780s date for the picture, indicating that he was a different ancestor with the same name, but from the previous generation (1777-98). His hair, styled long with a casual, short fringe, and his clothing - a low, open-necked shirt with wide, frilled collar, worn over a cream waistcoat, with a dark frock coat featuring large buttons - typify boys' fashions of the 1780s. He came from a wealthy Hampshire family but unfortunately died from yellow fever, aged only 21, whilst on a voyage to Jamaica.

Fig. 3 Watercolour Miniature (6.5cms x 5cms), c.1798-1805

This unsigned and undated miniature was painted in India, where demand for portraits flourished within the colonial community. Miniatures were easily shipped home to family during what were often long periods of separation, and conveniently transported on the frequent journeys and house moves within India experienced by both civil servants and the military. This young man was identified from an inscription on the back, written in 1848 by his sister, some years after he died in a shipwreck of 1809. Venturing to India as a young cadet in 1788, he had risen to officer rank with the East India Company's army in Madras, serving under General Wellesley in the Mahratta War of 1803. Here he wears military uniform, the high collar and his fashionable, short curled hairstyle suggesting a date in the late 1790s or early 1800s. The picture may have been painted to mark his promotion to Captain with the 12th Native Infantry Regiment in 1801, although only one epaulette (instead of the usual two for Captain) is visible in this side view.

Figs. 4(a) Pencil sketch and 4(b) painted silhouette (11cms x 8.5cms), c.1805-20
These portraits in different media are both undated but are clearly linked, perhaps being made at the same time, or the pencil sketch possibly a preliminary study. Profile portraits were popular during the Regency era as, looking rather like classical busts, they emulated the antique statuary then in vogue. Such head and shoulders compositions are not very closely dateable as the style of men's upper wear changed little during the early 19th century. The prevailing fashion, seen here, was for the coat collar to be worn very high, the points of the shirt collar obscuring the jaw line, and hair swept forward onto the cheeks in neo-classical mode. A broad date-range of c.1805-20 for the pictures would make this ancestor (1777-1860), aged somewhere between his late 20s and early 40s. He lived in India until 1807, although he may well have sat for these portraits following his return.

Fig. 5(a) Watercolour miniature (7.5cms x 6cms), c.1810-1818

These three unmarked family miniatures seem to have been identically framed in the 19th century, suggesting they were regarded as a set, although 5(a) is clearly the work of a different artist to 5(b) and 5(c). This gentleman is identifiable as an ancestor (c.1761-1818) who was born into an established Essex landowning family. Being a younger brother and also cut out of his father's will through family manipulations, he inherited little money, but had minor landholdings and evidently lived fairly well. This portrait is difficult to date very closely: the distinctive 'M-notch' lapel of his high collar confirms a date of at least 1800 while the dark coat and waistcoat teamed with white linen shirt and cravat are broadly early 19th century in style, although his hair, long about the ears, does not follow the fashion for close-cropped hair and sideburns. Portrayed candidly here with facial lines and a slightly ruddy complexion, he looks to be aged in his late 40s, or even 50s, suggesting that this was painted c.1810-18.

Fig. 5(b) Watercolour miniature (7.5cms x 6cms), c.1818-22

This lady, presumed to be the wife of the man in 5(a), was born in 1760 and died in 1855, outliving him by many years. Her portrait, also unsigned and undated, is clearly painted by a different, less accomplished artist and exhibits a rather naïve quality, although the details of her clothing and accessories are carefully depicted and offer a close date around the turn of the 1810s and 1820s. Her waistline is still high but the 'historical' ruff-like neckline of her white *chemisette* demonstrates how simple neo-classical elegance was giving way to novelty and decoration. Her frilled white cap - characteristically tall in shape at this time - identifies her as a married lady (or widow), and her shawl, a fashionable accessory, is worn modestly covering her shoulders. The date range suggests that this portrait and 5(c) were perhaps made after her husband's death and displayed together, with his earlier image, as a family set.

Fig. 5(c) Watercolour miniature (7.5cms x 6cms), c.1818-22

This miniature seems to have been painted by the same artist as 5(b), probably at the same time, and is presumed to depict one of the couple's four sons. Born between c.1791 and 1798, they were the first generation of the family in 300 years to inherit no land, and consequently they all went into trade. This young man may be the eldest son, born c.1791, who was recorded in the 1841 census as a 'Tailor and Draper' and if so, could well have been serving his apprenticeship at the time of this portrait. Tailors generally kept abreast of the latest clothing styles and he certainly presents a very up to date appearance here: his double-breasted coat, featuring a high collar, is worn with a stylish striped waistcoat, while his hair, cropped and worn forward, together with prominent sideburns, was the height of fashion in the years around 1820.

Fig. 6 Watercolour Miniature (6cms x 4.5cms), c.1821

This is a glossy, well-executed painting, the most skilled area being the head, the focus of the picture, while the body is dealt with more sketchily. Being unsigned and undated, some years ago the miniature was shown to a curator at the Ashmolean Museum in Oxford who, judging from its appearance and from a label on the reverse giving a partial name, 'Roch..', suggested that the artist may have be Simon Jacques Rochard (1788-1872). This miniature is, however, probably a copy, the original, perhaps by Rochard, now thought to be in the Argentine. The lady is thought to be an ancestor born in 1804, who was painted when aged 17, and accurate dating of her appearance confirms that a date close to 1821 is likely. The belted waist of her dress, still worn high under the bust, is characteristic of the late 1810s or early 1820s, as are the low neckline and wide shoulders which suggest the burgeoning *gigot* sleeves. Her hairstyle, centrally-parted and curled at the temples, is also typical of the era.

Fig. 7 Oil on canvas (74cms x 61cms), c.1826-37

This imposing oil painting has been passed down through successive generations of the family, although the true identity of the subject was only established when another version of the portrait appeared onscreen in an episode of BBC TV's 'Who Do You Think You Are?' in 2009 featuring Davina McCall. This ancestor (1787-1860) trained as a stonemason, becoming King's Master Mason to George III in 1808, in which role he carried out major renovations to Windsor Castle. He went on to run a successful building and property development company and was elected to the New Windsor town council in 1835, later serving as Mayor 1846-7 and in 1854. This portrait is unsigned and undated but is dateable, chiefly from the puffed sleeves of his tailored coat, to c.1826-37, a period coinciding with his rising career. It may possibly have been commissioned in 1835 to mark his election to the council. In recognition of the picture's local significance, its owner has donated the painting to the Royal Borough of Windsor and Maidenhead (RBWM), who aim to display it in the Guildhall Mayors' Parlour, alongside other mayoral portraits, following restoration work.

Figs. 8(a) & (b) Paired pencil drawings (10cms high), c.1828-36
These companion drawings by a competent draughtsman are unsigned and undated and are, judging from their height, effectively miniature portraits. Their estimated date range is based mainly on the woman's appearance, in particular the wide *gigot* sleeves which are the most fashionable element of her dress. The identity of these ancestors is certain, the man born c.1783 and his wife c.1785. Initially he worked as an apprentice cook in the kitchen at Windsor Castle but later became a wine merchant and served on the New Windsor council 1835-39. These portraits representing the couple in their middle years, presumably at a high point in his career, were perhaps commissioned in 1835 to mark his election to the council, or possibly in 1836 to commemorate their 25th wedding anniversary. Note the significant difference in appearance between this older, married woman, who wears a matron's frilled cap and a modest, high-necked dress, and the younger, much more fashionable woman of the same era seen in Fig. 9.

Fig. 9 Oil on canvas (c.20cms x 16cms), c.1828-36

This unsigned and undated portrait is known to depict an ancestor born in 1811 but offers little information except a view of her appearance, which is broadly dateable to c.1828-36. Therefore the picture could well have been painted in 1832, to mark her 21st birthday, or alternatively perhaps around 1835, to coincide with her betrothal. In 1836 she married the man portrayed in Fig. 10, although clearly this is not strictly a companion picture to his. She may well have commissioned her own portrait, for she had inherited some money following the death of her father, a London veterinary surgeon, in 1832. Fashionably dressed in keeping with prevailing 'Romantic' aesthetic tastes, she wears a formal, low-necked gown featuring the full *gigot* sleeves of the era, her fabric belt fastening with a prominent buckle and a long chain being looped asymmetrically across her bodice. Her hair is styled into a version of the 'Apollo knot', a distinctive fashion from the late 1820s to the mid-1830s.

Fig. 10 Oil on canvas (c.20cms x c.16cms), c.1830-36

This interesting painting, expressive of the dramatic 'Romantic' era in the arts, depicts a boldly-attired young man in a contrived room setting with a picturesque landscape suggested beyond the window. Unsigned and undated, it is known to portray an ancestor whose dates are 1809-1874. His appearance, seen unusually clearly in this three-quarter length view, is very stylish, especially his fashionably tousled hair, prominent sideburns and well-tailored, colourful clothing, which suggests a date range of c.1826-36 for the portrait. However he is evidently an adult here, so it must date from at least 1830, perhaps being commissioned to mark his 21st birthday in that year, or possibly later, in 1835 or 1836, around his betrothal or marriage to the lady in Fig. 9. The couple married in London but afterwards returned to Boulogne where his family resided, along with many other genteel but struggling English families at that time who had moved across the Channel, finding the cost of living cheaper in France.

Figs. 11(a) & (b) Paired watercolour miniatures (3.6cms x 4.7cms), 1834

Unsigned and undated, these small pictures form a pair and mark the wedding of this young couple in New Windsor in May 1834. The bride, b.1808, was the eldest daughter of the gentleman in Fig. 7, while the groom, baptised in 1812, was the son of the couple seen in Fig. 8, so both came from successful and respected local families. Traditionally marriage portraits depicted the man and woman individually, which can make them hard to identify if they become separated, especially as brides of the era didn't ordinarily wear special white bridal gowns. Pale blue was, though, a popular bridal colour, this blue gown, worn over a white chemisette and with a fine, embroidered white stole, may well demonstrate the bride's actual wedding outfit. She does not wear the usual cap of a married woman, perhaps preferring to show off her glossy curls and elaborate 'Apollo knot', a fashionable feature which helps to support a likely 1834 date for the pictures. Her husband wears a smart tailored coat with stylish puffed sleeves, his black cravat being fashionable for men from the 1830s until the 1850s.

31

Fig. 12 Painted and bronzed silhouette (c.8.5cms x c.12cms, framed), 1840
This profile portrait or 'shade' is painted in black watercolour highlighted in bronze paint, 'bronzing' being very popular for silhouettes by the 19th century. Family believe the young lady to be an ancestor (1820-61) portrayed at the time of her wedding at East Chinnock, Somerset in July 1840 and the details of her appearance support that probability. Her long hair, drawn down from a central parting over her ears, follows the fashion of the later 1830s and 1840s although the usual ringlets are not visible here. Her neat, close-fitting cap, decorated with frills and ribbons, was the style of headwear usually worn by married women in the early Victorian era, so although she is young, this feature expresses visibly her newly-married status. Her close-fitting bodice with folds of fabric converging into a V in front and tight sleeves (just seen here) reflect the narrowing of the fashionable line by 1840. It is possible that a companion silhouette of the bridegroom once existed but is now lost.

Fig. 13(a) & (b) Paired oil portraits (93cms x 81cms), 1841

These substantial, unmarked oil portraits again represent the kind of paired pictures that were painted to commemorate a wedding in the pre-photography era. This couple married in July 1841 in Birmingham and their appearance here accords with such a date. The bride, aged 22, wears a formal black dress featuring the long, rigid bodice of the 1840s. Over her fashionable ringlets is a delicate lawn or muslin cap with trailing lappets, trimmed with frills and flowers about the ears, an accessory which denotes her married status. The groom, also 22, wears a smart black frock coat and black silk cravat, the usual style of the decade. He was a tea dealer living three doors away from the bride's family in Wellington, Salop, but was reputedly 'a gambler and a waster' and her parents opposed their relationship, so the couple eloped. The groom probably commissioned these paintings as neither parents could have afforded the expense, his father being a poor stone mason in Kircudbrightshire and the bride's father, once a wealthy farmer, having fallen into debt. In the circumstances the portraits must have made a bold statement, visual confirmation of the couple's controversial marriage.

Figs. 14 Paired watercolour portraits (24cms x 19cms), c.1843
These unsigned and undated watercolours are individual portraits framed together in a modern mount. The identity of these ancestors was known but the pictures were not linked to the occasion of their wedding in Islington, North London, in December 1843, until their appearance was dated, indicating that the couple were portrayed around the time of their betrothal or marriage. The man wears a smart frock coat with velvet lapels, tailored in the narrow style of the 1840s, with a vibrant waistcoat and black silk cravat. His fiancé or new wife wears a shimmering gown made from one of the pastel-coloured 'shot' or 'changeable' silks admired during the 1840s, the pale blue colour suggesting that this was perhaps her wedding dress. She is bareheaded here, her centrally parted hair and short curls or ringlets offering a fashionable dating clue. Neither was from a prosperous background: the bride, the daughter of an Essex shoemaker, had been a domestic servant and according to later censuses was illiterate, while the groom was the son of a baker; however he had succeeded in business as a jeweller and silversmith and by the time he married, aged about 33, was probably at the height of his career. Later the couple became less well off, two of their many children dying young and being buried in common graves.

Fig. 15 Oil on canvas (19cms x 15cms), 1845

This small but attractive oil portrait depicts an ancestor born into a propertied family. She was well educated and kept a personal diary over many years between 1836 and 1883 which provides a fascinating insight into her life. Although unsigned and undated, thanks to her diary notes her descendants know exactly when the picture was completed and also the name of the artist, who evidently stayed at her home outside Uttoxeter for several days while he was working on the portrait. Her diary entry for July 29th 1845 reads:

'I took my first sitting. I wore my ruby velvet. We found Mr Burton a quiet gentlemanly guest, he is an excellent artist & is noticed by a number of great people. He lives at Nottingham. He finished my picture by Saturday 2nd August & it was thought very like (me) by everyone in the house'.

Unfortunately her husband's aunts, who visited a few days later, had other ideas:

'They did not think my picture like me at all which mortified me very much and they abused it in every way.'

Here she is portrayed wearing the centrally-parted hairstyle with ringlets fashionable during the late-1830s and 1840s, her short-sleeved dress with a low décolletage being 'full' or evening dress, suitable for a formal social occasion.

Fig. 16 Crayon drawing (66cms x 55cms), c.1840-50

This recently inherited portrait was unfortunately not signed by the artist, although it is a fine drawing which resembles the style of other known mid-19th century portraitists. It depicts a distant ancestor (1786-1869), a newly-created baronet whose well-connected family originated in Scotland, then moved to Ireland, although his home by the time of this portrait was a family property in Suffolk. As yet, little else is known about this gentleman, although internet research reveals that he held a commission in the Life Guards. Undated, the picture looks to have been executed in the 1840s, judging from his black stock and bushy sideburns, both features characteristic of this period, and from his apparent age range here. The portrait may possibly have been commissioned to mark his 60th birthday in 1846.

Fig. 17 Crayon drawing (c.60cms x c.48cms), c.1848-9

This delightful group portrait, drawn in coloured crayons, shows three young sisters, the daughters of a prosperous civil engineer whose firm had been involved in building many of the railways in Yorkshire. Their birth dates of 1843, 1845 and 1847 helpfully confirm a close date-range of c.1848-9 for the picture, which is unsigned and undated. According to family tradition, the basket of flowers toppled over while the girls were positioning themselves and the artist decided to leave the blooms scattered as seen here. They are prettily-dressed in wide-necked dresses with full skirts which echo the ballooning dresses worn by women by the late-1840s, but, as always, made much shorter, and in the case of the older girls, layered over lace-trimmed drawers. The elder sister has her hair dressed in ringlets, following contemporary adult fashions, and all three seem to be wearing little coral necklaces, popular over a long period of time for small girls. The 19th century vogue for tartan fabric, inspired by Victorian interest in the Scottish Highlands, is also evident in the rug and the toddler's sash.

Fig. 18 Watercolour portrait (18cms x 11.5cms), c.1854-5

This charming watercolour depicting a father surrounded by eight children offers a good example of how accurate dating, further investigations and inspired guesswork can unravel the story behind a picture, revealing far more than is first apparent. The man was identified as an ancestor who lived 1806-1864, the picture initially assumed to post-date 1858, the year when his wife died, since she is absent from the scene. However professional analysis suggested a slightly earlier date, based on the styles of dress, this seeming more likely following the discovery that the eighth child (the toddler, far right) was born c.1853, and that a ninth child followed later. In view of the mid-50s date that was emerging it became possible that the painting may have marked the father's departure for the Crimean War: he was a career soldier, a Colonel with the 56th Regiment, who were involved in the later stages of the war at the Siege of Sevastopol (September 1854-September 1855). Having established a date of 1854 or early 1855 and the picture's probable purpose, one question remained: where was the mother? A hunch led to closer scrutiny of the portrait and on the back was found her name in faint writing: she was the artist who painted this intimate family picture.

**Figs. 19(a) & (b) Pastel or watercolour portrait heightened with white
(50.5cms x 39.5cms), c. 1850-58**

These paired portraits depict Scottish ancestors (the husband 1768-1858 and his younger wife c.1789-1864) who owned property and farmed outside Perth. The couple's appearance indicates a date in the 1850s, suggesting that the pictures were perhaps commissioned to mark their 50th wedding anniversary in 1856, just two years before the husband died. Their style of clothing follows fashionable lines but is practical and, in the case of the lady, who wears a substantial cap and shawl, is rather plain and modest, as might be expected of elderly country people. The pictures are well executed and although undated, they unusually bear a signature, which in this case is unfortunately difficult to decipher - possibly 'J. White' or 'J. Waite'. When these photographs were sent to the Scottish National Portrait Gallery in 2001 for analysis, the Chief Curator suggested some possible artist names but was unable to positively identify the artist. However she pointed out that the pictures are similar to the work of George Richmond (1809-96) who popularised this portrait style - half-length figures set against an empty background, executed in pastel/crayon and watercolour and heightened decoratively in white.

Figs. 20 (a) & (b) Watercolour miniature 7.5cms x 8.5cms and photograph, c.1869
This delicate watercolour miniature is dateable from the style of the young woman's dress, which features the square neckline and dropped shoulders fashionable during the late 1860s and seems to show signs of the bustle, in vogue c.1869-75. This ancestor lived 1848-1939, so her 21st birthday in 1869 would have been a perfect reason for a special portrait such as this. Unusually the picture is signed by the artist, Lambert Weston, who internet research indicated was a photographer working in Dover c.1856-1908, Dover being a few miles from the young woman's home. This is clearly an original painting, not a retouched photograph, although its fine detail suggests that it was copied directly from a photograph. The family researcher has recently found a photograph (20(b)) on which this picture seems to have been based. Since Lambert Weston entered photography early on, he may well have been one of the painters who made the transition to photography, to keep up with changing times.

41

TWO

CHAPTER TWO

Family Photographs - Formats, mounts and photographers

Photographs are amongst our most precious personal possessions - irreplaceable if lost or destroyed - and photographic images of ancestors or more recent relatives are to be found in every home. Whereas paintings and drawings are relatively rare survivals because only better-off forebears could afford to commission original artworks, photography became available to ordinary working people in the 19th century and family photographs have often been passed down the generations. Whether a collection comprises complete Victorian or Edwardian albums, or boxes of 20th century snapshots, old photographs provide today's family history researchers with a wealth of fascinating visual information about the past.

This chapter charts the invention of photography and development of photographic portraiture from the 1840s through to the 1940s, offering a framework for analysing over a century of family photographs. The following examination of the main photographic formats and their dates of production should aid recognition of the various different kinds of photographs that may occur in a family collection and assist with understanding their place in history. As family historians will already know, many old photographs are undated and unidentified, so dating these images accurately is essential for effective research. Further techniques that can be used to estimate the date of a photograph are discussed in detail here, including dating the style of the mount and how to research photographers and their studio operational dates. Other queries which may crop up during research are also covered, for example interpreting the handwritten information on the back of photographs and getting as much information as possible from surviving photograph albums. All these topics are illustrated in the chronological sequence of photographs at the end of the chapter, numbered references in the text linking to the images here and elsewhere in the book.

The invention of photography

For centuries men of science had been trying to find more accurate methods of representing life than through drawing and painting and eventually during the 1830s ways of combining chemistry and optics to mechanically reproduce and fix images were successfully developed. In France Louis Jacques Mandé Daguerre (1787-1851) had been working with Joseph Nicéphore Niépce (1765-1833) and following Niépce's death, Daguerre created his first permanent photographic image in 1837 - named a *daguerreotype*. In January 1839 he officially announced his discoveries, following which the Englishman William Henry Fox Talbot (1800-77), who had been experimenting since 1834 with a different photographic method, hastily publicised his own work. Therefore 1839 is the year generally recognised as marking the birth of the new technique of photography: one of the greatest inventions of the 19th century, photography as a mode of visual expression was to transform the way the physical world was viewed and recorded.

A new portrait medium

The two competing types of photograph pioneered by Daguerre and Fox Talbot both exhibited a unique beauty but produced very different visual effects and it was the sharp, well-defined daguerreotype that achieved commercial success, being regarded as the better of the two processes for producing portrait photographs. Within a few years of its development, the possibilities of the new medium were being realised in Europe, America and Australia, and a whole new industry was emerging. In Britain the entrepreneur Richard Beard (1801-85) was responsible for converting the scientific breakthrough into a business enterprise. In March 1841 he opened the first British commercial photographic studio in London's Regent Street, offering portraits using the new daguerreotype process. Shortly afterwards another daguerreotype studio was established in West Strand, London, by Frenchman Antoine Claudet (an example of whose work is seen in Fig. 1). Later that year several more studios opened in the provinces - Plymouth, Bristol, Cheltenham, Liverpool, Nottingham, Brighton, Manchester and Bath - towns and cities where the trade in portrait paintings already flourished (see Chapter 1). Further studios were established in Edinburgh and Dublin, and in 1842 Beard opened two more in London. By 1843 daguerreotype studios were operating in several more provincial centres including Truro, Exeter, Derby and Doncaster, some photographers covering a wide radius.

Professional daguerreotype photographers of the 1840s were competing directly with miniature painters, and inevitably met with opposition from within the artistic community. The new method of capturing a likeness was not universally accepted and it had its limitations: depending upon the season of the year and time of day, initially an exposure time of around at least ten minutes was needed, even up to half an hour if lighting conditions were poor. Nonetheless photography had a significant advantage over the average miniature painting as it combined precision with novelty, and once the exposure times were reduced, the portrait sitting usually only took a few minutes rather than the hours required for a painting. In particular, photography was welcomed by a rising middle class who may not have received a classical education teaching appreciation of the arts, but who were at the centre of the rapidly-expanding world of the mid-19th century and admired the immediacy and accuracy of the new medium. As portrait photography became more established, the demand for hand crafted likenesses declined rapidly and some professional painters found it necessary to learn the new technique in order to remain in business and keep up with changing times. During the 1850s further technical advances changed the practise of photography and new photographic formats followed in the ensuing decades. The history of early photography continues to interest enthusiasts today, and details of the various chemical processes, techniques and apparatus which shaped the medium are well covered in books and articles in photographic journals. Here the main concern is with portrait photography and its relevance to family historians.

Photographic heirlooms

A great number of photographs taken in the past appear to have survived the passage of time, a remarkable legacy for today's researchers spanning 170 years - around seven generations of many families. Some photographic heirlooms have been passed down the family line in their original albums, while others have been dispersed more randomly, split up amongst different relatives: many will have been stashed in boxes or tins and squirreled away in cupboards, garages and attics, to be found decades later when descendants are clearing out a family home. The source of any inherited or newly-discovered photographs should be recorded clearly at the time they are added to the wider collection, for, like family artworks, their history or provenance is a significant aspect of their survival. Since photographs are generally kept by those for whom they have a personal meaning, the hands through which different pictures have passed over the years offer a link between their origins and the present day and can be a relevant factor, especially when trying to identify unknown faces.

Accurate photograph dating

Many old family photographs exist in limbo, without a date or a name attached to them and, interesting though they may be to look at, their genealogical significance remains unrealised until they have been firmly assigned a historical context and attempts have been made to match them to names on the family tree. Taking the time to individually date and, from there, identify each photograph is fundamental to understanding and discovering more about them. This process can impact on an entire collection, for if a misleading date and identification is given to one image, this can lead to a chain of confusion affecting many other pictures. It is rarely possible to discover the precise year of an unmarked photograph, but a close *date range* of a few years is a realistic objective. This is adequate for connecting unidentified portraits with the appropriate generation of the family, while in those cases where identity is already certain, a close date range will reveal at what stage of life the ancestor or relative was portrayed. Determining an *accurate,* if approximate, time frame for a photograph may sometimes focus attention on a particular individual's name, perhaps singling them out as the most likely candidate out of several contenders. Dating often helps to confirm an existing theory about identity - or, as sometimes happens, it can positively disprove family tradition or ideas. Many researchers are confident that they already know who is pictured in a photograph, but have no firm historical evidence to support their theories, so ideally judgement should be reserved until all the evidence is in place. Establishing an accurate date range may at times produce disappointing results if, for example, it rules out the hoped-for ancestor, yet the process will inevitably suggest new names and may well lead to some unexpected discoveries!

Identifying and dating the format

As different photographic processes were developed over the years, they produced varying types - or formats - of photograph, each having its own physical characteristics and remaining fashionable for a certain time period. Identifying the formats of individual family photographs will therefore lead to a greater appreciation of these pictures as artifacts and will also help to establish approximately when they were produced.

(1) Daguerreotypes 1841-c.1865 (most common c.1845-55)
The daguerreotypes which first entered the British portrait market in 1841 were photographic images made directly onto a silvered copper plate. Surviving daguerreotype photographs may be recognised from the highly-polished, mirror-like surface of the metal plate, the reversed picture (as noticed from the buttoning of garments) and their ability, when tilted at certain angles, to fluctuate between a

negative and a positive image. The image quality may look rather faint but the details are usually well-defined and these portraits may be delicately coloured in places, as they were often re-touched by hand, using paint, once the photographic process was complete. Plates can either look silvery or golden in tone as they were sometimes gilded to give a warmer effect to the metal and they may be tarnished with a bluish tinge, especially around the outside of the picture, as seen in Fig. 2. The plate may also bear fine scratches as the surface was vulnerable and easily damaged. Being fragile pictures, daguerreotypes were protected under glass and sealed with a paper binding, before being placed in a frame suitable for hanging on the wall, or bound in a gilt frame and fitted into a case. Usually cases were made of red leather-covered wood and opened on hinges like a book, with a padded red plush (cotton velvet) lining facing the picture inside, as seen in Figs. 1 & 2. The photographer's name and address was sometimes embossed in gold lettering on the front of the case (Fig. 1).

Daguerreotypes were unique, one-off pictures and the earliest examples were expensive products. Authorities on early photography who have consulted original advertisements and other documents note that initially Beard charged £1 8s 6d, or £1 13s 6d for a daguerreotype, while Claudet charged around £1 3s 6d, and conclude that most operators in the early 1840s priced their daguerreotype portraits at around one guinea each. Such figures amounted to more than the average urban weekly wage and were comparable to the cost of a hand-painted portrait miniature - hence these early photographs were the preserve of the wealthier classes. Towards the mid-1840s prices began to lower, particularly in the provinces, where cased daguerreotypes could be purchased for between 12s 6d and 14 shillings by 1844, while a growth in the number of studios in the later 1840s and increased competition encouraged a steady lowering of prices. However daguerreotypes essentially remained luxury portraits which ordinary working people could not afford and they also pre-date the major boom in commercial photography, so they occur only rarely in today's family collections. Most surviving British examples date from between the mid 1840s and mid 1850s, for by then a new photographic format was becoming popular which rendered the daguerreotype virtually obsolete in Britain by the early 1860s.

(2) Ambrotypes c.1852-1890s (most common c.1855-65)

In March 1851 a new photographic process using transparent glass plates was introduced by an Englishman, Frederick Scott Archer (1813-57). The wet collodion or wet plate method, faster and more sensitive than earlier techniques, was welcomed by portrait photographers, although its commercial use was limited initially due to patent restrictions, these being effectively lifted in 1854/5. The glass plate could be used as a negative from which to make positive prints, and some photographers followed this path, but the majority adopted the method devised by

Scott Archer in 1852, converting the original plate into an apparently positive image by bleaching the negative and blacking the back of the glass. The resulting one-off glass photographs were known as *collodion positives* in Britain, but were patented in the United States as *ambrotypes* and this is the name now generally used to describe them. Ambrotype portraits embodied something of the elegance of daguerreotypes but they were much cheaper to produce, inspiring a surge in commercial photography that led to a rapid increase in the number of photography studios during the 1850s. The first ambrotypes retailed at 10s 6d but prices plummeted with increased commercial competition and by 1857 they were being sold for as little as one shilling - this lowering further to 6d (plus 2d extra for a case) by 1858. It was the affordable ambrotype that finally ended the trade in inexpensive silhouette portraits (see Chapter 1) and which opened up the possibility of photography to more working people.

Surviving ambrotype photographs may possibly be confused with daguerreotypes. Many ambrotypes are reversed images, although this depended upon which side of the glass was blackened and some do appear the right way round. The black backing used was generally shellac (varnish) - or very occasionally velvet. Some ambrotypes show signs of deterioration, cracks or patches of clear glass appearing where the shellac has flaked away (see Fig. 3) and this is a helpful identifying feature. Ambrotypes were commonly retouched by hand using paint to add depth and render the portrait more life-like, so there may remain a hint of blush on cheeks, bright gilding on buttons and jewellery and traces of colour on fabrics (Figs. 4, 5 and Ch 4 Figs. 7 & 31). Ambrotypes being fragile images, they may also be presented similarly to daguerreotypes (see Figs. 4-6 and 13 and further examples in Chapter 4). The glass plates were sometimes protected by another layer of glass and were usually mounted in a decorative surround of brass or cheaper pinchbeck (a gold-coloured alloy of copper and zinc). Some were sold uncased but had a metal ring or loop of thread at the top for hanging the picture on the wall (see Ch 4 Fig. 7). Others were housed in hinged cases of leather or substitutes such as wood, papier-mâché and leather cloth, and inside a single picture might face a pad of velvet or plush, as in Fig. 5, although double photographs also occur (Fig. 6). Late in 1854 a new moulded casing made from an early form of plastic was patented in the United States - the Union Case (see Fig. 5). Such cases were used in Britain from c.1855 through to the mid-1870s, the more ornate the moulding, generally the later the date of the case. Occasionally the photographer's studio details, printed on a label, were attached to the back of the case or frame.

Not all family picture collections will include ambrotypes, although many more survive than daguerreotypes, since working class ancestors could afford to try out these cheaper photographic portraits. Evidence indicates that most family ambrotypes set in a studio date from between c.1855 and the early 1860s: they were still being produced in the 1870s (see Fig. 13) and even until around 1890 by itinerant photographers working outdoors, although such late examples are uncommon. Their main period of production was brief, for by the turn of the decade another new photographic format had appeared which was to exceed in popularity any other kind of photograph.

(3) Cartes de visite, c.1859-1919 (most common c.1861-1908)
In November 1854 the Parisian photographer André Adolphe Eugène Disdéri (1819-89) patented a new type of portrait photograph created using several small negatives on one large photographic plate. The process produced multiple photographic prints which were pasted onto card mounts, each the size of a visiting card, and named the *carte de visite*. Measuring approximately 10cms x 6.5cms, the small cartes became fashionable in France from c.1856 onwards and finally arrived in Britain in around 1858/9. They were slow to catch on at first, a few being produced in 1859, but interest was growing and the August 1860 publication of John Mayall's 'Royal Album', a collection of 14 cartes de visite portraits of members of the royal household, seemed to confer royal approval on the new format. The book sold hundreds of thousands of copies but ultimately cartes were most desirable as individual photographs. The public wanted not only 'celebrity' pictures of the royal family and of other famous people of the day, but also portrait cartes of themselves and their families. As demand soared during 1861, many more photographic studios opened in London and throughout the provinces, and by October of that year cartes de visite were said to be the most popular type of portrait. 1862 was the year of greatest commercial success, and sales remained high in 1863, before settling down in 1864. The craze which seized Britain in the early-1860s was known as 'cartomania', as consumers avidly bought, collected, exchanged and gave away photographic cards on an unprecedented scale. Before long, purpose-designed albums with pre-cut apertures were produced for containing and arranging the card collections and these were proudly shown to friends and family and displayed in the home (see below for more on photograph albums).

Unlike daguerreotypes and ambrotypes, both unique photographic plates which did not easily reproduce, cartes de visite were mass-produced prints which conveniently enabled customers to buy in bulk what they had previously only been able to acquire as one-off portraits. Cameras usually took eight carte de visite photographs at a time and several copies might be purchased at the time of the original sitting, although the negatives were generally kept by the studio, so that further copies could be ordered later on. For customers wanting a more decorative coloured effect, the photographic prints could be artistically re-touched by hand using watercolour paint, for an additional fee (Fig. 12). In 1862 the average carte de visite cost around 1s 6d, but by 1864, as the number of studios continued to rise and commercial competition forced price cuts, some 'cheap jack' photographers were charging as little as 5 shillings for twelve copies. At these sorts of prices, many ordinary working families could afford to visit the photographer, if only to mark a special occasion (see Chapter 4), and so it was the carte de visite that finally brought photography to the masses. Cartes dominated Victorian portrait photography: they were the principal format of the 1860s and 1870s and remained popular throughout the 1880s, only facing serious competition by the 1890s from the larger cabinet print. Any family collection including 19th century photographs is therefore likely to include cartes de visite, which are easy to identify from their standard, neat size (Figs. 7-12, 14-20, 22, 26-27 & 29). Early 20th century cartes may also survive, as they were still being produced in the early 1900s and, in much smaller numbers, until the 1910s.

(4) Cabinet Prints c. 1866-1919 (most common late 1870s-1910)
As the initial rush on cartes de visite waned, photographers welcomed any innovations which might boost the market. Early variations on the carte format included the Diamond Cameo (1864), an arrangement of four tiny portraits on a carte-sized mount, each showing a different view of the sitter's face, although these were not widely popular and relatively few examples survive. In 1866 the cabinet photograph was introduced, another photographic print pasted onto card, but, measuring around 16.5cms x 11.5cms including the mount, over twice the size of the carte de visite. Despite its active promotion, in Britain there was initially little interest in the new format, but demand picked up gradually during the 1870s and by the 1880s cabinets were a popular choice, finally rivalling the smaller carte towards the end of the century (Figs. 23-25, 28 and 31). Cabinet prints, like cartes, were still being produced in the early-1900s (Fig. 32) and even into the 1910s, although most surviving examples will be pre-1910 in date. Along with cartes, cabinets dominated the market for portrait photography in the Victorian and Edwardian eras, so both types of photograph are likely to occur in early picture collections.

(5) Unusual card-mounted formats, 1870s-early 1900s
Following the launch of the cabinet print, further photographic card formats were trialled in an attempt to ring the changes and encourage further demand. For example, the Victoria, introduced into Britain from America in 1871, was sized between the carte and the cabinet, while other new formats were larger than the cabinet, like the Boudoir (approximately 20.5cms x 13cms) and the Imperial (around 21.5cms x 16cms), both sizes introduced in 1875. Further novelties were promoted during the 1880s, for example the Mignon (1883), which was even smaller than the carte at around 2.5cms x 1.5cms. Other card formats appeared in

the ensuing decades, but none attained anything like the popularity of the carte de visite and the cabinet print. Researchers should, though, be aware of their existence as collections may occasionally include examples of some of these photographs.

(6) Tintypes (ferrotypes) In Britain 1870s-1940s

The cheapest of all photographic portraits was the tintype, or ferrotype, an image produced directly onto enamelled tin plate using the wet collodion process. The technique was patented in the United States in the mid 1850s and was developed for the use of itinerant photographers, with all the operations taking place inside a special, multi-lensed camera. Some cameras could produce as many as 36 exposures on one plate, the plate being processed quickly, removed from the camera, cut up with scissors into separate tintypes and presented, still wet, to the customer. Like daguerreotypes and ambrotypes, the pictures were unique, but they only cost a few pence and their cheap price was generally reflected in their inferior quality. Tintypes, popular over a long time period in the United States, met with criticism in Britain and were scarcely recognised until 1872 when an American ferrotyper, Thomas Sherman Estabrooke, accepted the agency of the Phoenix Plate Co. in England and opened the first ferrotype studio in London's Regent Street. Despite the importation of instruction manuals, equipment and plates from America and enthusiastic promotion, tintypes were generally seen as low-status, poor quality images, although they were welcomed by the travelling photographers who pedalled on-the-spot photographic souvenirs at the seaside, fairgrounds and on the street. The higher class of photographer would have nothing to do with the cheap novelties, although some local studios catering for the popular end of the market began to introduce ferrotypes during the later 1870s in areas including Bristol, London, Liverpool, Birmingham, Manchester, Glasgow and Edinburgh. By around 1880 there was also a market for gem tintypes, which were the smallest commercially produced portrait - the so-called American Gem being a postage stamp-sized photograph which retailed at around nine for 7 ½ d.

Sometimes a tintype or two will occur in a family collection. If un-mounted or unframed, tintypes are easily identified as they have a murky, metallic appearance, and are essentially photographs on a thin, sharp-edged, blackened piece of metal. They are also usually fairly small - often no more than 6.5cms x 3.5cms (Fig. 18). Some examples may be more difficult to recognise as, like other one-off pictures, they could be mounted or framed. Tiny gem tintypes were often inserted into standard carte de visite-sized mounts or other types of card, including versions with an open aperture bordered by a decorative printed or embossed frame. Being easily cut to size, they were also suitable for fitting into jewellery, so may be found, for example, in a locket or brooch. Tintypes might be presented under glass in a gold-coloured pinchbeck frame, as seen in Fig. 21, although the metal back is generally clear. If in doubt about the material, a gentle magnet (like a fridge magnet) can be applied as this will attract a tintype without causing damage, whereas it will not attract a daguerreotype, ambrotype or paper print. Obvious signs of deterioration may also include rusting of the metal or the flaking or bubbling of the coating of photographic emulsion. While tintypes may depict ancestors posing formally in a studio, as in Fig. 18, more often they will have been taken outdoors, and therefore show forebears in more casual settings, for example on the beach (Fig. 21). The earliest tintypes remaining in family collections are likely to date from the late 1870s and many will have been taken some time between the 1880s and WWI, although examples as late as the 1930s or 1940s may survive.

(7) Portrait postcards c.1902-1940s
Postcards offered a new kind of card format for photographic portraits at the beginning of the 20th century. The first picture postcards had appeared in 1894, when postcards became an authorised form of postal communication, and during the Edwardian era quite independently they became a popular format for portrait photography. Initially on regular postcards the whole of the blank side of the card was reserved for the address, so if a postcard was to be sent through the post, any message had to be written across the picture, but in 1902 the divided back (with a line running down the centre) was introduced, offering separate spaces on each half of the back for the address and for a short written message. It was probably this new, more convenient arrangement that first inspired commercial photographers to use the postcard for portraits. Photographic postcards could certainly be posted like any other postcard, but often the photograph was never intended for the post and was put straight into an album. Some studios may have been using the postcard format as early as 1902 or 1903 (Fig. 34 is an early example), although most surviving examples date from after the mid-decade, 1906 and 1907 being the first years of significant production (Fig. 35). Visually the images look like any other studio photograph, complete with the usual background and props of the time (see Chapter 3 for more on these aspects). Postcards became the standard professional format of the 1910s (Figs. 36 & 37), reaching their highest peak by the end of WWI, although they remained popular throughout the 1920s, 1930s and into the 1940s for both indoor and outdoor photographs (Figs. 45, 46 & 49). Postcard-style cards were also used for amateur snapshots until at least WWII, in some cases later. Photographic paper in the form of a postcard was being manufactured in the United States by 1899 and the No.3A Folding Pocket Kodak, a camera designed for postcard-sized film, launched in 1903, allowed the general public to take pictures and have them printed on postcard backs (Fig. 39). Other makes of camera followed suit, and the industry developed further postcard products that appealed to the new generation of amateur photographers.

Family collections of early 20th century photographs are sure to feature some professional studio postcard portraits and may also include some amateur shots printed onto postcards. Most photographic postcards measure a standard 14cms x 9cms, the size introduced for postcards in November 1899, although slight variations may occur. If by chance a postcard was actually posted and the postmark is legible, the date of postage should logically be fairly close to the year of the picture. If the postmark cannot be read then the head on the postage stamp will at least show which monarch was on the throne at the time: Edward VII ascended the throne in 1901, George V in 1910, Edward VIII in 1935, George VI in 1936 and Elizabeth II in 1952. The reigning monarch and the monetary value of the postage stamp offer combined clues which should help to narrow the date range further. The inland postal rate for postcards was ½ d until June 1918 and from then, until June 1921, it remained at 1d. From then the cost rose to 1½ d, but dropped again in May 1922 to 1d.

Many surviving portrait postcards were not posted, although they may still offer helpful clues. The unstamped stamp box in the right hand corner can sometimes be dated approximately from its style, which may comprise a small, decorative motif or may denote a manufacturer's name or initial (see Web Resources for a useful online guide to identifying stamp boxes). Otherwise unmarked postcards can sometimes be broadly dated from the arrangement and wording of the printed instructions on the back. As mentioned above, the divided back confirms a date of at least 1902, while the explanation 'For Inland Postage ONLY, this space may now be used for communication' (Fig. 34) was common immediately following the introduction of the new style, especially in the years c.1902-6. However this is only a loose guide as some postcards had dropped the 'now' as early as 1904, while it may occur as late as c.1909. The precise wording of postcard instructions varied, but by the 1910s it was often fairly simple, usually being reduced to 'Correspondence' on the one side and 'Address' or 'Name and address'- or words to that effect - on the other (Figs. 36 & 37). If the postcard is a professional photograph the studio name may also occasionally be printed on the back: researching photographers' operational dates is explained in more detail below.

(8) 20th century card-mounted studio photographs

Commercial photographers were kept busy in the early 20th century, at least up until the First World War as, despite the growing popularity of amateur photography (see below) the formal studio portrait was still regarded as a superior product. They were still producing the traditional cartes de visite and cabinet prints until the 1910s and the newer postcard portrait until at least the Second World War but some early 20th century studio photographs in family collections will not fit into any of those familiar formats, as the professional photographer's repertoire also included larger mounted prints. Quarter plate (10.2cms x 12.7cms) was a standard size, but larger pictures were always possible and were especially well suited to the family group portraits of the Edwardian era. The taste in mounted photographs was for a stout matt card in sober colours - off-white, beige, shades of grey, sludgy browns and dusty greens. Mounts were often much larger than the picture, and this offered scope for subtle detailing: for example a series of borders or a decorative surround might be pressed into the card, framing the print. Photographs mounted onto a thick card of pale or muted colour continued after the First World War and throughout the inter-war era although, as photographic papers became sturdier, the need for a robust mount lessened and sometimes photographs were instead slipped into a protective folder. During the 1920s and 1930s the fold-over card became popular: this had pre-cut slots in its back half for containing the photograph, while the front folded over to protect the image. Many folding cards are rather plain, offering few dating clues, although the style of a decorative motif may suggest a particular period, while deckled or scalloped edges became especially popular during the 1930s (Fig. 44). The folding card method of presenting photographs remained popular throughout much of the 20th century.

(9) Amateur snapshots
Amateur photography - as distinct from professional, commercial photography - was practised from the earliest days, although for several decades it remained essentially a genteel pastime for the wealthier, leisured classes who could afford to buy expensive, elaborate apparatus and had ample time to experiment with the medium. From around the mid-1880s, various innovations gave a significant boost to amateur photography. New ready-made gelatine plates were much faster and more convenient than the old wet plate method and price reductions in photographic supplies and products made photography more affordable for middle-class hobbyists. In the United States, George Eastman (1854-1932) was also trialling gelatine-coated paper-backed film which could be used in roll form in a specially-designed camera. In 1888 he launched the Kodak No.1 camera - a relatively simple box camera loaded with a 100-exposure roll of film that was sent back to the Eastman factory when it was finished, to be reloaded and returned to the customer while the first roll was being processed. Although traditional glass plates were still used by professionals and serious amateurs for many more years, for the casual 'snapshooter' taking photographs no longer required advanced technical skills, artistic ability or complex equipment, and snapshot photography gained momentum. New models of camera introduced in the late 19th and early 20th centuries provided further encouragement and eventually helped to bring amateur photography to the masses. After the First World War the camera became a familiar gadget in many homes and by the 1920s and 1930s taking snapshots was a regular part of family life.

Photographs were taken by the family photographer to record special occasions and everyday scenes and any family photograph collection will include amateur snapshots. A few researchers may be fortunate to possess mid-19th century amateur photographs taken by affluent ancestors who were keen photographers, but these are very rare: surviving Victorian snapshots are most likely to date from the later 1880s onwards, when the middle-classes became more involved in photography. Fig. 30, dating from the 1890s, is one image from a collection of late-Victorian photographs, taken by an ancestor who was an early amateur photographer: further 19th century examples can be seen in Chapter 6, although the vast majority of family snapshots will date from the 20th century. Some may have originated in the early 1900s, like Fig. 33, although evidence shows that many more occur from the 1910s onwards (Figs. 38 & 39) - the decade when snapshots and studio portraits begin to jostle for position in the family album. By the 1920s amateur snapshots are more common than professional photographs and dominate family collections from this period onwards (Figs. 42, 43, 47, 48 & 50 and see also Chapter 6).

Photographer information

Family photographs taken in a professional studio often bear the name and address of the photographer and this provides significant historical evidence. Early photographs in the daguerreotype and ambrotype formats may have a studio name and address embossed on the protective leather case, as in Fig. 1, or printed on a label stuck to the back of the case or frame, although unfortunately photographer's details are often absent from these fragile metal and glass plates, and from tintypes - also photographs on metal. More positively, the majority of family photographs surviving from the Victorian and Edwardian eras are printed pictures on card mounts - cartes de visite, cabinet prints and the occasional non-standard sized mount. These card-mounted photographs, produced in quantity from 1861 onwards, provided commercial photographers with an ideal medium for identifying their work and advertising their business. Often the photographer's name and studio address were printed in neat lettering on the front of the card, as seen for example in Figs. 8, 12, 16, 17 & 27-29, but the reverse offered a larger area and this was used to publicise the details of one or more studios, to elaborate on the photographic services offered and to promote any other features likely to impress clients. Relatively few 19th century photographs were left blank on the reverse and the practise of identifying card mounts drifted over into the new century, as seen in Fig. 32, although by then new formats were beginning to take over and those were generally less explicit in their details. Many photographic postcard portraits made no mention of the photographer, although sometimes a studio name was printed on the back, as in Figs. 35, 45 & 46, and occasionally an address also (Fig. 34). Trade information was also patchy on early 20th century card-mounted photographs and folding cards, a line with the studio or photographer name sometimes being printed in small lettering at the bottom of the mount, as seen in Fig. 44: the back was usually left blank, although occasionally a label was attached.

When studio details occur on a family photograph, they provide a helpful geographical setting and also offer researchers the potential for dating the picture. Naturally photographers specified the town or city in which they operated and this important nugget of information immediately suggests the place of residence for the ancestor(s) represented in the photograph, as customers desiring a professional photograph usually visited a studio close to home (or their nearest town, if they lived in a rural area without a resident photographer). There may be exceptions to this general principle: for instance an ancestor who moved around with their job may have visited a photographer's studio whilst studying or working away from home, as in Fig. 19, or families may have had a photograph taken while enjoying a day trip or holiday, as was perhaps the case with Fig. 24, taken in a studio in the popular tourist resort of Southend-on-Sea. Researchers cannot, of course, expect to know about every journey ever taken by family members in the past, but may have formed some idea of their usual movements. Ultimately the geographical origin of a studio portrait always provides evidence that the ancestor or relative who posed for their photograph was, at some point, connected with that area, and this knowledge should help when considering possible candidates for an unidentified photograph.

Photographer details may be very significant when it comes to dating a photograph, as establishing exactly when a named photographer operated at the stated address confirms the time period within which the picture must have been taken. If a photographer is only known to have run a particular studio for a few years, as in the case of Figs. 8-10, clearly this suggests a close date-range for the image; however if he or she operated from the same studio for many years, as did the photographers named on Figs. 7 and 12, then this can only offer a broad circa date for photographs taken at that address and a narrower time frame will still need to be ascertained using other methods. Photographers who expanded their business and took over more studios generally lost little time in reprinting their card mounts to include details of additional branches. When two or more studio addresses are specified on a photograph, as with Figs. 19 and 31, it is necessary to find out when both were operating simultaneously; since some branches were ultimately short lived, the period of multiple studios may have been relatively short, so this can also help to narrow down a photograph's date range.

Researching photographers and studios

Discovering more about a 19th or early 20th century studio named on a photograph may take time, or can be surprisingly easy, depending upon whether accurate data is easily accessible. Photographic history generates significant interest nowadays and old photographs are collectible items (besides being family heirlooms), so a great deal of information has been compiled about past photographers and their operations. Institutions like the National Portrait Gallery, London (www.npg.org.uk) emphasise the work of eminent society photographers such as Alexander Bassano (1829-1913), James Lafayette (1853-1923) and famous studios like Hills and Saunders (established in 1852 and still operational today). Such notable portrait photographers, patronised by the social elite, may possibly have photographed prosperous and well-connected ancestors: if so researchers will find much written about them and their studios in books, gallery and exhibition catalogues and photography websites. However, most family historians will be concerned with investigating names from amongst the thousands of popular commercial photographers who operated high street studios across the country in the Victorian era and early 20th century. Some transient photographers seem to have left little trace of their activities, but many others were recorded on census returns and may have advertised their businesses in local trade directories and newspapers, making it possible to trace their operations over a period of time as they expanded their business to include additional branches, joined up with new working partners or moved between different locations. Sometimes it may be necessary to consult these original sources to find out when a photographer was recorded at a specific address: using newspapers and trade directories is discussed in Chapter 1, while the census returns dating from 1851 onwards may be relevant when looking for photographers, especially the 1861 and later censuses. If using primary sources, it is important to bear in mind their limitations: census returns will only show a place of residence every 10 years and, while trade directories and newspaper notices are very useful, not all photographers advertised regularly in the press, so dates of individual advertisements found may not show the full picture. Local libraries and record offices may also hold details of photographers who worked in their area and can be a good source of information. Some local organisations have published guides to past photographers in their city or county and these are listed in the Bibliography at the end of the book.

Online resources

As with many aspects of genealogy, the internet is a valuable tool and may well provide the best method of determining dates and addresses for a photographer or studio named on a photograph. A simple search should produce any online references to the individual or studio at the location named. Typically the results of a search may include random forum discussions and eBay photograph sales, as well as copyright records held by The National Archives at Kew detailing photographs intended for publication which were registered (originally at Stationers' Hall) by photographers from 1862 onwards. More specifically, an internet search will also reveal whether research into the photographer under investigation has already been carried out, and the results recorded for others to view, on a specialised photographer website or database. At present there exists no complete national online directory of 19th and early 20th century commercial photographers, and there are no known plans to undertake such a mammoth project in the near future; however several important photographer indexes and databases have been compiled by various national institutions, regional organisations, local and family historians and independent collectors and specialists. Most of these cover studios from a specific city or geographical area, giving A-Z photographer listings with dates of operation at each address, some entries also including additional biographical details. Again, researchers need to be aware of the limitations of the data, which usually derives from census returns, trade directories and newspaper advertisements. Some databases and indexes do not claim to supply complete operational dates: some cite details of the original sources of information used, and in these cases researchers can at least judge for themselves their scope and reliability. The principal searchable online indexes available at time of writing are listed in the Web Resources section at the end of the book: in general, they offer a very useful short cut and if any cover the town or city of the photographer under investigation, they should provide a guide as to when he or she was in business. However data for some areas of the country has not yet been compiled, so if a photographer's dates cannot be found on an existing index, or anywhere else on the internet, and research in person using censuses and trade directories is not an option, researchers may wish to apply to a specialist website offering photographer information for a small fee: such services are also listed in the Web Resources.

Dating the card mount

Identification of a photograph's format and discovering the photographer's operational dates can sometimes suggest a close time frame for a photograph. However the main card formats spanned several decades, and a photographer may have run a particular studio for many years, so in some cases additional dating techniques may also need to be applied to obtain a more useful date range. Collections of cartes de visite and cabinet prints demonstrate not only the obvious size difference between these two card formats, but also further variations in their appearance - the shape of the corners, the thickness of the card, the colour of the mount, and the design on the reverse - physical features which all changed over the years. The mounts used by a particular photographer may not always have represented the very latest style, especially if he or she needed to finish existing stocks before beginning a fresh supply, but in practise it was rare for an active photographer to use very old cards. Therefore recognising the characteristics associated with different time periods can also aid dating of card mounted photographs and this technique works well in combination with analysing other types of evidence. The reverse views of the card-mounted photographs illustrated in this chapter show some of the different mount styles which may feature in family collections, offering a dating guide. Since many different designs were used over the years, researchers may also find it helpful to look at further examples displayed on some of the websites listed in the Web Resources.

The earliest cartes de visite always have square corners, as seen in Figs. 7-12, 14-17 and 19, and the card tends to be quite thin and flexible, bending easily. The square-cornered shape prevailed from the beginning of the 1860s until the late 1870s: at this time rounded corners began to be used, although they did not become common until the early 1880s. Cartes de visite and larger cabinet prints dating from the 1880s until the early 1900s usually have rounded corners, as seen in Figs. 22-27, 29, 31 & 32, although square corners did reappear at times, so a square-cornered photograph could, conceivably, date from these years. The card used by the late 19th century was generally thicker and sturdier than that used for earlier mounts, a development that facilitated bevelled edges which were often finished in silver or gold. In the 1880s and 1890s some cartes and cabinet photographs were also protected by a flyleaf - a covering of fine protective tissue which was usually pasted along the top edge of the reverse and folded over the front of the photograph. Usually the tissue has not survived (often it was removed when the photograph was placed in an album) but signs of its original presence may remain on the back of the mount, offering another dating clue.

The colour of photographic mounts is a more visible feature, easier to judge by eye than card quality. Mounts from the 1860s are usually pale in colour - ivory, cream and slightly pinkish tones - and these neutral shades continued into the 1870s, although during this decade there emerged a new vogue for coloured card, especially bright turquoise, gold-yellow (Fig. 19) and sugar pink (used for both male and female subjects), a colour which remained popular throughout the 1880s. In the mid-1880s there developed a marked taste for deep colours, especially bottle green (Figs. 24 & 29), black also being used, but less common: these dark shades were fashionable for mounts from around 1884/5 and throughout the 1890s, until the early 1900s, although strong creams and beiges were also common in the late 1880s and 1890s (Figs. 25-28). Bright and dark red-coloured mounts enjoyed a brief vogue in the later 1880s and early 1890s (Fig. 23), while different shades of grey, from pale to dark, were common during the late 19th and early 20th centuries, often being used around the turn of the century (Figs. 31 & 32).

Occasionally cartes and cabinet photographs were left blank on the back, as in Figs. 24 & 29, but more often the reverse was, as already discussed, used for promoting the photographer's details. The style of the lettering and accompanying designs changed significantly over the 50-odd year period of their production, in general becoming increasingly elaborate as the 19th century advanced, then growing a little more subdued again by the early 20th century. Some designs dovetailed with others or spanned more than one decade and various styles were popular at any given time, although some were especially common, the same basic cards being used by many different photographers. The earliest cartes were printed or stamped neatly with the photographer's name and address and a crown or royal coat of arms if the studio boasted royal patronage (Figs. 7-9), the details placed usually in the centre of the mount, or very occasionally at the bottom. After the mid-1860s the text began to expand outwards from the centre, often incorporating flowing font styles, while from c.1865 an additional advertisement for copies was sometimes printed at the bottom of the mount (Figs. 10 & 11). By the late 1860s additional design features were also beginning to appear, especially delicate filigree scrollwork and ribbon-like banners, these both continuing throughout the 1870s (Figs. 15 & 17). Also popular during the 1870s were crests and coats of arms (Figs. 16, 17 & 19), while medals denoting photography exhibition prizes also became more common (Fig. 12). The year of any awards won by the studio provides a firm *post quem* date.

In general printed details became progressively more elaborate and often covered much of the card by the 1870s, three or four different font styles also being common. A typical later 1870s style, which continued into the 1880s and may crop up at the beginning of the 1890s, displays the studio name sprawled diagonally across the mount, bordered by ornate filigree work, the text embellished with a decorated capital letter (Fig. 22). 1880s mount designs were usually highly complex, large lettering and expansive decoration usually filling the whole of the back. Another recognisable style, first seen in the later 1870s, is the card with an elaborate border, the text and other motifs contained within (Fig. 25), the style of these borders varying greatly. A feature also noticed on many mounts of the 1880s and 1890s is the active promotion of photographers' artistic skills, the mention of 'Artist', 'Art photographer' or similar descriptions reflecting a concern to emphasise superior professional status in the face of growing competition from amateur photographers (Figs. 25, 26 & 31). Reinforcing the artistic theme, many mounts from the early 1880s until the mid-1890s incorporate pictures, favourite subjects including easels and paint palettes, and scenes depicting swimming or flying water birds amongst reeds or bamboo: these might also be accompanied by exotic fans and parasols in the corners, expressing the contemporary vogue for Japanese imagery (Figs. 26 & 28). Classically draped female figures, cherubs and fairies may also occur on mounts of the mid-1880s through to the later 1890s (Fig. 23). Meanwhile a printed detail noticed on some 1890s cards is the promotion of 'electric studios' or 'electric lighting': such references may very occasionally occur on 1880s mounts, but they usually date from at least the 1890s - the decade when many towns and cities received their first supply of mains electricity (Fig. 27). By the later 1890s mounts are beginning to lose some of their exuberant decoration and around the turn of century are often more 'modern' in their appearance: font styles are usually plainer, sometimes displaying shaded effects, while bunches of flowers and other botanical motifs are especially popular (Figs. 31 & 32).

Manuscript information

Although relatively few family photographs surviving from past eras have anything at all written on the back, hand-written information does occasionally occur - perhaps a name, or name and date, which may helpfully identify the subject and record the year when the photograph was taken. Photographs of minors in particular may bear an inscription giving the age of the child or 'teenager' when photographed and perhaps also their date of birth (see Figs. 19 & 24 and Ch 4 Fig. 11). Postcard photographs are also more likely to have handwritten notes on the reverse as they were originally designed for this purpose (see Figs. 35, 37 and 39). When considering handwritten information, be aware that some comments may not be entirely accurate. In general, the earlier the inscription, the more trustworthy it may be, as it is more likely to have been added during the lifetime of the photograph's subject, or by someone who personally knew them. The age of the inscription can be judged to some extent from the style of handwriting and from whether ink, pencil or biro has been used (biros and ballpoint pens were not in common use before the late 1940s). Information 'helpfully' added by later generations will always be more suspect: dates and identities may rely on memory, hearsay or unsubstantiated personal opinion and even the most seemingly reliable source may have been misinformed or unwittingly gave ambiguous information. Establishing a firm date range for the photograph will always indicate whether any names and dates written on the back are likely to be accurate.

Often a carte de visite, cabinet print or other card-mounted photograph will also have a reference number written on the back in pencil or ink by the photographer, as seen on the reverse of Figs. 7-10, 16, 22, 25, 27, 28 & 32. The number may be scribbled in a corner or in a designated area printed with the words 'No.' or 'Neg. No.' This refers to the number of the negative - the glass plate which was kept in store by the photographer for some years after the photograph sitting, in the hope of further orders from the customer. Where a collection includes several photographs taken by the same studio, the ordering of such negative numbers can provide a helpful sequential ordering for the photographs. Successful commercial photographers typically took several hundreds of portrait photographs a month when business was brisk; annual output could easily amount to three or four thousand photographs, or many more, if some accounts are to be believed, so high negative numbers on photographs are common, especially if a photographer was in operation for many years. If his or her studio dates at a particular address have already been discovered, then the negative number may also give a rough indication of how early or late within that period the photograph was taken. Unfortunately very few business records or negative holdings survive today from the many thousands of Victorian and Edwardian photographic portrait studios that once existed. Early glass plate negatives took up much storage space and were also very heavy, plates stacked in the attic literally causing some studio buildings to collapse. When studios changed hands the new incumbent might advertise prints from his or her predecessor's negatives but after or a year or so, those which weren't selling would be disposed of, and if a photographer died, quite commonly their whole collection of plates was destroyed. Glass being a valuable commodity, during the wet-plate era negatives could also be recycled, the photographic emulsion being washed off and the glass re-used. By the early 20th century it was standard practise to cull negatives every five years or so and many more were destroyed between the First and Second World Wars. Generally when studio negatives were discarded, so too were any accompanying written records - card files or studio registers, the log books listing customers' names and corresponding negative numbers. Therefore even if a negative number is recorded on a photograph, unfortunately the chances are very slim indeed of discovering a name, date or anything more. That said, there are some important collections of glass negatives from the studios of well-known photographers in public institutions such as the National Portrait Gallery, while a handful of early photography studios are still in operation today, for example Hills and Saunders, mentioned earlier, and Edward Reeves in Lewes, East Sussex, businesses which often maintain archives of old images and negatives. A standard internet search should reveal whether the photographer or studio under investigation is still in existence, or whether any surviving negatives from a dissolved company have been transferred elsewhere, for example to a local city museum or county archive.

Family photograph albums

Some families may be fortunate in possessing original 19th century or early 20th century photograph albums compiled by earlier generations. The early-1860s craze for collecting cartes de visite inspired the production of the first purpose-designed photograph albums and the availability of albums in turn encouraged the taking of more carte de visite photographs. In fact in the earliest years of their production, cartes were known as 'album portraits', demonstrating the close relationship between these popular photographs and the fashion for displaying them in albums. (Any printed reference to album portraits occurring on the back of a surviving carte will immediately indicate that the photograph was taken in the early 1860s). The first purpose-designed albums were produced in France but photograph albums were being advertised in Britain by 1861. Looking externally very much like the traditional family bible, the first albums had heavy leather bindings and sturdy metal clasps, as seen in Fig. 53(a). Inside it was customary to include a 'page one' carte de visite - a frontispiece with (often humorous) verses addressed to family and friends about to look through the album (Fig. 53(b)), while the main album pages featured pre-cut carte-sized apertures for the convenient arrangement and display of growing collections of photographic cartes. These substantial albums made ideal gifts at Christmas and for special birthdays, especially for ladies, and they rapidly became a fashionable ornament in the middle class home. Later albums usually featured two sizes of apertures for both cartes and cabinet prints, especially by the 1880s and 1890s once the larger cabinet cards had become a more popular photographic format, and this can help to date surviving Victorian albums. The styles of album bindings also changed over the years, as seen by comparing Fig. 53(a) with Fig. 54(a), while the pages inside grew more elaborate as fashionable taste veered increasingly towards the ornate: in many late-Victorian albums some of the apertures were framed with watercolour paintings (Fig. 54(b)). Albums, like photographs themselves, gradually came down in price and over the years they became affordable for more families. In the early 20th century plainer, slimmer albums were popular for displaying amateur snapshots and, naturally, many more of these will survive in family collections (see Chapter 6).

Photograph album collections were generally started by one person then passed down through the family, later generations often adding more photographs to the compilation already begun. Surviving Victorian albums may then include quite an assortment of photographs spanning four or more decades. Sometimes it may be necessary to temporarily remove photographs from their apertures to study any information on the back and to scan them, but they should afterwards be returned to their original locations. The positioning of photographs within an album may at first appear random, but their organisation offers important evidence. There was usually a purpose to their initial arrangement: in particular, portraits of husbands and wives were typically displayed alongside each other, and on the same or adjacent pages were inserted pictures of any children, while photographs of other family members branched out further throughout the album. The family relationships expressed in the different photographs may take some time to unravel, but at least respecting their organisation within the album will preserve the original connections and these may well prove a useful starting point when attempting to identify unfamiliar ancestors. The next chapter describes in more detail how to date, analyse and link up these fascinating yet often baffling images from the past.

Fig. 1 Cased daguerreotype, c.1847-8

This well-preserved daguerreotype survives in its original red leather case, a velvet pad facing the vulnerable metal plate inside. On the front is embossed a studio name and addresses: 'Claudet's Daguerreotype 18 King William Street Strand & Colosseum'. The online database www.photolondon.org.uk records that the well-known photographer Antoine Claudet operated simultaneously from both of these studios only for a short time, from April 1847 until December 1850, providing a close date range. The middle-aged lady is thought to be the wife (1791-1848) of the ancestor seen in an earlier oil painting (Chapter 1, Fig. 7) and probably also in Fig. 2 here. If her identity is correct, her death in November 1848 narrows the picture's date even closer to 1847 or 1848. Her appearance here reflects her comfortable middle-class status and expresses a taste for good clothing in keeping with her age. Her fine day dress is made of pale-coloured silk satin fabric, in vogue during the 1840s, and her tight-fitting bodice attached to a wide skirt follows the fashionable line of the decade. Other characteristic features are her narrow sleeves and the fan pleats converging from the shoulders towards the bodice centre, although the elongated front point was rather outmoded by 1847/8, so, like many older women, she was slightly behind the times. Her elaborate white day cap incorporates long lace lappets and is close-fitting, trimmed with flowers and other ornamentation at ear level - the fashionable style of the late 1830s - 1850s.

Fig. 2 Cased daguerreotype, c.1847-55

This daguerreotype is housed in a padded leather case, although the front bears no photographer's stamp, so any clues about date and identity rely on the visual image. The composition, like Fig. 1, is typical of very early photographs when single subjects were usually shown close up, seated at a cloth-covered table. The blurred cloth looks similar to that seen in Fig. 1 so this photograph could also have originated in Claudet's studio although it seems unlikely that the eminent photographer would not have identified his work. This gentleman is thought to be the ancestor (1787-1860) seen in an earlier oil painting (Chapter 1, Fig. 7). Although likeness can be hard to judge, visual comparison suggests that he could be the same man, now thinner-faced and probably aged here in his 60s. The picture was passed down from the same source as Fig. 1 which also supports a likely link between these two subjects. He is dressed in the fashionable style of the 1840s and 1850s, his slender frock coat worn with matching, narrow trousers, a deep V-fronted waistcoat and the wide black cravat customary during those decades. His tall 'stove-pipe' top hat has, as usual for photographs, been removed and rests on the table.

Fig. 3 Ambrotype, c.1854-5

This unlabelled ambrotype, a fragile photograph on glass, has lost its original frame, judging from the oval outline around the edge of the picture. The subjects are sisters, the eldest born in 1843 and the younger either in 1845 or 1847 - the eldest and one other of the three girls portrayed in an earlier crayon portrait (Ch 1 Fig. 17). The apparent age of the older sister (about 11-12) suggests that the photograph was taken c.1854-5, although 1855 is most likely since ambrotypes are rare before that year. The studio setting is typical of the 1850s, featuring the familiar boldly-patterned cloth-covered table, the draped curtain a feature also present sometimes from around mid-decade. Both girls wear good frocks which follow the close-bodiced, full-skirted style of the era. The older sister's more adult dress is made in a plainer, more sedate fabric and with a longer skirt, while the younger wears the tiered, knee-length dress of childhood which reveals her frilled drawers or *pantalettes* beneath, her wide neckline and short, puffed sleeves usual for younger girls. Both sisters' hair is dressed in the long ringlets still worn by girls during the 1850s.

Fig. 4 Ambrotype, c.1856-60

This ambrotype is framed in an oval surround of brass or pinchbeck, and an outer frame of leather or leather cloth. As usual for an early photograph, the subject is posed against a blank studio background, her elbow resting on an unseen table. Although undated, a close date range of the later 1850s or 1860 is suggested by her appearance. Her centrally-parted hair, draped over her ears into a low chignon behind, follows the style of the era, while her fashionable day dress, also typical of these years, features the characteristic folds of fabric arranged over the bodice and decorative white collar. One of the best dating clues is the shape of her open 'Chinese' or *pagoda* sleeves, which came into vogue during the 1850s: after mid-decade they were often very wide and sometimes layered, as here. This unmarried ancestor was a professional dressmaker, so she may well have made her outfit for the photograph. Her bracelet and brooch are highlighted with the bright gilding that was often applied to jewellery and buttons in ambrotype photographs.

Fig. 5 Ambrotype, c.1860

This ambrotype has survived in its original case although unfortunately the photographer is unidentified. This is a Union Case, used in Britain from c.1855, the relatively plain moulding on the front suggesting an early date. A printed sheet of paper (not shown) concealed beneath the velvet pad identifies the case makers as A.P. Critchlow & Co. and an additional announcement concerning their patenting of the 'Embracing Riveted Hinge' in October 1856 indicates the earliest likely year for the picture. The composition and other visual clues here are compatible with the evidence attached to the case. The lady's appearance narrows this down to the late 1850s or very early 1860s. Her bodice, with its folds of fabric and wide outer sleeves, is typical of these years, as is her hairstyle, centrally-parted and draped low over her ears. Her black dress, worn also with black under sleeves, and narrow black head dress with lappets suggests that she is in mourning. Although she is not firmly identified, she was related to an ancestor who died in February 1860, a year which would fit the photograph well (see Chapter 4 for more mourning images).

Figs. 6(a) & (b) Ambrotypes, c.1860

This leather case contains two framed ambrotypes, both depicting siblings who lived in Calcutta, where their father ran a cabinet making and upholstery firm. The family made regular trips back to London and Carmarthen on business and to visit friends and relatives during the 1860s. The case bears no photographer's details but the photographs were probably taken in London c.1860, judging from the apparent ages of the children. Fig. 6(a) shows the youngest girl, born in 1857, sitting in the lap of her half-sister, born in 1845. The little girl wears the full-skirted, knee-length dress made with short, puffed and ribbon-trimmed sleeves fashionable for small girls between the 1850s and 1870s. Her half-sister's appearance is approaching that of an adult, as seen from her very wide pagoda sleeves and her 'grown-up' hairstyle, the hair drawn down into a decorative net or caul; however her skirt fabric, pulled from beneath her and draped over her knees, is clearly not supported by the crinoline frame worn by women at that date. Fig. 6 (b) depicts another sister, born in 1850, who wears a youthful version of adult dress, her bodice fashionably pleated, but uncorseted, and her full flounced skirt ending just below her knees, revealing drawers or *pantalettes*. The brothers, born 1852 and 1854, wear the belted tunics and loose trousers fashionable for young boys before the knickerbocker suit was introduced in the 1860s.

HENNAH & KENT,
108, King's Road,
BRIGHTON.

Fig. 7 Carte de visite, c.1860-62

This carte de visite is a very early example of the new format, judging from a combination of dating clues. The style of the reverse is typical of the early-mid 1860s, the photographer's details printed neatly in a small area in the centre of the mount. The online resource www.spartacus.schoolnet.co.uk/Brighton-Photographers.htm shows that Hennah & Kent operated a studio at 108 King's Road, Brighton between 1854 and 1884 - a long time period which does not aid close dating, but in this case the visual image offers a very firm date range. The studio setting with its draped curtain and plinth is characteristic of 1860s cartes, as is the full-length composition. The appearance of the unidentified lady suggests a date around the turn of the 1850s and 1860s, although 1860 seems the earliest likely year. Her hair, draped over her ears and secured into a low chignon behind, perhaps contained in a net or caul, was the prevailing style of these years, the plait an additional feature. Her formal silk day dress displays a tight-fitting bodice and vast skirt worn over a crinoline frame, the circular shape typical of c.1860, while another fashion clue is the wide pagoda sleeves, still worn until around 1862, but rarely afterwards.

Fig. 8 Carte de visite, c.1863

This carte de visite is thought to date from c.1863, and this is supported by online research into the Southwell Brothers, for www.photolondon.org.uk notes that these photographers only operated simultaneously from both 16 and 22 Baker Street during 1862 and 1863. The design on the reverse is also characteristic of the early-mid 1860s, the printed details contained in the centre of the mount. This wealthy ancestor (1799-1878), who came from a family of coach masters and had married well, is portrayed here as a distinguished elderly gentleman. Photographed in full-length, as usual in the 1860s, he poses in a very elaborate studio with a painted Gothic Revival backdrop and ornate furniture - a setting reflecting the status of the Southwell Brothers, who photographed royalty and the social elite. He wears the newly-fashionable lounging jacket, fastened only by the top button, in the manner generally seen at this date. It is worn with a matching waistcoat but paler-coloured trousers, a popular 1860s combination. Note too the customary top hat placed on the table. His walking stick or cane was a fashionable accessory and, being of mature years, he wears a full beard.

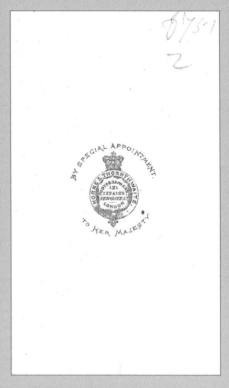

Fig. 9 Carte de visite, c.1863-4

This carte de visite is undated but research into the photographers, Horne & Thornthwaite, using the online London database www.photolondon.org.uk, records their operational dates at 121-123 Newgate Street as only 1863 and 1864, so this photograph is of comparable date to Fig. 8. As expected, the corners of the mount are square and the small, centrally-placed printed design on the reverse of the mount is typical of early-mid decade. This unidentified ancestor is photographed in full-length, as usual during the 1860s, and poses in a more conventional studio setting featuring the customary draped curtain and a chair and table. Like the older man in Fig. 8, he wears the new lounging jacket, this version slightly longer and looser, and appearing distinctly untailored. Again it is teamed with a matching waistcoat and contrasting trousers, their soft fabric demonstrating the rather shapeless look noticed during this decade. Being aged perhaps in his early twenties, he is clean shaven. His silk top hat, worn with the lounge jacket during the 1860s, rests on the table.

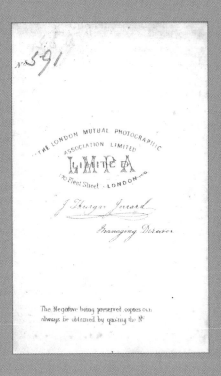

Fig. 10 Carte de visite, 1866

An 1860s date is immediately suggested for this undated carte by the full-length composition and the studio setting showing draped curtain and plinth, on which the subject leans. Photographer research using www.photolondon.org.uk has proved enlightening as it appears that the London Mutual Photographic Association operated for only a few months between March and July 1866, providing an exact year for this photograph. The reverse of the mount has changed, the text now beginning to occupy a larger area and also featuring extra information at the base. The young lady's appearance is very up to date for 1866: the fashionable line has slimmed down and the crinoline is no longer circular but displays the flatter front and backward sweep that became more pronounced after mid-decade. The bodice sleeves are made in the closed style which was usual from the early-1860s onwards, the detailing around the shoulders also a common feature by this time. Another major fashion clue is her hairstyle, now drawn well away from her face and the chignon worn higher.

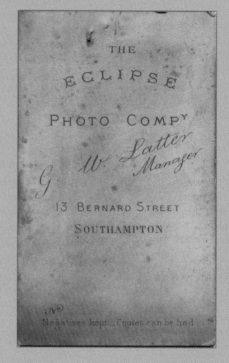

Fig. 11 Carte de visite, c.1869-70

This undated carte de visite exhibits the usual studio setting and full-length pose of the 1860s, the draped curtain as usual present on one side, although the velvet chair with a rolled back and fringing offers an additional pointer as this style of furniture first occurs in photographs in the later 1860s. The ancestor, born in 1850, married a station porter in 1871, also having a baby in that year, so this portrait probably pre-dates her pregnancy and wedding, judging from the absence of a ring. Her appearance is in fact closely dateable to c.1869-70, especially the shape of her skirt, which has lost any crinoline support but has acquired the layered arrangement typical of the period c.1869-75, when the overskirt was drawn up over a bustle; the back projection here is very modest, however, suggesting an early phase in its development. This ancestor was also rather poor, which may partly explain the plain nature of her outfit, although her hair is dressed fashionably in the high chignon of the late 1860s and early 1870s. Online research produced no studio data but the reverse of the mount is also compatible with a late 1860s or later date, the printed details now more complex.

74

Fig. 12 Carte de visite, c.1869-71

Photography was practised in Australia since the early 1840s and this carte de visite from Launceston, the capital of Tasmania, was taken by Cawston's, who local research revealed operated from these premises between 1862 and 1886. The reverse of the mount shows the busier design usual by the later 1860s, the mention of the medal won in a photography exhibition of 1866 offering the earliest possible year for this image. In fact the young woman's appearance confirms a date of at least 1869, for her layered clothing demonstrates the *polonaise* mode fashionable c.1869-75 when the drapery behind was supported by a bustle, although the modest back projection here may, like Fig. 11, suggest an early phase of the style. Her ornate outfit comprises an overdress worn over a flounced skirt, the velvet fabric and fringed trimmings both popular around the turn of the decade. Her hair is also styled into a fashionably elaborate chignon and worn with a decorative comb, one of several personal items later passed down within the family. Her portrait has been re-touched using watercolour to enhance the image, the curtain and tassels painted crimson, and her eyes, cheeks and lips accentuated, giving her a doll-like appearance. This ancestor, the daughter of a cordwainer, is believed to have been born in Australia c.1849-52.

Fig. 13 Ambrotype, c.1870

This framed ambrotype would have been quite an unusual choice by 1870 since the format had been
largely superseded by the popular carte de visite, but its survival is a reminder that late examples do
exist. There is no photographer's information on the frame and children's dress can be difficult to date
very closely, but the identity of these two brothers and their sister is known and their birth dates indicate
the likely year of this picture. The girl, probably aged 3, wears a 'best' dress shaped with a fitted bodice,
short puffed sleeves and a full, knee-length skirt, all features typical of the 1850s-early 1870s, although
the boldly contrasting sleeve ribbons and braid decorating the bodice and outlining the skirt panels helps
to narrow the date, since this trimming was fashionable between the mid-1860s and early 1870s. The
younger brother, aged around 5, wears a version of the knickerbocker suit, devised in the 1860s for little
boys. The older brother, aged 11 or 12, is dressed more like a young adult in full-length trousers,
waistcoat and a version of the male lounge jacket.

Fig. 14 Carte de visite, c.1870-75

The family historian researching this carte de visite has only seen this front view, so the photographer's details and the style of the reverse are absent and we only have the visual image for analysis. Significant here is the long half-length composition, this length and slightly longer three quarter-length views being characteristic of the 1870s and 1880s. The pose is also of note, being common during the 1870s when women were often photographed leaning over the back of a fashionable padded velvet chair. Fortunately the lady's distinctive appearance offers an accurate date range of c.1870-75, for this was the period of the bustle (seen here behind her left arm), while the velvet fabric of her dress was also fashionable during the 1870s. Her elaborate hairstyle is also typical of the period, when coiffures sometimes combined complex, high-piled chignons with long tresses of (probably false) hair. This ancestor (1832-1901) was the wife of a London importer and bottler of olive oil, the family being well off for a time. Although not very young, she is dressed in the height of fashion.

Fig. 15 Carte de visite, c.1871-75
This is another carte of three quarter-length composition, indicating a likely 1870s or 1880s date. There is no accessible online record of a G McLean operating in Penge, although data supplied by www.cartedevisite.co.uk confirms that a George McLean was working in Norfolk from 1875 to 1883. Assuming this is the same photographer, he probably worked in Penge before he moved to Norfolk, judging from the reverse of this image: the fine scrollwork was popular from the late 1860s until the late 1870s, while the neat, central placing of the design suggests an earlier, rather than later, date within this time frame. The bare studio setting offers no further clues, but this unidentified ancestor's appearance also supports a date in the early 1870s. By this date, all three pieces of the suit usually matched and early in the decade the lounge jacket typically featured wide lapels, as noticed here, the silk braid binding on the edges also a common feature. Another clue is the bowler hat: first worn in the 1860s, it appears more frequently in photographs of the 1870s, teamed with the lounge suit.

 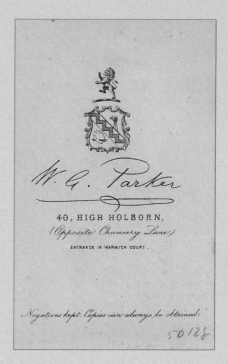

Fig. 16 Carte de visite, c.1873-75

This carte de visite from the early 1870s may seem unusual for it does not follow the usual three quarter-length composition of the era, but photographic evidence confirms that some sitters, especially women, sometimes preferred a full length view. The outfit worn by this middle-aged lady clearly dates from the period c.1870-75, judging from the prominent bustle projection behind the skirt. Her jacket bodice has a vent at the back to accommodate the drapery, while the skirt front displays rows of gathered frills, often used as trimming in the early 1870s. Her hair is dressed into a high chignon, the usual mode of the late 1860s and early 1870s, and also incorporates a plait, a common variant. Notice too the padded velvet chair with cord fringing, often present in photographs of this era. The reverse of the mount illustrates another popular 1870s design - various different fonts combined with a shield. Online research using www.photolondon.org.uk suggests that W G Parker operated from 40 High Holborn between 1873 and 1889, so here the fashion clues and photographer records dovetail nicely to produce a very close date range of c.1873-5 for this undated image.

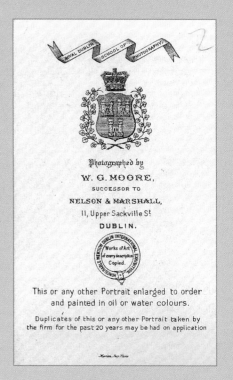

Fig. 17 Carte de visite, c.1876-80

Another 1870s carte portraying a female ancestor in full-length, this example shows an elaborate outfit dateable to the second half of the decade. The main stylistic clue is the shape of the skirt, for in around 1875/6 the bustle quite literally collapsed, the full back drapery, now unsupported, cascading downwards into a sweeping train. The skirt front, flatter by c.1876, is drawn across the legs in horizontal folds or gathers; on a younger woman this elongated 'Princess' line would appear more fitted and sheath-like but elderly ladies often preferred a looser arrangement. The trimmings around her hem and on her cuffs demonstrate the late-1870s and early-1880s vogue for minutely-pleated ornamentation and her decorative bonnet of middling height, tied with ribbons under her chin, was a matronly late-1870s style. Note the ribbon-like banner and a shield motif on the reverse of the mount - both common during the 1870s. Little is known about the Dublin photographer, W G Moore, except that he took over this studio some time after 1868 (information provided by www.cartedevisite.co.uk).

Fig. 18 Tintype, c.1876-80

This tintype, an image on a thin metal plate, typically bears no photographer's details, so the visual image often offers the only dating clues. Fortunately the fashionable outfit worn by this young woman is closely dateable to c.1876-80: her appearance may not seem very similar to the lady in Fig. 17, of comparable date, but the narrow, vertical silhouette, in vogue from c.1876, is apparent in both pictures. Her jacket bodice, extending smoothly over the hips, demonstrates well the longer *cuirass* line which now underpinned garments: the fall, or puffs, of fabric noticed at the back of the skirt indicates the drapery retained for a few years following the collapse of the bustle, while the decorative fringing and narrow pleats were both popular during the later 1870s and 1880s. Her headwear is also very up to date: her curled fringe was a new hairstyle at this time, while her feathered hat was a style favoured by younger women. She is dressed in the latest fashions and yet was not a well-off ancestor: her father was a Hampshire shepherd who was later buried in an unmarked grave, and her husband was a signal linesman for the railway; she married in 1878 so the absence of a ring here suggests that the photograph may just pre-date her wedding.

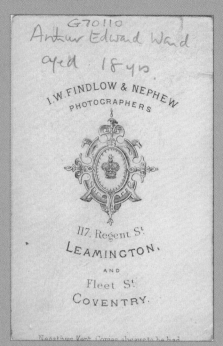

Fig. 19 Carte de visite, c.1876

A typical three quarter-length composition from the 1870s, this carte shows a young man aged 18, according to a pencilled note on the back. There is no reason to doubt this information as he is the same ancestor seen in an earlier ambrotype (Fig. 13), who was born in 1858. The likeness between the boy there and this young adult seems reasonable, although naturally he has matured in six years. By 1876 he was a plumber and decorator and had this photograph taken while working in the Coventry area. His appearance belies the nature of his trade as he looks very stylish and businesslike here in a smart suit of finely checked fabric, seen often during the late 1870s and 1880s. His sloping morning coat was a fashionable option for semi-formal wear and his distinctive necktie is the Ascot cravat - one of several styles worn during the 1870s. The card is bright yellow, following the vogue for coloured photographic mounts from the 1870s onwards, and the design on the reverse, featuring a shield-like motif, is highly characteristic of the 1870s. The online listing of Victorian photography studios in Birmingham and Warwickshire, www.hunimex.com/warwick/photogs.html, does not give full operational details for I.W. Findlow and Nephew, but confirms that they were operating in Regent Street, Leamington during the 1870s.

Fig. 20 Carte de visite, c.1878-82

Only the visual image is available for this carte, which illustrates the usual three quarter-length composition of the 1870s and 1880s. Here is the same ancestor seen in Fig. 14, but now aged in her late 40s or perhaps even 50, and still dressing very fashionably and elaborately. Her appearance is completely different here, the contrast between this and her earlier portrait demonstrating strikingly the stylistic changes that have occurred since the mid-1870s. She wears a formal afternoon or semi-formal evening ensemble, as confirmed by the low neckline (not worn for regular day wear) and 'dressy' accessories including a fan - very popular by the late 1870s and often seen in photographs. Her silk bodice shows clearly the elongated, figure-hugging *cuirass* line, well-developed by now, and suggests a late-decade or early 1880s date, as does her rather severe hairstyle with its fashionable tousled fringe. We cannot see the full shape of her skirt but its horizontal bands of satin, fringing and minute pleats towards the hem were fashionable in the late 1870s and early 1880s.

Fig. 21 Tintype, c.1880-83

This metal tintype photograph, unlike Fig. 18, is protected under a layer of glass and mounted in a decorative frame - probably made of pinchbeck, a gold-coloured alloy. This image, typical of 1880s tintypes, which were often taken outdoors, shows a group of young people enjoying a day out on the beach in their heavy layers of clothing. Although there are no photographer's details to investigate for dates, the style of the women's outfits dates this to the early 1880s. We see tight-fitting bodices and dark, pleated skirts, the pleats a prominent feature at this time. The women do not yet seem to be wearing the bustle, first worn in 1883/4. The lady on the right sports a fringe, popular from the later 1870s until the late 1880s and all three wear fashionable feather-trimmed hats with small brims. The men are dressed in the usual narrow lounge suits of the decade, one made in a pale colour, suitable for summer.

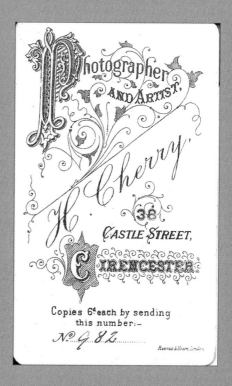

Fig. 22 Carte de visite, c.1883-4

Three fashionably-dressed young women pose for their photograph, the wooden fence a prop often used during the 1880s when 'outdoor' studio sets attempted to look more natural and often included bark-covered gates and fences. They all wear the dark, rather plain outfits usual for day wear during the 1880s, their close-fitting bodices with tight sleeves still following the long, narrow *cuirass* line that prevailed until c.1883/4. Their skirts are fairly narrow and are enlivened by the pleats and rows of ruches that were popular ornamental details in the early 1880s. Their hats are another fashionable 1880s style of headwear - the *tocque*. They may have been celebrating a special occasion, judging from their floral corsages and flower posies, although these could have been studio props. The reverse design shows how mounts were becoming more ornate, the pronounced initial letter and slanting text a common late-1870s and 1880s style. The photographer, Henry Cherry, moved around a great deal and was not operating in Cirencester before 1883, according to information supplied by www.cartedevisite.co.uk , although this still ties in well with the dress clues.

85

Fig. 23 Cabinet print, c.1887-9

Nothing is known about this undated photograph but the design of the mount, the photographer's dates and the various clues contained within the image all combine very well to offer a close date range of just a few years - c.1887-9. The cabinet format was more common by the 1880s, the colour of the bright red mount in vogue from c.1885-95 and the elaborate pictorial design featuring a classically-draped figure used between c.1884 and c.1899. Photographer data supplied by www.cartedevisite.co.uk shows that W H Prestwich advertised at 155 City Road from 1873 until 1893 and from High Road Tottenham between 1888 and 1908. Even extending the year back to 1887 (when the 1888 directory was probably compiled) we are left with a very useful date range of 1887-93 for the two studios operating simultaneously. The clothing seen here narrows this even further: the mother's dress is typical of the 1880s, especially her tight-fitting bodice, broad white collar and pleated skirt. The sailor suit worn by the little boy (back) was also coming into vogue at that time, while the two daughters wear the narrower dresses with pleated skirts that were fashionable for girls from c.1880. Another visual clue is the shaggy rug, a studio prop first seen in the 1880s.

Fig. 24 Cabinet print dated July 1888

This is another cabinet print, a format introduced in 1866 but only used regularly by the 1880s. The dark green card also reflects the vogue for dark-coloured mounts between c.1885 and c.1905. The photographer's details are printed on the front of the mount but the back is completely blank, except for a handwritten note stating that this little boy was photographed in July 1888, aged 3 years and 8 months. Photographers working in coastal resorts often used a beach or marine setting in their studios and this child poses against a textured 'rock' in front of a painted backdrop depicting the sea. The nautical theme is continued in the ropes - a studio prop - and in his outfit, a miniature naval uniform complete with sailor collar, lanyard and sailor's cap. These garments may also have belonged to the studio, or they could have been the boy's own clothes, as sailor suits were very popular for small boys from the 1880s onwards.

Fig. 25 Cabinet print, c.1889

Another cabinet print, this shows the three quarter-length composition still common in the 1880s. This ancestor was married in 1889 and she wears a wedding ring here: in fact this may be one half of a pair of wedding photographs, as a date any later than 1889 is unlikely, judging from the style of her outfit. In particular there is a prominent bustle at the back of her skirt, a fashionable feature that was becoming outmoded during 1889 and is rarely seen after that year. Other dating clues attached to this rather stark look are the close-fitting bodice with pointed front, high, uncomfortably tight collar and narrow, shortened sleeves. Her severe hairstyle, an alternative to the fringe, shows the hair drawn up high into a neat coiled chignon on top of the head - a mode continuing into the early 1890s. Little data appears online for the photographer, J Laing of Shrewsbury, but the image is already closely dated, while the busy reverse design, with its decorative border, is typical of the late 1870s and 1880s.

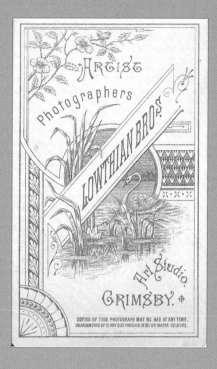

Fig. 26 Carte de visite, c.1889-92

The carte de visite format used for this photograph is of limited help, as it spanned several decades, while the hazy studio setting and style of chair, seen periodically from the 1860s until the 1890s, are not very useful either. Children's appearance can sometimes be difficult to date closely too, so requires careful analysis. The little girl wears a curly fringe, popular during the 1880s and 1890s, while the velvet fabric of her dress was fashionable during the 1870s and again around the turn of the 1880s and 1890s. The best dating clue may be her broad waist sash, also becoming common for small girls by around 1890. In this instance the photographer's operational details, combined with the design on the reverse offer the closest dates. Information obtained from www.cartesdevisite.co.uk confirms that Lowthian Bros advertised from this Grimsby address between 1889 and 1893. The reverse of the mount incorporates pictures, fashionable by the mid-1880s, but this specific design, also used by other photographers, is unknown after 1892, leaving a likely date range of c.1889-1892.

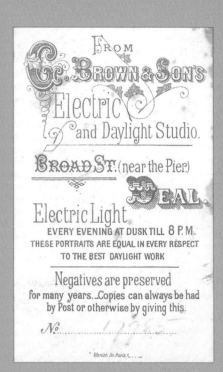

Fig. 27 Carte de visite, c.1890-92

This family group photograph is undated but the image offers a close date range, especially the fashionable appearance of the young woman. The sleeves of her close-fitting bodice display a well-developed vertical puff, a feature typical of the early 1890s and signifying the early 'leg-o'-mutton' style. Aged 16-18 in 1890-2, this relative poses with her two younger brothers, aged 14-16 and 11-13, the trio being the youngest three of twelve children. They may have been celebrating a special occasion together, judging from the corsage and floral buttonholes (see Chapter 4 for more on this subject). Another 1890s visual clue is the palm leaves, often seen in studio sets of this decade, while the busy style of the reverse is also characteristic of the late-19th century. The description of 'Electric and Daylight Studio' and assurance of the merits of portraits taken by electric light suggest that this was a new service being offered by G Brown & Sons. Such references on photographs often date to the 1890s.

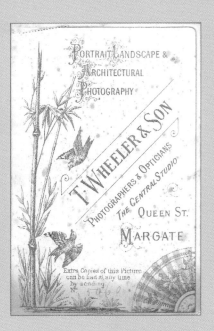

Fig. 28 Cabinet print, c.1893-4

This photograph in the popular late-19th century cabinet format is closely dateable from the visual clues. Studio settings of the 1890s and early-1900s often featured a plant on a stand, while painted backdrops sometimes included a paned window, surrounded by a decorative arch or frame. The lady's appearance narrows the date much closer to a likely range of c.1893-4. The sleeves of her bodice show how the early vertical puff has expanded, becoming fuller on the upper arm to form the *gigot* or 'leg o' mutton' style, but has not yet attained the width of mid-decade, while her hair is dressed in the high, coiled chignon of the late 1880s and early 1890s. This unidentified ancestor is clearly in mourning, judging from the crape trimmings on her bodice (see Chapter 4 for more on mourning dress). Her husband wears the usual three-piece lounge suit, still narrow in cut during the 1890s and often teamed with the long, knotted tie. His beard and moustache are clipped in the neat style fashionable throughout the decade. The reverse design reflects the 1880s-early 1890s vogue for artistic, Japanese-inspired motifs, this particular style of mount not seen after 1893/4.

91

Fig. 29 Carte de visite, c.1895-6

This undated photograph is mounted on dark green card, fashionable from the mid-1880s until the early 1900s, while its head and shoulders oval vignette composition was especially popular during the 1890s. Although offering only a limited view of dress, the image is closely dateable from the young woman's bodice, particularly her puffed sleeves which display the *gigot* or 'leg-o'-mutton' style, fashionable c.1893-8. They appear to be very full here, suggesting a date of c.1895-6 when these sleeves were at their widest. Her hair is dressed in a smooth style but shows the rolled front sometimes noticed by mid-decade. The card is blank on the back but the photographer is named on the front and online research using www.spartacus.schoolnet.co.uk/Brighton-Photographers.htm confirms that Mora worked from 127, Western Road, Brighton from 1891 until at least 1910.

Fig. 30 Amateur snapshot, c.1896 or 1897

This early 'snapshot', a paper print, exemplifies the kind of late-Victorian amateur photograph which may occasionally occur in a family collection. Taken by an ancestor who was a Lancashire mill worker, this picture depicts three generations of the family while on holiday in the summer of 1896 or 1897. The back is annotated 'Hardcastle Woods', thought to be Hardcastle Crags, a wooded valley near Hebden Bridge in West Yorkshire. The site is now administered by the National Trust, whose website records a little of its history, confirming that it was a popular beauty spot in the 19th century. The two ladies wear attractive but practical outfits comprising blouses and skirts, the usual combination for everyday wear by the 1890s, their cotton blouses displaying the puffed 'leg-o'-mutton' sleeves of the decade. The little boy, aged 3 or 4, wears the customary knickerbockers suit, the frilled shirt collar one of several collar styles current in the 1890s and early 1900s.

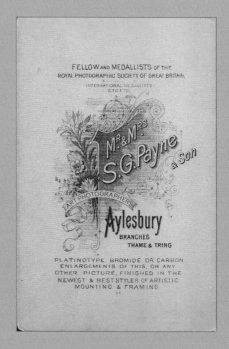

Fig. 31 Cabinet print, c.1897-1902

This undated photograph shows the head and shoulders oval vignette composition that was popular in the 1890s and spilled over into the early 20th century. The appearance of the young man is also compatible with this period, especially his high, starched collar, worn with the long knotted tie - most common during the 1890s but still worn a few years into the 1900s. Grey card mounts were used broadly between the 1870s and around 1915, but were most fashionable during the 1890s and early 1900s. The style of the reverse, with its shaded design and more 'modern'-looking font was typical of the turn of the century, and perhaps offers the best dating clue for this picture. A general internet search led to www.hertfordshire-genealogy.co.uk, a website that included a biography of Samuel Glendening Payne and his wife, who were both photographers. Without providing complete operational dates, the details given confirmed that the third studio mentioned here, at Tring, was recorded between 1895 and 1907 only, dates which support the visual evidence and style of card mount.

Fig. 32 Cabinet print, c.1901-04

This cabinet print depicts an ancestor, a Hampshire-born domestic servant, posing in her 'Sunday best' outfit, a formal matching bodice and skirt. Its style is a modest version of the hour-glass silhouette fashionable in the late 1890s and early 1900s. The loose panel on the bodice front accentuates the bust, while the tailored skirt is shaped to fit the waist and hips closely, before flaring out towards a flounced hemline. An even closer dating clue is offered by her sleeves, which are narrow in the upper arm then widen above the wrist before gathering into a tight cuff - a shape characteristic of the years c.1901-04. Her hair is waved or frizzed in the usual soft Edwardian style. The studio setting is also compatible with this time frame, the plant on a stand a popular prop in the 1890s and early 1900s, while the elaborate cane seat was a style of furniture fashionable during those decades. The photographer's dates are of little help since Debenham & Smith worked from this address for many years between 1885 and 1918, according to data provided by www.cartedevisite.co.uk . The dark grey mount and reverse design are, however, typical of the turn of the century.

Fig. 33 Amateur snapshot, c.1901-4

Amateur photographs become more common after 1900 and this is a snapshot, although it is posed rather like a professional portrait. The back of the paper print is blank, revealing no identity for this ancestor, no location and no idea of who photographed her, although from the visual image we can deduce that this was taken between around 1901 and 1904. The style of her outfit is remarkably similar to that worn in Fig. 32, even though the two images are very different. We notice again a smart, early-Edwardian blouse featuring a high neckline, loose, decorative front panel and narrow sleeves widening below the elbow before gathering into cuffs at the wrist, worn with the usual tailored skirt shaped with flared panels. Her hair is fashionably waved and loosely drawn up into a neat chignon, the characteristic style of these years. The natural flowers pinned to her bodice are a feature often seen in outdoor photographs of the late 19th and early 20th centuries - perhaps picked on a walk.

Fig. 34 Studio postcard, c.1902-6

The postcard portrait became the dominant format of the early 1900s, the divided back of this card confirming a date of at least 1902, while the instructions printed on the left (usually expressed in this way when this style of postcard was new) suggest a likely date range of c.1902-6. Taken by a professional photographer, the cloudy backdrop and weathered plinth are both features typical of studio sets of the early-1900s. The relative standing left was born in 1881 in Manchester, the son of a charwoman and builder's labourer from Ireland, but he rose from his working class origins, acquired a law qualification and later became the Irish High Commissioner in London, 1930-49. He and his companion are both well-dressed in smart three-piece lounge suits, their starched, turned down shirt collars with rounded edges, worn with the 'modern' long, knotted tie, typical of the early-1900s. He sports a straw boater, a popular hat for summer in the Edwardian era. Both young men are clean shaven, as was usual by that time.

Fig. 35 Studio postcard dated 1907
This photograph has been annotated with a record of the year - 1907 - and there is no reason to doubt this information as the ancestor portrayed was born in 1893, making her age around 14 here. She is fashionably dressed in the smart blouse and skirt combination that was well established for everyday wear amongst older girls and women by this time. Her blouse is high-necked in the usual Edwardian mode and features modest detailing on the front, while her plain tailored skirt is made with the customary flared panels. Her dark straw hat decorated with silk bows is a fairly simple style, suitable for ordinary wear. The studio setting features the stone wall and cloudy or hazy backdrop often noticed in photographs during this decade and the 1910s. Internet research revealed the USA Studios to be a chain with many branches.

Fig. 36 Studio postcard, c.1910-14
This professional photograph bears no studio name, although this is not unusual, for few postcard portraits were printed with these details. The visual clues are more helpful, for the setting includes a stone balustrade and hazy, vaguely leafy backdrop, both features familiar from the early-1900s that drifted over into the early 1910s. The appearance of this unidentified relative offers a closer date range of c.1910-14. Her practical blouse and skirt combination was still usual for regular every day wear, many 'modern' young women adopting this severe version in the years prior to WW1: an unadorned white shirt, worn with a tie and teamed with a plain tailored skirt echoed male attire and was suitable for work and sporting pursuits. The most useful dating feature is her hairstyle, the hair centrally-parted and drawn up into two swathes above the ears being most fashionable between around 1910 and 1914.

Fig. 37 Studio postcard dated July 1912

Another postcard photograph, this has a handwritten message on the back dating it to July 1912, although unfortunately nothing is known about 38 year-old Kate, who had a brother named Jack. She wears a relatively feminine and 'dressy' outfit for that date, as might be worn for a day out, although her lightweight cotton or linen summer day dress is simple in shape, following the new, natural lines of the early-1910s. The elbow-length sleeves, broad waist sash and deep lace collar or insert are all features that contributed to the fashionable look. Her crocheted or macramé reticule bag on a long cord was a new accessory around this time, while her dainty footwear demonstrates how shoes were beginning to take over from boots. Her ornate, broad-brimmed hat with a wide crown would also have been very fashionable in 1912.

Fig. 38 Amateur snapshot, 1913

This informal snapshot shows young parents and their small children relaxing outdoors somewhere in the Manchester area. The man is the same relative seen in Fig. 34, aged here in his early 30s and still affecting a rather pretentious mode of dress, as seen from his formal winged collar and bow tie - more suitable for evening wear than a day in the park. By this time he was father to two sons, born in August 1910 and July 1912, their birth dates suggesting a summer 1913 date for this photograph. The older brother wears the tunic top and shorts which became popular for little boys during the 1910s, while the baby wears the skirts still common for male infants at that time. Their mother wears an attractive day dress with elbow-length sleeves which follows the same basic shape as the dress seen in Fig. 37, while her hairstyle, drawn up at ear level, on either side of a central parting, is also typical of the early-1910s.

Fig. 39 Amateur postcard dated 1915

By the mid-1910s amateur photography was becoming more popular, as noticed from the larger numbers of snapshots occurring in family collections from this date onwards. Amateur photographers sometimes used postcard-style mounts for their pictures, and this casual snapshot, printed onto a postcard, is signed 'H.H.' on the back, confirming that it was taken by the same ancestor responsible for Fig. 30. Dated 'September 1915', it depicts his wife, aged here in her early 50s, sitting reading in the garden of their home in Burnley, Lancashire. She wears the usual everyday blouse and skirt outfit, the blouse featuring the prominent collar which became fashionable in around 1915 and helps to pinpoint undated photographs of mid-late decade.

Fig. 40 Studio portrait dated 1920

Professional photographs were still recognised as superior products in the early 20th century, and during and after the First World War there evolved a trend for studio portraits presenting a close-up head and shoulders view of their subjects. These intimate images were sometimes commissioned as personal gifts and this attractive photograph, signed on the front 'Thine Doras' and dated 1920, is thought to have been given by the young woman to her fiancé. She appears not to have cut her hair into a short bob, as did many of her generation at the time, but follows the alternative option of slightly longer hair pinned back behind the head. She wears a fashionable loose blouse with a long pointed collar, a popular style in the post-war years.

Fig. 41 Amateur snapshot dated June 1920

This outdoor group photograph, printed onto paper, is helpfully annotated on the back: 'Glenview Hotel, Glen of the Downs, Co Wicklow, June 1920.' The relative seated centre front, also seen in Figs. 34 and 38, was by then aged 39 and Assistant Secretary at the Treasury. The identity of his companions, perhaps political colleagues, has not yet been established, but this may have been a significant gathering. Meanwhile the scene offers a good range of post-WW1 war dress styles for men. The three-piece lounge suit was slender in cut for most of the 1920s, as before the war: long lapels now shape the jacket, while narrow trousers often show centre-front creases and turn-ups by this date. The older man, front right, wears old-fashioned leather boots, common before the war but more often replaced by shoes by 1920. Various hats were current at the time, the flat cloth cap still very popular but the felt homburg and trilby hats considered more stylish. At least one man smokes a cigarette, a social habit rarely seen in photographs before the 1920s.

Fig. 42 Amateur snapshot, c.1926-30

Amateur snapshots become plentiful by the 1920s and this example from a family album is, like many, blank on the back, so the location is unknown, although the young woman is recognisable as a relative born in 1907. The picture can be dated closely from her appearance here, which reflects the simple, uncluttered lines of the 'flapper' era - c.1926-30 - during which time young women, especially, wore their hemlines very short, at around knee-level. The minimalist simplicity of this look was expressed in shift-like dresses for summer, as seen here, while newly-revealed legs were set off with flesh- or pale-coloured stockings. The string of beads and low-heeled bar shoes were both fashionable accessories of mid-late decade, while her short bobbed hair was the style worn by most women by the late 1920s.

Fig. 43 Amateur snapshot dated 1930

Many snapshots offer few visual clues, except the clothes worn by the subject(s) and this photograph from a family album would be difficult to identify and date if the Liverpool location and the year, 1930, were not already known. Children's dress is often hard to pin down closely and this small girl, dressed for summer, could conceivably have been photographed any time between the 1920s and 1950s. The basic features of this popular look for female toddlers, as seen here, were a short white dress, the hemline worn well above the knee, teamed with short white socks and leather bar shoes, the strap worn high up on the foot. Short sleeves could be puffed or straight, bodices were sometimes ornamented with smocking, and the skirt section could be flounced or plain. Although it was, by 1930, becoming fashionable to acquire a sun tan, infants' heads were often protected by a cotton sunbonnet.

Fig. 44 Studio portrait, c.1931-34

This attractive image shows the interwar vogue for professional portraits depicting their subject(s) close-up, careful attention being paid to pose and lighting. The relative is the same lady seen in a snapshot taken around 20 years earlier (Fig. 38). Although this photograph is undated, her fashionable appearance indicates a date in the early-1930s, suggesting that this special photograph may have marked her 50th birthday in 1934. Here the dating clues are her short, waved hair and her soft 'Beanie'-style hat, which typifies the close-fitting headwear popular in the early-1930s. Fur was very fashionable c.1920s-1940s but this deep fur collar, worn high at the back of the neck, is characteristic of the 1920s and early 1930s. Often studio mounts of this era are blank, although the photographer's details may appear on the front, as here. Online research using www.photolondon.org.uk confirms that Navana Ltd operated from 124, Oxford Street, W1 between 1929 and 1937, dates that support the fashion clues.

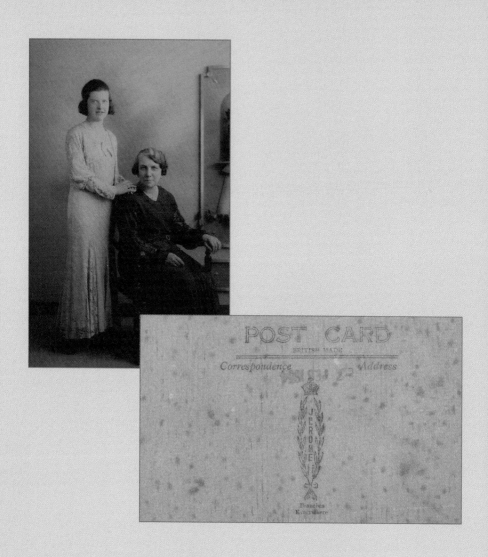

Fig. 45 Studio postcard dated February 1934
This professional studio portrait was taken by Jerome photographers who claimed to have 'Studios everywhere' in the 20th century and who helpfully stamped the date on the back - Feb 1934. This shows a daughter, aged 19, and her mother, aged 55, posing in full-length, the image offering a good view of early-1930s formal fashions. Fluid, draped dresses were worn to low calf length during these years, fabric often being cut on the bias to achieve a smooth fit and hemlines falling into soft folds. Women's hair was worn short in the early-1930s, following 1920s trends, but was usually more shaped and waved. These early-1930s fashions are very distinct from those of late-decade, when hair was worn longer and clothing was more tailored.

Fig. 46 Studio postcard, c.1934-36

This photograph looks like an amateur snapshot taken outdoors, but, judging from the postcard back, was photographed by Jerome studios again. This ancestor, born in 1877, was station master at Waverley Station, Edinburgh and descendants recall him retiring from work before he was 60, suggesting that this photograph was taken before 1937. Interwar and 1940s photographs of men can be difficult to date closely although a good guide is the cut of the suit which, after decades of narrow tailoring, was worn much wider by the 1930s. This suit is not very stylish but the loose fit of the trousers suggest a date of at least 1930. Other elements indicate that he is dressed in his work attire, especially the bowler hat, now worn mainly for business, and the very formal, conservative high-standing starched collar. The watch chain is also rather old-fashioned as it had been largely replaced by the wrist watch by the 1930s. Research using www.edinphoto.org.uk reveals that Jerome opened their Leith Street, Edinburgh studio in 1934, data that helpfully narrows the range of this photograph to 1934-1936.

Fig. 47 Amateur snapshot, c.1936-9

This amateur snapshot, like many from family collections, is undated but is known to represent the same relative seen in Fig. 44. Although aged in her early-mid 50s here, she clearly kept up to date with new fashions, her appearance suggesting a close date range of c.1936-9 for this picture. Her smart, tailored jacket with square, padded shoulders reflects the significant change in women's styles by the later 1930s, fashions being much sharper and more tailored, pre-empting the rather severe modes of the war years. By now, the fashion for fur was often expressed in a narrow fox fur stole, as seen here, or a fitted shoulder cape. Her hat is also typical of late-1930s headwear - now more structured and angular and worn with a brim.

Fig. 48 Amateur snapshot, 1938 or 1939

This undated snapshot of a large family gathering was taken in a Hampshire garden before the Second World War. A late-1930s date is suggested especially by the outfits of the younger women, whose dresses display the square padded shoulders and short hemlines of these years. Two men wear the very broad pinstriped three-piece suits fashionable during this decade while the young man centre back is dressed more casually without a waistcoat or tie, his shirt collar laid open over his shoulders in the manner often seen in 1930s photographs. The older man beside him wears wide plus-fours, a country or sporting style popular between the wars. The older ladies are conservatively dressed in blouses, pleated skirts and jackets - a plain style which would still be worn by women of their age-group after the war.

Fig. 49 Street photograph, 1943

This photograph annotated 'Paignton, May 1943' on the back, is a partial postcard and from its appearance was probably taken by one of the many street photographers who worked the seaside promenades in the early 20th century, even up until the 1960s. These relatives first met in Chelmsford, where the soldier was previously stationed and where the lady worked in a munitions factory, and they married in 1942. By 1943 they were based in Bovington in Dorset, so their visit to Paignton may have been a day trip from there, or a longer holiday. He served with the RAC (Royal Armoured Corps) during the war and by the time of this photograph was a sergeant, as confirmed by the three stripes on his uniform. His wife wears the plain, utility-style clothing which influenced fashion in the 1940s - a knee-length skirt, narrow, slim-fitting tailored jacket, coat with padded shoulders and hard-wearing laced leather shoes.

Fig. 50 Amateur snapshot, 1949

This photograph of the author's parents enjoying a day out in an unidentified location was taken in 1949, judging from a pencilled note on the back of the print. Her father had served with the Royal Engineers throughout the war and, like many men who had spent years in military uniform, welcomed the return to civilian dress. His lounge suit is worn without a waistcoat, as was usual by the 1940s, and his sharply-creased trousers demonstrate the wide, tailored style fashionable from the 1930s through to the 1950s. The outfit worn by her mother, aged eighteen here, typifies the relaxed but smart separates which became popular after the war, especially with the younger generation. Clothing was still rationed in Britain in the late 1940s and her tailored skirt with front pleats echoes narrow wartime shapes, although footwear was becoming more varied and young women often wore high sandals with wedges and ankle straps. Her hair is worn long, partly reflecting her youth and also following the 1940s vogue for glamourous, waved hairstyles.

Fig. 51 Memorial cabinet portrait: 1850s copied in the late 1890s/early 1900s

Dating and analysing this photograph indicated that it is in fact a memorial portrait because the image is very much earlier in date than both the photographic format and the photographer's operational dates. The ancestor portrayed here (1822-1880) probably sat for this photograph in the 1850s, judging from both his apparent age and from the style of his narrow frock coat. The original photographic portrait was therefore either a daguerreotype or an ambrotype - the only formats commonly used in the 1850s - while the current picture is a cabinet card, a format popular between the late 1870s and 1910s. Online research shows the photographer, Alfred Calvert, operating from this address in the 1890s and early 1900s, confirming that this early photograph on a metal or glass plate was copied and printed in the late 19th or early 20th century, some ten or twenty years or more after the subject of the photograph had died, and some 40 or 50 years after he visited the photographer's studio.

114

Fig. 52 Memorial carte de visite: photograph of a late 1820s/early 1830s painting
Initially this unusual photograph was believed by the family to represent an ancestor whose dates were 1820-61, but professional analysis and dating revealed a photographic reprint of a much earlier image that must have been a painting from the pre-photography era. The flat, 'painted' quality of the picture is very evident here, and also shows signs of 20th century retouching, especially about the face: essentially, though, the striking hairstyle and dress worn by the woman here confirms a date range of c. 1827-32. This reassessment now suggests that the subject is an ancestor from the previous generation (1792-65), the wife of a prosperous Somerset farmer/landowner, who would have been aged in her 30s or possibly 40 when she sat for her portrait. This memorial photograph was displayed in an album alongside a memorial portrait of her husband (1790-1866), copied not from a painting but from a photograph taken shortly before his death: naturally his identity was also revised following dating.

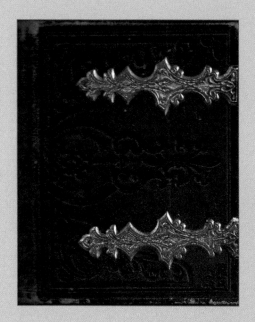

Figs. 53(a) & (b) Family photograph album, presented in 1863

This Mid-Victorian photograph album was presented to an ancestor in December 1863 as a 30th birthday gift, as confirmed by an inscription inside the cover, and was later passed down through several generations of the family. Its style is typical of the earliest purpose-designed photograph albums, which often resembled family bibles with their heavy, embossed leather bindings and stout, decorative metal clasps. All the pages inside have carte-shaped apertures, as to be expected in 1863 since the carte de visite was the only card-mounted photograph then being commercially produced. Here the carte-sized frontispiece takes the form of a photograph depicting ornate vases and a photograph album (Fig. 53(b)), the message warning that the album was only open to viewers prepared to contribute their portraits. The back of the frontispiece bears the details of Ashford & Co., Photographic Publishers of 76, Newgate Street, London, a company specialising in printing and distributing celebrity cartes and photographic novelties to stationers and other retail outlets. It is dated 1864 in pencil, suggesting that the album's first owner soon set to work filling the album pages with portraits of her family, some of which are featured in this book.

Figs. 54(a) & (b) Family photograph album, presented in 1886

This Late-Victorian album was purchased second-hand so its provenance is unknown but an inscription inside the front cover states that it was presented by one lady to another in 1886. The leather bindings are embossed with angular and botanical motifs, echoing the style of ornamentation seen on the reverse of many photographic card mounts from the mid-1880s onwards. Late-19th century aesthetic taste was more ornate than that of mid-century and, like many photograph albums of the 1880s and 1890s, this example is also very elaborate inside: several of the pages are embellished with painted flowers and greenery which frame the images (Fig. 54(b)). Unlike the earlier album seen in Fig. 53, the apertures here are of two sizes, to accommodate both cartes de visite photographs and the larger cabinet prints which were becoming more popular during the 1880s. The photographs themselves are all dateable to the later 1880s and 1890s, so in this instance the album was filled with new photographs.

THREE

CHAPTER THREE

Family photographs
- The visual image

The progress of commercial photography and, later, the popularity of amateur photography, along with changing tastes and new fashions shaped how earlier generations were portrayed at different times, determining what we may now observe from their images. As shown in Chapter 2, photographic formats, styles of card mount and photographer's operational details can provide a very useful time frame for many photographs, yet there may remain areas of uncertainty and there is no guarantee of a close date range even once all these forms of evidence have been combined. This chapter focuses on dating and analysing the visual image, which will invariably offer many helpful and interesting historical clues. It is, after all, the picture on the front of a photograph which especially interests family historians, and to skim over the pictorial details is to miss the most important evidence of all. No photographs are included in this chapter, but all of the points covered here are illustrated in numerous images reproduced throughout the book, so the text provides picture references wherever relevant.

Dating the visual image

Judging and interpreting visual evidence is different to other research processes. It may seem an imprecise method to some genealogists accustomed to working with documentary records and other factual printed material, but pictures too can be 'read' and their contents analysed and applied to family history research. Analysing a photographic image and, particularly, estimating its date, requires an understanding of what visual features to look out for and how to place them in an accurate historical context. This means not only studying the person or people portrayed, but also carefully scrutinising every other visual element of the picture, especially its setting and the clothes which ancestors and relatives are wearing. Surroundings and dress are both stylistic features which changed over time to embrace new fashions and aesthetic trends, and so these aspects provide significant dating clues. Costume is always a valuable dating guide, whatever the type of photograph, and this subject is covered in detail later in this chapter. Some family photographs were taken outdoors and show people in authentic settings: these photographs have an important documentary function and are discussed further in Chapter 6. However most Victorian and Edwardian photographs, and some later portraits, were set in a studio and the following sections explain how the commercial photography studio operated and how to recognise the compositions and formal settings popular in different eras.

The photographer's studio

Professional photographs feature in all family collections and most of these portray their subjects not in a real-life environment but in a studio setting contrived by the photographer. In particular, Victorian and pre-First World War photographs reveal a set rather like a theatrical stage, involving a painted backdrop and 'props' which aimed to create a three-dimensional effect and enhance the portrait. Drapes, furniture, painted architectural mouldings and moveable indoor accessories produced an idealised drawing room setting, while rocks, greenery, fences, gates and pergolas positioned against a rustic backdrop suggested an outdoor landscape. On the one hand the setting for photographs needed to be anonymous (as the same set was to be used for many different clients), but equally it was intended to convey a sense of good taste, financial security and status. Elite portrait studios patronised by royalty, the aristocracy and upper classes (which inevitably charged higher prices) provided the most elaborate and elegant studio settings, as seen in Ch 2 Fig. 8, whilst at the other end of the market inexpensive portrait studios catering for the lower classes offered more basic surroundings (Ch 2 Figs. 11, 15 & 37). Accessories kept by the studio were placed with the sitter so as to reinforce the genteel ambience: quality toys such as dolls, spinning tops, drums and tambourines were kept for small children to clutch (Ch 2 Figs. 23 & 26 and Ch 4 Fig. 35), while adults often held a book, implying literacy at a time when not everyone had received the benefit of an education (Ch 2 Figs. 1, 5, 16, 25, 28). Personal items could be used for photograph sittings on occasion, but were generally only permitted if they carried positive associations and enhanced the portrait.

Following established artistic tradition, the photographer took control of clients when they entered the studio, composing them in a pleasing manner, manipulating facial expression, angle of the head, stance and placing of the legs, arms and feet to best advantage. Until the 1880s, when faster dry photographic plates came into common use, thus reducing the exposure time needed for the photograph, posing stands were regularly used to help sitters maintain their pose: some were free-standing, while others were attached to chairs, and some involved uncomfortable head clamps. Women's full skirts usually covered the bases of the stands effectively although close inspection of men's and children's portraits may reveal the stand behind the feet (Ch 2 Fig. 13). Studios used multi-lensed cameras and usually took up to four different poses at the time of the sitting: once proof sheets had been printed, these were shown to the customer who could then choose which portrait(s) they wished to have finished and mounted. The resulting pictures expressed the photographer's skills and professional reputation and they also reflected the fashionable photographic conventions which prevailed at the time - changing ideas about composition and tastes in backdrops, furniture and other complementary props. These shifting elements can help with dating the visual image.

Dating the composition and setting

Whatever the date, groups of 2 or more people always appear full-length (or almost full-length) in a studio photograph, as the camera had to move back to include everyone in the frame - seen for example in Ch 2 Figs. 3, 6, 13, 22, 23, 27, 28, 34 & 45). In 1840s and 1850s daguerreotypes and ambrotypes, single figures are usually depicted close-up, next to a cloth-covered table (Ch 2 Figs. 1, 2, 4 & 5 and Ch 4 Fig. 7). By the 1860s, for which decade photographs survive in greater numbers, a completely different composition and studio setting was being used. In early cartes de visites, single subjects are usually posed full-length in a mock drawing-room interior, nearly always with a draped curtain to one side and standing with elbow or hand resting on a strategically-placed piece of furniture (Ch 2 Figs. 7 & 9-12 and Ch 4 Figs. 13 & 25). Middle-aged or elderly sitters, meanwhile, usually appear full-length but seated at a table (Ch 2 Fig. 8 and Ch 3 Title Picture). Solid architectural devices - plinths and pedestals, classical columns, urns and balustrades and staircases - often crop up in studio sets of the 1860s and early 1870s (Ch 2 Figs. 6, 7, 10, 12 and Ch.4. Fig. 27). A painted backdrop may also be present: Fig. 8 is an unusually elaborate example, but a more common 1860s theme was a painted window, door or archway, perhaps offering a glimpse of a 'landscape' beyond (Ch 4 Figs. 13, 21 & 25).

The convention for whole-length single figures in a room setting drifted over into the early 1870s and recurs from time to time throughout the decade, as seen in Ch 2 Figs. 16 & 17. However usually during the 1870s and 1880s, the camera moved in closer toward the subject and took three-quarter length views in which the lower legs and feet are cut off (Ch 2 Figs. 14, 15, 18-20 & 25 and Ch 4 Figs. 5, 11 & 19). Figures may be seated, perhaps at a table, and sometimes hold a book or another personal accessory (Ch 2 Figs. 15 & 20), while standing subjects usually lean in a relaxed manner on, or over, the back of a chair, if the setting is a room interior (Ch 2 Figs. 14 & 19) or support themselves on a fence or balustrade in the case of mock outdoor settings (Ch 4 Figs. 5 & 19). Since less background appears in the frame of close-up photographs, furniture features more prominently in the foreground and these props can help to some extent with dating. The velvet padded chairs with a rolled back seen in Ch 2 Figs. 14 & 19 and in Ch.4 Fig. 4, and a similar velvet chair with fringing noticed in Ch 2 Fig. 16, represent a style of seat which first appears in the late 1860s and is very common in studio sets of the 1870s, being used less by the 1880s. During this period, chairs in general are solid and often upholstered in fabric or leather and ornamented with fringing, tassels and pom poms (Ch 2 Fig. 20; see also Ch.4 Fig. 11 and Ch.5 Fig. 7)

1880s photographs present a more varied array of scenes. Interior settings remain fashionable, (Ch 2 Figs. 23 & 25 and Ch 5 Figs. 9, 11 & 12) but there is also a new vogue for more naturalistic 'outdoor' studio settings, sometimes featuring a painted rustic-looking backdrop, while in the foreground bark-covered fences and gates, 'weathered' masonry, imitation grass underfoot and ferns are all common (Ch 2 Fig. 22 and Ch.4. Figs. 5 & 19). Marine themes - mastheads, ships' decking, ropes, rocks and painted backdrops depicting the sea or beach - are also popular, these settings especially favoured by studios in tourist seaside resorts (Ch 2 Fig. 24). Other 1880s props which offer quite specific dating clues are swings suspended on ropes - popular for young ladies in early 1880s 'outdoor' scenes - and shaggy rugs, used either on the floor (Ch 2 Fig. 23) or draped over a chair (Ch 5 Fig. 9). From the later 1880s onwards and, especially, throughout the 1890s, plant stands and potted plants may crop up in interior room sets (Ch 2 Fig. 28 and Ch 4 Figs. 20 & 30). As usual, late-century group photographs of two or more people are posed in - or almost - full-length (Ch 2 Figs. 27 & 28 and Ch 4 Figs. 14, 15, 23, 24 & 33). Following 1870s and 1880s trends, single subjects are often photographed in three-quarter length during the 1890s (Ch 4 Figs. 20 & 30); however a very popular composition current between the end of the 1880s and beginning of the 1900s - one which almost dominated the 1890s - is the head and shoulders oval vignette, in which the central portrait fades away around the edges into a blank background (Ch 2 Figs. 29, 31 and Ch 4 Figs. 6, 8 & 16).

In early 20th century studio photographs single figures are usually represented full-length or long three quarter-length (Ch 2 Figs. 32 & 35-7). Many late-19th century features continue into the beginning of the 1900s: potted palms or other plants and ornate wicker or cane furniture in the *art nouveau* style are popular props (Ch 2 Fig.

32 and Ch 5 Fig. 17). As the Edwardian decade advanced and during the early 1910s, painted backgrounds are often cloudy and indistinct, vaguely suggesting shrubbery and leafy glades, while in the foreground clients pose by realistic-looking stone plinths, pedestals and balustrades (Ch 2 Figs. 34-36). Studio room sets of the 1910s are plainer than during the Victorian and Edwardian eras, reflecting more modern tastes in interior decoration: typically they show blank-walled or wood-panelled rooms, often featuring painted bookshelves and curtained, small-paned windows and simpler furniture - long bench seats and solid-looking wooden chairs (Ch.4 Figs. 2, 36). Hazy backdrops and plain styles of furniture continue into the 1920s: groups may still be photographed in full length (Ch.4 Figs. 37 & 38) but the distinguishing trend with small groups and single portraits from the late-1910s onwards, continuing throughout the 1920s, 1930s and 1940s, is for close-up head and shoulders shots focusing on the head and upper body, with close attention paid to camera angle and lighting (Ch 2 Figs. 40 & 44 and Ch.4 Figs. 9, 17 & 39).

Fashion in photographs

Identifying different compositions and studio settings takes care of one aspect of dating the visual image, when the photograph is a professional indoor portrait, but these clues are not present in open-air photographs and for these images it is usually dress that offers the best evidence of date. In any old photograph, whatever the format, it is very often the style of the clothing worn that strikes us most - the appearance of garments which, even when fashionable only 60 or 70 years ago, look so different to modern styles and vividly evoke a sense of the past.

From the earliest days of portrait photography, it was understood that clients visiting the photographer's studio would arrive dressed in their finest, most fashionable clothing. Even ordinary working-class ancestors donned their 'Sunday best' for the occasion as they wished to create a good impression in the special portraits which would be proudly shown to family and friends. Picture researchers often wonder whether poorer forebears would have looked very up to date or fashionable in photographs, so it is useful to consider the concept of 'fashion' and what it meant to past generations. By the time photography reached the masses in the 1860s, the notion of fashion was already well-established. Information about new styles was widely available from the pictorial fashion plates and paper patterns for home dressmaking which featured in magazines and also from the photographs of the rich and famous in wide circulation. In addition, it was the job of professional tailors, dressmakers and milliners to keep abreast of fashionable innovations and to stock the latest fabrics and trimmings. Since relatively few female garments were available ready-made in the shops in the 19th and very early 20th centuries, in Britain there operated numerous affordable independent seamstresses and dressmakers who catered for the lower-middle and working classes, while many women made some clothes at home. So, when ancestors bought, made, or ordered new garments, they could update their personal image according to the most recent style, and when garments grew outmoded, if still wearable they were re-made according to the latest fashions. In the past, families spent comparatively more of their income on clothing than most of us do nowadays and took good care of their clothes so that they would last. The material was the most expensive part of an outfit and different fabrics were available to suit different pockets, so it was the quality of the fabric and extravagance of the trimmings that distinguished the dress of the wealthy from that of the working classes - not, in general, its shape or cut. Thus the notion of what *looked* fashionable was understood across the social spectrum and even poorer ancestors able to finance a visit to the photographer could equally afford to follow the prevailing fashionable style. This means that in most conventional studio photographs our forebears are wearing fairly up to date garments, more or less in keeping with the times.

The various fashions worn in the past having been well researched and their period of popularity carefully charted, it is possible to identify and date these successfully where they occur in old photographs. Essentially it is the shape, or silhouette, of clothing on the body which defines the styles of a given era. The fashionable female silhouette during the period of photography was formed by the corsets, crinolines, bustles and other under-structures worn beneath clothing, which produced a succession of very distinctive, dateable 'looks', while male styles derived from more subtle shifts in tailoring which created either a slender or bulkier silhouette. At any time the basic image was completed by important elements such as sleeve shapes, neck wear, ornamental trimmings and complementary accessories and hairstyles (and facial hair for men). Children wore garments which followed certain juvenile conventions but also mirrored adult styles to a degree, their clothing becoming more 'grown-up' as they grew older. Boys dressed as men by their early 'teens' (a word not used until the 20th century), or in some cases earlier, while girls progressively lowered their skirts and finally wore floor-length hemlines and put their hair up like women at some point between the ages of fifteen and eighteen. Predictably, in photographs young adults in their late teens and twenties are usually the most fashionably-attired, although many mature and middle-aged ladies did maintain a keen sense of style, as seen for example in Ch 2 Figs. 14 & 20 and 44 & 47. Female fashions altered regularly in the past and consequently the dress worn by women in photographs can often be dated to within around five years, sometimes less. Men's styles evolved more gradually and, male garments being essentially more uniform, in some cases their images may only be placed accurately within a decade. Elderly ancestors and relatives are usually dressed most conservatively since they were generally slower to adopt new styles and may have modified certain extreme fashions, although certain elements of older ladies' dress, especially headwear, are recognisable and dateable in their own right. In general, in mixed group photographs, it is the clothing of younger people, especially of young or young-ish women, that will offer the closest date range for a photograph.

Location may sometimes have a bearing on dress, as there would have been a slight time lag between new fashions first appearing in cities and spreading to rural areas: the length of the delay is difficult to judge precisely as it varied according to the place and the person, although it is rare to see very outmoded styles in formal studio photographs. Some minor regional clothing variations existed in the 19th century and early 20th centuries, for example in Wales and Ireland, although Britain has not the strong tradition of folk dress which survived in many European countries. Specific local styles are only very occasionally evident in family photographs and when they do occur tend to be expressed in distinctive headwear and other accessories, while main garments generally conform to the prevailing fashions and can be dated in the usual way. Similar issues apply to photographs taken abroad depicting ancestors who were born in other countries, or had emigrated from Britain or were posted overseas temporarily with their jobs (see Ch 2 Fig. 12 and Ch 4 Fig. 18). Certain differences did emerge between the clothing worn in the outposts of the British Empire or in newly-settled areas of the world and that worn at 'home', but by the era of photography such variations were not as great as we might imagine. Settlers leading outdoor, rough and ready lifestyles no doubt adopted plain and practical garments for everyday wear, but if they did visit a photographer's studio they followed convention by wearing respectable, fashionable 'Sunday best'. By the second half of the 19th century, although news and supplies might take several months, or even a year or two to reach outlying areas, on the whole regular postal and personal communications, newspaper advertisements and shipments of goods kept overseas communities abreast of the main fashionable developments in Europe. To summarise the point about possible variations in dress, where a family's geographical location, or a subject's age or status suggests that they may not have been very up to date in their dress, an extension of a few years to the usual date range should effectively cover most deviations from the fashionable norm.

Occupation is sometimes apparent from the clothing seen in photographs, for example if the subject is wearing a civilian uniform, like a nurse's, postman's or fireman's regulation outfit, or special work attire such as domestic servants' livery, which is an archaic form of dress. Often a new job or a promotion at work inspired forebears to wear occupational garments to the photographer's studio, to express their new role, or perhaps they appear in a 'team' or group photograph with their work colleagues (Ch 6 Figs. 16 & 19). Military uniforms are another, distinctive type of clothing, common in wartime photographs (Ch 2 Fig. 49 and Ch 4 Fig. 17) but also worn by career servicemen at other times (for example Ch 5 Figs. 19 & 21). Uniforms are best dated and analysed by military specialists whose expertise lies in identifying badges, medals, and the changing forms of army, naval and air force dress (for books on this subject see Bibliography). Practical work gear may be glimpsed in casual amateur snapshots which captured spontaneous everyday situations, although when working-class ancestors visited the photographer's studio they usually wore their best fashionable outfits, which usually give no hint of their line of work (see for example Ch 2 Fig. 19). Occasionally 'fancy dress', as worn for parties and theatrical productions, or other picturesque forms of clothing occur in photographs, for example novelties picked up as souvenirs on trips to Eastern countries, and these unfamiliar garments can present a challenge. However the wearers will usually still have their hair dressed in the fashionable style of the era. Hair is always very sensitive to fashion, so in general, even if dress appears irregular and difficult to pinpoint, if nothing else, hairstyles will generally offer an accurate time frame.

Many family historians are interested in costume history and may already have some idea of how their forebears would have looked at different times. However for those who are not familiar with fashions from the past, there are various books written by dress historians covering fashion in paintings, photographs and so on, as listed in the Bibliography. Certainly a detailed visual survey of Victorian and early 20th century fashion ideally warrants a whole book, while here space only permits a brief summary of the main developments: however the following tips, based on both specialised dress history knowledge and experience of dating and analysing the clothing seen in many thousands of family photographs, aim to offer a practical guide to the kinds of fashion features which researchers will encounter in their own inherited photographs. Each visual clue mentioned here is referenced to relevant photographs wherever they appear throughout the book.

Dating women's dress 1840s - 1940s

1840s-1868
Between the 1840s and mid-1860s, essentially the fashionable female silhouette comprised a tight-fitting bodice attached to a full, bell-shaped skirt, which became even wider following the introduction of the circular crinoline frame in 1856 (Ch 2 Figs. 1, 4, 5 & 7, Chapter 4 Figs. 13, 21, 31 & 32, Ch 5 Fig. 1 and Ch 6 Fig. 1). By 1860 skirts were vast in circumference, but soon after this they began to loose their bulk and progressively the front of the skirt grew flatter while the fullness became concentrated increasingly at the back, as seen especially in photographs after mid-decade (Ch 2 Fig. 10, Ch 4 Fig. 25 and Ch 5 Fig. 2). For most of the 1840s, sleeves were narrow and tight-fitting (Ch 2 Fig. 1) although by late-decade wider sleeves

were becoming fashionable; the flared *pagoda* style prevailed throughout the 1850s (Ch 2 Fig. 4, Ch.4 Fig. 31 and Ch 6 Fig. 1) and may still be seen at the beginning of the 1860s (Ch 2 Figs. 5-7). The closed *bishop* sleeve, fitted at the cuff, was an alternative style popular from around 1860 and after c.1862 this was the usual shape (Ch 2 Fig. 10, Ch.4 Figs. 13, 21 & 25 and Ch 5 Fig. 1). Sometimes stylish outdoor garments are seen in photographs and for much of the 1860s short, wide jackets complemented the full crinoline skirts (Ch.4 Figs. 25 & 32 and Ch 6 Fig. 25).

The principal hairstyle of the early-mid 1840s was curled ringlets, as seen in artworks in Ch 1; between the late-1840s and beginning of the 1860s hair was usually centrally-parted and drawn down smoothly over the ears into a low chignon worn at the back of the neck (Ch 2 Figs. 4, 5 & 7, Ch 4 Fig. 31 and Ch 6 Fig. 1). The hair may, though, be partly concealed in photographs showing older or mature married ladies wearing an indoor cap, as was customary in the mid-19th century (Ch 2 Figs. 1 & 5, Ch 4 Fig. 7 and Ch 6 Fig. 1). During the early 1860s the hair was beginning to be drawn back behind the ears (Ch 4 Figs. 13, 21 & 32), while occasionally one or two coils of hair were brought forward over the shoulders (Ch 5 Fig. 1). From mid-decade onwards, the chignon was worn noticeably higher and the hair continued to rise during the later 1860s (Ch 2 Fig. 10 and Ch 4 Fig. 25). Bonnets were the usual outdoor headwear until around 1860 and they remained fashionable, especially for older and conservative ladies (Ch 6 Fig. 25) although during the early-mid 1860s younger women often wore neat round 'pork pie' hats, or straw hats, trimmed with feathers, flowers or ribbons (Ch.4 Figs. 25 & 32).

1869-75
A new female silhouette is evident in many photographs by c.1869, skirts having become progressively flatter in front during the later 1860s and the crinoline frame eventually discarded in favour of a crinolette or half-crinoline, worn behind the waist, which produced a slight back projection: by the end of the decade this had developed into a pronounced bustle and photographs generally show skirts and long bodices layered or draped up in swathes, *polonaise*-style, to accommodate the new style (Ch 2 Figs. 11 & 12, Ch 4 Fig. 27 and Ch 5 Fig. 3). Often bodices and overskirts were trimmed with decorative fringing at this time, while prominent jewellery and large neck bows were becoming fashionable (Ch 2 Fig. 12, Ch 4 Fig. 27 and Ch 5 Fig. 3). The exuberant and feminine look was fully established by 1870 and this remained the height of fashion until c.1875. Photographs of the early 1870s show skirts draped up over a curvaceous bustle, the bodices featuring either high collars or low, square necklines, ornamented with frills and bows, and made with open or closed sleeves (Ch 2 Figs. 14 & 16, Ch 4 Fig. 26, Ch 5 Figs. 5 & 6 and Ch 6 Figs. 2 & 26). The distinctive silhouette of these years is seen best in full-length or standing figures such as Ch 2 Fig. 16 and Ch 5 Fig. 6; the bustle may not be so

obvious when women are seated, or portrayed in three-quarter length, as is often the case, but the layered and flounced skirts and fashionable ornamentation on the bodice are generally clear. Hairstyles were also especially elaborate, being worn high on the head and sometimes incorporating plaits (Ch 2 Figs. 14 &16) or long tresses (Ch 2 Fig. 14 & Ch 5 Fig. 6). The high-piled hairstyles demanded a different style of hat and during the early 1870s jaunty brimmed hats perched forward over the chignon, the crowns trimmed with feathers or flowers (Ch 6 Fig. 26).

1876-83

Fashion divides the 1870s into two quite distinct halves, with a transitional period occurring in around 1875. By c.1876 photographs usually show the effects on clothing of the new, long *cuirass* bodice, a rigid corset which moulded the body and extended in an unbroken line over the hips, forcing the early-1870s bustle downwards. The fashionable narrow line now evolving was either expressed in a hip-length bodice (or jacket) and skirt (Ch 2 Fig. 18) or a slender, front-buttoning one-piece 'princess' dress (Ch 2 Figs. 17 & 20 and Ch 5 Figs. 7 & 8). From c.1876 until around 1880, photographs show narrowing skirts wrapped or gathered across the legs at the front while initially the collapsing bustle cascades into a swathe of drapery at the back of the skirt, ending in a long train until c.1880 - a style most easily recognised in full-length photographs like Ch 2 Fig. 17 and Ch 5 Figs. 7 & 8. Three-quarter length views do, though, demonstrate the elongated, figure-hugging bodice and the vogue for bands of decorative fringing and narrow pleats decorating the skirt (Ch 2 Figs. 18 & 20). By 1880 the long skirt train had largely disappeared from daywear and the narrow, sheath-like silhouette continued into the early 1880s, slightly shorter skirts worn just off the ground and typically ornamented with gathers, ruches and rows of pleats (Ch 2 Figs. 21 & 22, Ch 4 Fig. 19 and Ch 5 Fig. 9). Outdoor garments, when seen, followed the narrow, minimalist line with short shoulder capes or the long slender *pelisse* coat (Ch 5 Fig. 9).

Headwear, which changed frequently, may offer a close dating guide: in photographs of the later 1870s the bonnets still worn by mature ladies and the stylish hats favoured by younger women followed the vertical silhouette by growing taller in the front (Ch 2 Figs. 17 & 18 and Ch 5 Fig. 8). By the early 1880s, hats were more rounded in shape, either made in the soft *tocque* style without a brim, or with a small brim, these often trimmed with feathers (Ch 2 Figs. 21 & 22 and Ch 5 Fig. 9). Meanwhile some fashionable women began to wear curled or softly-waved fringes in the later 1870s, a hairstyle which extended into the 1880s (Ch 2 Figs. 18 & 20, Ch 4 Fig. 19 and Ch 5 Fig. 9).

1884-9

In around 1883/4 fashion decreed a return of the bustle and by 1884 signs of the new style are usually evident in photographs. Initially this may be glimpsed from extra drapery appearing at the back of the skirt (Ch.5 Fig. 10). Once established, this second bustle was worn with a skirt featuring a horizontally-draped apron front, the fabric behind being bunched up over the projection: teamed with a very close-fitting front-buttoning bodice with narrow sleeves and high, tight neckline this produced an uncompromising effect commonly seen in photographs from c.1884/5 until c.1889 (Ch 2 Fig. 25, Ch.5 Fig. 11 & Ch 6 Fig. 3). At the same time, fashionable hairstyles became sleeker and more severe: sometimes a fringe-like effect was retained but otherwise hair was drawn off the face and dressed tightly to the head, a small chignon being wound neatly on the top (Ch 2 Fig. 25, Ch 4 Fig. 5, Ch 5 Fig. 11 and Ch 6 Figs. 3 & 4). Other 1880s stylistic clues include circular, frill-like white collars, worn sometimes c.1883-8 to enliven plain bodices (Ch 2 Fig. 23, Ch 4 Fig. s19 & 28), while at the end of the decade, from around 1888, more complex styles of bodice appear, featuring *plastron* fronts with inserts, mock waistcoat fronts with V-necklines and lapels and other arrangements with panels of contrasting fabrics (Ch 4 Fig. 5, Ch 5 Fig. 12 and Ch 6 Fig. 4). By c.1889 fashionable women were discarding the bustle, their skirts still slightly padded around the hips but no longer draped in front and generally worn with a pointed bodice (Ch 4 Fig. 5). Headwear changed again: as the decade progressed, all types of hats and bonnets grew taller, a narrow, towering style very much in evidence by the end of the decade (Ch 4 Figs. 1 & 8 and Ch 5 Fig. 12). Only older ladies wore a matronly white day cap, some elaborate examples of the 1880s being made of lace and featuring trailing lappets (Ch 6 Figs. 3 & 4)

1890s

Early-1890s photographs continue the styles of the previous years: plain skirts - slightly padded around the hips - worn with tight-fitting panelled bodices combining velvet with woollen cloth or using other contrasting fabrics (Ch 4 Figs. 14 & 23 and Ch 5 Fig. 13). A significant dating clue relating to the bodice, seen between around 1890 and 1892, is a small vertical puff at the shoulder - a subtle but important feature which represented the beginnings of the puffed *gigot* or 'leg-o'-mutton' sleeve (Ch 2 Fig. 27, Ch 4 Figs. 14 & 33 and Ch 5 Fig. 13). Changing sleeve shapes, which offer a very helpful dating guide for this decade, are seen most clearly in the formal, more structured bodices usually worn for studio portraits. Increasing fullness is generally noticed in the upper arm by c.1893-4 (Ch 2 Fig. 28), while photographs of 1895-6 tend to demonstrate the widest sleeves, as well as some of the most decorative dress bodices (Ch 2 Fig. 29, Ch 4 Fig. 6, Ch 5 Fig. 14 and Ch 6 Fig. 6). Sleeves might still appear very full and rounded in 1897 (Ch 5 Fig. 15 and possibly Ch 4 Fig. 34), although the puff was already beginning to withdraw up the arm and, in other photographs of the same year, it may be seen deflating and changing shape (Ch 4 Figs. 29 & 30). Finally, in photographs taken between c.1898 and 1900 the sleeve is generally narrow but retains residual detailing at the top of the arm towards the shoulder - a small puff, frill, epaulette or rows of tucks (Ch 5 Figs. 16 & 17). (Note that exceptions to these sleeve shapes may be noticed on the white cotton blouses which were often teamed with plain skirts as more practical outfits, for these tended to retain their full sleeves until around 1900 (Ch 2 Fig. 30 and Ch 6 Figs. 6 & 27-29)). Meanwhile by late decade a curvaceous *art nouveau*-inspired silhouette was also evolving, the waistline of the jacket or bodice nipped in tightly while the skirt clung closely to the hips before flaring gently outwards toward the hemline - lines seen best on standing figures (Ch 4 Figs. 20 & 30).

Hairstyles and headwear are also very sensitive to fashion. During the early 1890s, hairstyles were tightly dressed, drawn high off the face and often featured the neat chignon on top of the head, familiar from the late 1880s (Ch 2 Figs. 27 & 28 and Ch 4 Fig. 33). From around mid-decade onwards younger women in particular are often noticed wearing a lower chignon behind the back of the head, while the front hair may be slightly frizzed, waved or rolled softly back off the face (Ch 2 Fig. 29, Ch 4 Figs. 6, 20, 29 & 30, Ch 5 Fig. 14 and Ch 6 Fig. 6). The tall headwear of the late 1880s rapidly lowered, fashionable styles of the 1890s ranging widely from delicate confections of lace, ribbons, feathers and flowers pinned to the hair (Ch 5 Fig. 14), through straw boaters for summer wear and brimmed hats with solid crowns, ornamented with bows or feathers (Ch 4 Fig. 20). By mid-decade the elaborate hats worn for formal occasions such as weddings rested plate-like on the head, heaped with bows, flowers and feathers (Ch 5 Fig. 14); these hats grew larger and more extreme by the year so that by the turn of the decade they were very wide-brimmed and bore profuse ornamentation (Ch 5 Figs. 16 & 17).

1900-09

The fashionable lines of the late 1890s continued into the early 1900s as an exaggerated hourglass silhouette: this was demonstrated strikingly in lavish evening wear - rarely seen in family photographs - but a modest version of the style is evident in day wear. Formal dress bodices or blouses were puffed in front to emphasise the bust and were decorated variously with ornamental frills, lace bands, inserts or collars and rows of tucks, while plain skirts were expertly tailored with panels to create a small waist and smooth fit over the hips, flounces often accentuating the sweeping hemlines (Ch 2 Figs. 32 & 33, Ch 4 Fig. 35 and Ch 6 Fig. 7). Blouses and bodices were generally high-necked for most of the Edwardian era but sleeve shapes can, again, help to narrow the date. Between around 1901 and 1904, sleeves were are usually narrow in the arm, sometimes fitted at the wrist (Ch 6 Fig. 30) though more often showing a fullness at the wrist where they gathered into a small cuff (Ch 2 Figs. 32 & 33, Ch 4 Fig. 35 and Ch 6 Fig. 7). Moving forward, between c.1905 and c.1908, the elbow area tended to be emphasised with deeper cuffs, three-quarter length sleeves, or puffs or flounces around elbow level (Ch 2 Fig. 35 and Ch 5 Figs. 19-21). While elaborate blouses and bodices were worn for special occasions, plainer versions were usual for ordinary wear and during the later 1890s and early 1900s, many younger - and some older - women adopted a combination of plain, full-sleeved white blouse, worn with a tie or bow tie (Ch 6 Fig.s 6 & 27-29).

Photographs of the early 1900s show hairstyles becoming softer and fuller, a small 'cottage loaf' bun or knot sometimes glimpsed on top of the head early in the decade (Ch 2 Fig. 33 and Ch 6 Fig. 7). Fashionable headwear includes summer boaters and other straw brimmed hats (Ch 2 Fig. 35 and Ch 6 Fig. 30), while very ornate styles are worn for weddings and formal events. The shape of hats can often help to narrow down the date of an Edwardian photograph. The late-1890s plate-like edifices heaped high with bows and feathers were still fashionable early in the decade (Ch 5 Fig. 17) but by around 1904 were giving way to wide, flat styles in which crown and brim appear to merge (Ch 5 Fig. 19); by c.1906/7 the crowns were rising and appear almost as wide as the brim, creating a gateaux-like effect, while neater, brimless tocques, trimmed with fabric and ostrich feathers were also popular (Ch 5 Figs. 20 & 21).

1910-1918
Fashions of the new decade were characterised by a more natural shape and a decline in fussy ornamentation. The evolution of a slimmer, less cluttered, slightly high-waisted line may be glimpsed in photographs as early as 1908/9 but is noticed more from around 1910 onwards. In the early-1910s standing views may show fairly narrow skirts and, when the woman is portrayed in full-length, a shorter hemline can be seen, ending at around ankle level (Ch 2 Figs. 36 & 37). Between c.1909 and 1914, one-piece dresses were typically caught in at the waist, or a little higher, and might be layered, tunic-style, an elbow-length overdress often being worn over a long-sleeved under dress, or contrasting fabric used to suggest separate layers, or a *chemisette* (blouse) worn beneath a lower-necked garment (Ch 2 Fig. 38, Ch 4 Fig. 2 and Ch 5 Figs. 22 & 23). A high, choker-style Edwardian collar still occurs during the early 1910s (Ch 6 Fig. 31), but from around 1911, slightly lower, rounded necklines appear more often, especially on younger women, offering a useful dating clue (Ch 2 Figs. 37 & 38 and Ch 5 Fig. 22). For everyday wear, the plain blouse and skirt combination was usual, a white shirt-like blouse and tie combination remaining popular with younger women and also being worn by older schoolgirls (Ch 2 Fig. 36 and Ch 6 Fig. 9). A smart tailored jacket was worn outdoors and these separates were even acceptable for special social occasions (Ch

5 Fig. 23). In 1915 a major change occurred in the fashionable silhouette as much fuller, shorter skirts came into vogue: this development may be hard to discern, especially in photographs of older or seated subjects (Ch 2 Fig. 39), but the new style calf-length, flared skirt is often evident in both one-piece dresses and tailored skirts. At around the same time, blouses and bodices acquired a V-neckline with a pronounced collar or flat reveres, and together these fashion details help with dating most photographs taken between c.1915 and c.1918 (Ch 4 Fig. 36, Ch 5 Figs. 24 & 25 and Ch 6 Fig. 20).

In the early-1910s, formal hats were still decorative, wide brims ornamented with sweeping feathers or ribbon arrangements and often worn tilted on the head (Ch 2 Fig. 37 and Ch 5 Figs. 22 & 23), while hats worn for ordinary occasions were more modest in their size and decoration (Ch 6 Fig. 31). Photographs of c.1910-13/14 usually show the hair drawn up in wide swathes above the ears on either side of a centre parting (Ch 2 Figs. 36 & 38 and Ch 4 Fig. 2), but from around 1914/15 onwards, styles begins to look smoother, a parting sometimes worn in the middle or to one side and the length of the hair drawn back more naturally (Ch 4 Fig. 36, Ch 5 Figs. 24 & 25 and Ch 6 Figs. 9 & 19). Meanwhile from mid-decade onwards, formal hats become plainer, often made with very wide brims and rounded crowns trimmed with a simple hatband (Ch 5 Figs. 24 & 25) while neater styles were worn for every day wear (Ch 6 Figs. 20 and 43). Older ladies at this time often favoured close-fitting, narrow-brimmed hats or soft, brimless tocques (Ch 5 Fig. 25)

1919-30
Post-WW1 photographs show that fashion favoured loose, draped styles that tend to look rather shapeless. Dresses of c.1918/19-22 when seen in full length typically display a barrel-like silhouette, the waistline placed just a little higher than natural level and the folds of fabric bulging outwards towards a straight, low calf-length hemline (Ch 5 Fig. 26 and Ch 6 Fig. 10). Another dating clue is the vogue for large collars on blouses and dresses, which may still be a prominent feature in the early 1920s (Ch 2 Fig. 40, Ch 5 Fig. 26 and Ch 6 Figs. 10 & 11). Coats of this period appear loose and capacious and reveal a fashion for broad fur collars (Ch 6 Fig. 33). With amateur snapshots becoming more common after the war, we begin to see a wider range of occasions being depicted in photographs. For example, in summer beach scenes swimwear may be glimpsed, demonstrating the modest bathing suits with short sleeves and legs that were still worn for most of the 1920s (Ch.6 Fig. 35). Many young women had cut their hair short during the later war years, or did so soon afterwards: this provides a dating clue as bobbed hair is unlikely to occur in photographs before around 1916 or 1917 but is more common by the new decade. A popular alternative was for slightly longer hair to be neatly pinned back (Ch 2 Fig. 40). Headwear was very varied in the early 1920s, both wide and narrow-

brimmed hats usually displaying deep crowns, while helmet-like hats with small peaks and squashy brimless beret- or tocque-style hats made in velvet or other soft fabrics were also fashionable (Ch 5 Fig. 26 and Ch 6 Figs. 11 & 33).

Blouses and skirts remained popular as ever, but as 1920s styles evolved a distinctive dress style is seen in photographs from c.1923 onwards - straight, untailored garments left unbelted or secured loosely with a fabric belt at low waist level: made now without a collar, typically the neckline is low and rounded, the plainer neck area invariably set off by a string of pearls or beads (Ch 4 Figs. 37 & 38 and Ch 5 Fig. 28). Where figures are seen in full-length, the hemline offers a very important dating clue for the 1920s. Until 1925 hemlines were long, always ending at mid-low calf level (Ch 4 Figs. 37 & 38 and Ch 5 Figs. 26-28), but in photographs of between c.1926 and 1930, the new fashion for much shorter skirts is evident. Young women of this so-called 'flapper' era wore the shortest dresses and skirts, ending on or just below the knee: the fashion extended to smart suits, bridal wear, narrow coats and simple shift-like dresses for summer, worn with pale or flesh-coloured stockings and bar shoes (Ch 2 Fig. 42, Ch 5 Fig. 29 and Ch 6 Fig. 36). Short bobbed haircuts also become more apparent in photographs as the decade advances (Ch 2 Fig. 42, Ch 4 Figs. 37 & 38, Ch 5 Figs. 28 & 29 and Ch 6 Fig. 36). Hats often have wide brims, especially for summer, but from c.1925, until after 1930, the close-fitting cloche hat, pulled down low is the most characteristic style (Ch 5 Fig. 28 and Ch 6 Fig. 36).

1930s
Although this decade may be within living memory for some family historians, the appearance of relatives in snapshots and studio photographs of the era can sometimes be difficult to date accurately. As in the 1920s, hairstyles, hats (when worn) and hemlines provide some of the most useful pointers. In the early-mid 1930s fashionable hairstyles were still short, but often appear softer, more waved than previously (Ch 2 Figs. 44 & 45, Ch 4 Figs. 9 & 39, Ch 5 Fig. 30 and Ch 6 Fig. 24), although older women's hairdressing was not always up to the minute and in some spontaneous photographs showing everyday occasions their hairstyles are hard to date closely (Ch 6 Fig. 12). In the early-1930s stylish hats were often neat, continuing the close-fitting cloche shape of the late 1920s or introducing soft beret or pull-on beanie styles (Ch 2 Fig. 44 and Ch 5 Fig. 30) although the 1920s vogue for wide-brimmed picture hats continued for formal occasions and summer wear (Ch 5 Fig. 30). Coats and jackets of the early-1930s might still feature the luxurious deep fur collars of the 1920s, worn high at the neck (Ch 2 Fig. 44 and Ch 5 Fig. 30).

Full-length photographs show that by around 1930 some women's hemlines were already becoming slightly fuller and longer, and from c.1932 until at least 1936, there was a return to calf-length hemlines and a preference for soft, draped fabrics. Formal dresses were often cocktail length, worn almost to the ankle (Ch 2 Fig. 45) and this also influenced bridesmaids' styles (Ch 5 Fig. 30). Some of the fashion features that help to date photographs of the early-mid 1930s are V-necklines, lace or embroidery decoration (for 'best'), draped, layered outfits comprising long jackets and loose, knitted cardigans, scalloped edgings, brooches and buckled belts (Ch 2 Fig. 45, Ch 4 Fig. 9 and Ch 6 Fig. 12). From around 1936 onwards signs of a changing silhouette may be evident, for a sharper, more tailored look was evolving, the new style being well established by the outbreak of war in 1939. Late-decade photographs reveal young and stylish older women adopting padded shoulders, smart fitted dresses, lapelled jackets and shorter hemlines again, and in some cases fuller and longer hairstyles (Ch 2 Figs. 47 & 48 and Ch 5 Fig. 32). Hats of the later 1930s are also more structured, sometimes asymmetrical in shape, usually made with brims and worn at an angle (Ch 2 Fig. 47 and Ch 5 Fig. 32)

1940s

The Second World War and its aftermath dominated dress during this decade. Civilian garments were rationed between 1941 and 1949 and the Utility clothing scheme (1942-1952) influenced the design and production of garments and cloth, restricting amounts of fabric and trimmings (including buttons) and inspiring a severe and economical, yet essentially smart female style. Material being in short supply, women's and older girls' dresses and skirts were relatively short, ending just below the knee, and slightly A-line in shape, plain in style or featuring modest pleats (Ch 2 Figs. 49 & 50, Ch 5 Figs. 34-36 and Ch 6 Figs. 13 & 41). Dress bodices were slim-fitting and featured no applied decoration but could be enlivened by a draped cowl neckline (Ch 5 Fig. 34) or ruching of the fabric; dresses (including bridal and bridesmaids' wear), coats and jackets usually demonstrate square padded shoulders until the late 1940s, even after 1950 in some cases (Ch 2 Fig. 49, Ch 5 Figs. 35-38 and Ch 6 Figs. 41 & 42). Wartime footwear had to be practical and hardwearing and the usual everyday style was a sensible leather laced shoe with a small heel, and for summer substantial sandals (Ch 2 Fig. 49 and Ch 5 Fig. 34), more attractive court shoes or open-toed sandals with higher heels being kept for special occasions (Ch 5 Figs. 35 & 36). By the late 1940s style and variety had returned to footwear, ankle-straps, wedges and peep-toes all being fashionable design elements (Ch 2 Fig. 50 & Ch 6 Fig. 41).

Headwear was not rationed and was an important element of dress during the 1940s: practical headscarves were an everyday sight but in most posed photographs fashionable hats are to be seen - soft hats worn to the back of the head or neat, jaunty hats in the pillbox and other angular styles, often tilted at an angle (Ch 2 Fig. 49 and Ch 5 Figs. 34-37). Hair had been growing longer since the late 1930s and was curled, waved or rolled off the face during the 1940s, presenting a glamourous image (Ch 2 Fig. 50, Ch 4 Fig. 40, Ch 5 Figs. 34-37 and Ch 6 Figs. 42 & 48), although women in the armed forces had to keep their hair shorter, off their collars. In late-decade photographs may be glimpsed elements of the 'New Look', launched in 1947, which introduced more feminine garments characterised by softer, more rounded shoulders and fuller skirts (Ch 4 Fig. 40). The post-war youthful generation was also influenced increasingly by progressive American fashions and so young women are often seen wearing casual but smart separates - slim-fitting, shaped sweaters and stylish skirts, or even trousers, rarely worn before the war (Ch 2 Fig. 50 and Ch 6 Fig. 48). After the war people soon returned to the seaside for their holidays once more and so bathing costumes and summer beachwear crop up frequently in photographs of the later 1940s (Ch 6 Fig. 40).

Dating men's dress 1840s - 1940s

1840s & 1850s
The male three-piece suit was well-established by the time of the earliest family photographs, the 1840s and 1850s suit being narrow in cut and usually comprising a dark knee-length frock coat, slim-fitting trousers and a deep V-fronted waistcoat that exposed the shirt front; neck wear completed the outfit and a broad black cravat was the usual choice (Ch 2 Fig. 2, Ch 4 Fig. 31 and Ch 6 Fig. 1). Deviations from this formal style may occasionally be seen, for example in photographs of manual or outdoor workers, or those living in hot climates, variations including light-coloured sack coats and more casual styles of scarf, necktie or cravat (Ch 4 Fig. 18). Until the mid-1850s facial hair usually consisted of prominent side burns (Ch 2 Fig. 2), but from around 1856 onwards mature men were beginning to wear beards, a fashion reputedly introduced by soldiers returning home from the Crimean War. Offering a helpful dating clue, these distinctive early beards usually appear as an extension of the sideburns under the jaw and chin, the hair not yet grown around the mouth (Ch 4 Figs. 18 & 31 and Ch 6 Fig. 1). Men usually removed their hats for photographs, the tall 'stove-pipe' top hat, which accompanied the mid-century frock coat, often held or placed on a table (Ch 2 Fig. 2).

1860s
Men's clothing became more diverse during this decade, various casual styles coming into vogue for different occasions. Especially popular by the early 1860s was the new comfortable lounging jacket - a short (hip-length), relatively untailored garment made with small, high lapels and usually worn fastened by only the top

button, a semi-formal style which worked well with the looser fitting trousers of the 1860s. The new easy-fitting lounge suit appears in many photographs of this decade, the lounge jacket either worn with matching trousers and waistcoat, or darker jacket and waistcoat teamed with lighter trousers (Ch 2 Figs. 8 & 9, Ch 4 Fig. 32, Ch 5 Fig. 1 and Ch 6 Fig. 25). The open jacket of the 1860s sometimes revealed a gold watch chain, the chain perhaps suspending a seal, while the watch itself was concealed in a waistcoat pocket (Ch 2 Fig. 8). This symbol of the Victorian businessman was common throughout the 19th century and was still worn by the conservative until well into the 20th century. The more elegant and capacious frock coat with generous lapels, waist seam and thigh- or knee-length skirts is also seen often in 1860s photographs - a traditional style often favoured by older ancestors and still required for formal occasions (Ch 4 Fig. 21, Ch 5 Figs. 2-4 and Ch 6 Fig. 25). Photographs of this decade usually show the familiar top hat accompanying both the lounge suit and frock coat (Ch 2 Figs. 8 & 9, Ch 5 Fig. 2 and Ch 6 Fig. 25) although occasionally the new, less formal bowler hat may be seen (Ch 4 Fig. 32 and Ch 6 Fig. 25). Very young men might still go clean shaven (Ch 2 Fig. 9) but most mature men grew facial hair, either moustaches or beards, or both, beards often very full by now and demonstrating a wide variety of styles (Ch 2 Fig. 8, Ch 5 Figs. 1-4 and Ch 6 Fig. 25).

1870s & 1880s
By the 1870s and 1880s the lounge suit was the customary outfit for everyday wear, and worn for 'best' by the working classes. Photographs of this era show that all three suit pieces often matched, and sometimes the jacket edges are bound with silk braid binding (Ch 2 Figs. 15 & 23). In the early-mid-1870s, the lounge jacket typically featured wide lapels, offering a useful dating clue (Ch 2 Fig. 15, Ch 5 Figs. 5 & 6 and Ch 6 Fig. 2), whereas by the late 1870s and during the 1880s the lapels are usually much neater and smaller, as seen in Ch 2 Fig. 23. There was a general paring down of the suit style at this time and in photographs of the 1880s the lounge suit often looks very narrow in cut (Ch 2 Fig. 21, Ch 5 Fig. 10 and Ch 6 Figs. 4 & 15). The new, slender lines are also seen in another garment, the stylish morning coat, distinguished by its cutaway front edges. First noticed in the 1870s (Ch 2 Fig. 19) this version of the morning coat (there had been earlier styles) remained very fashionable during the 1880s (Ch 5 Figs. 9 & 11). The correct headwear with the lounge and morning suits was the now-popular bowler hat, the crown of the bowler becoming noticeably taller by the mid-1880s and offering another dating clue (Ch 5 Fig. 10 and Ch 6 Fig. 15), although more casual hat styles may be seen in some photographs of the 1870s and 1880s (Ch 6 Figs. 15 & 26). The longer, stately frock coat also occurs in 1870s and 1880s photographs, this conservative garment preferred by some older men and still customary for solemn and formal occasions, a narrower version becoming fashionable at the end of the 1880s (Ch 4 Fig. 26 and Ch 5 Figs. 8 & 12).

During the 1870s shirt collars were often worn turned down (like modern collars), becoming higher again during the 1880s, when a winged collar was popular (Ch 2 Fig. 21, Ch 5 Fig. 11 and Ch 6 Fig. 4): throughout both decades the long 'four in hand' tie, resembling today's knotted tie, may be seen (Ch 2 Fig. 21, Ch 5 Fig. 6 and Ch 6 Fig. 2), other popular styles of neckwear including the Ascot cravat (Ch 2 Fig. 19 and Ch 4 Fig. 26). Another gentlemanly accessory was the handkerchief worn in the top jacket pocket, this becoming a common feature in the 1880s (Ch 2 Fig. 21, Ch 5 Figs. 9-11 and Ch 6 Fig. 15). Styles of facial hair varied widely during the 1870s and 1880s: beards and moustaches could be worn together (Ch 2 Fig. 21, Ch 4 Fig. 26, Ch 5 Fig. 8 and Ch 6 Fig. 15); a beard or bushy whiskers worn without a moustache (Ch 2 Fig. 15 and Ch 6 Figs. 2 & 26); moustaches might be worn on their own (Ch 2 Fig. 23 and Ch 5 Figs. 10-12), while very young men are often clean shaven (Ch 2 Fig. 19 and Ch 5 Fig. 9).

1890s

Photographs of the 1890s can sometimes be difficult to pin down from men's dress alone as there is little that firmly stands out as being typical of this decade in particular. Following 1880s trends, lounge suits were generally fairly narrow in cut at the beginning of the 1890s (Ch 2 Fig. 28 and Ch 4 Fig. 23), while the elegant morning coat worn with narrow grey trousers was a combination that spanned the 1880s and 1890s (Ch 4 Fig. 33). The suit became slightly easier in fit as the decade advanced, made with wider shoulders and, in some cases, longer lapels, as may be noticed in some photographs (Ch 2 Fig. 31, Ch 5 Fig. 15 and Ch 6 Figs. 5, 6 & 17). Again, usually all three suit pieces matched, although contrasting trousers might be worn (Ch 4 Fig. 34 and Ch 6 Fig. 6). Other 1890s features to look for are a white handkerchief in the breast pocket - now a common accessory - or a gold watch chain strung across the waistcoat front (Ch 2 Fig. 28, Ch 4 Fig. 34, Ch 5 Fig. 15), although these were not unique to that decade. Sometimes helpful clues may be gained from smaller details of dress. The formal winged collar - usually worn with a bow tie - and the very high, stiffly starched collar, which was generally teamed with the 'four-in-hand' long knotted tie, were both popular styles of neckwear throughout the decade (Ch 2 Figs. 28 & 31, Ch 4 Fig. 16 and Ch.5 Figs. 13, 14 & 16) although turned down collars may also be seen, worn with the long tie (Ch 4 Figs. 23, 29 & 34 and Ch 5 Fig. 15). Facial hair was still usual, at least for mature men, a moustache often being worn alone (Ch 4 Figs. 29, 33 & 34 and Ch 5 Figs. 13, 14 & 16) or with a beard. The 1890s beard is more easily dateable than those of earlier decades, as by now it is usually very closely trimmed and is sometimes shaped to a neat point, following the style worn by the Prince of Wales (later Edward VII) (Ch 2 Fig. 28, Ch 5 Figs. 14-16 and Ch 6 Figs. 6 & 27). Fashionable young men sometimes wore a pronounced hair parting by this time, the hair oiled flat on either side (Ch 2 Fig. 31, Ch 4 Fig. 33 and Ch 5 Fig. 13). When seen in photographs, hats of the decade range from the silk top hat, still worn for formal occasions (Ch 5 Figs. 13 & 16), through bowler hats, worn for work and working-class 'best' wear (Ch 6 Fig. 17), to more casual felt hats suitable for leisure and sporting activities (Ch 6 Fig. 27).

1900-1919

Men's appearance altered subtly in the new century, remaining fairly static until after the First World War. The regular lounge suit was usually worn in three matching pieces, and in photographs tends to present a neat, somewhat stark appearance. The lounge jacket is typically quite long, made with straight or curved front edges, the lapels generally short in the early 1900s (Ch 2 Fig. 34, Ch 4 Figs. 24 & 35 and Ch 5 Figs. 17 & 18) but often appearing longer by the 1910s - a feature which can help with dating (Ch 2 Fig. 38, Ch 4 Fig. 2, Ch 5 Figs. 22, 24 & 25 and Ch 6 Fig. 31). Throughout the period, trousers (when fully visible) often look rather narrow and may feature distinct centre front creases and turn-ups (Ch 2 Fig. 34, Ch 4 Fig. 2 and Ch 5 Fig. 18). The high starched shirt collar of the 1890s drifted over into the early 1900s, as seen in some Edwardian photographs (Ch 4 Fig. 35, Ch 5 Figs. 18, 19 & 21 and Ch 6 Fig. 18). Standing collars, including winged styles, remained a conservative and formal option in the 1910s, often worn by older men and for special occasions such as weddings (Ch 4 Fig. 24, Ch 5 Figs. 23-25 and Ch 6 Fig. 9). However the more comfortable turned down collar, worn with the long, knotted tie, gradually became established as the norm and this is the style seen most often in early-20th century photographs. Sometimes collars display 'modern'-looking points, especially for casual wear (Ch 6 Figs. 7-9, 29 & 30), although more often the Edwardian and early-1910s collar had distinctive rounded points (Ch 2 Fig. 34, Ch 4 Fig. 2, Ch 5 Figs. 21 & 22 and Ch 6 Fig. 31). From the mid-1910s onwards, softer un-starched collars also begin to occur in photographs, these becoming common after the war (Ch 5 Fig. 24 and Ch 6 Fig. 33). Family photographs of young men in civilian clothing are naturally sparse during the war years (1914-18), wedding photographs of this era usually showing the groom wearing military uniform (Ch 5 Figs. 24 & 25).

Fashions in facial hair also changed in the early 20th century and can assist with closer dating. Young men were already adopting a modern appearance by going clean shaven (Ch 2 Figs. 34 & 38, Ch 4 Fig. 35 and Ch 5 Figs. 17 & 22), although moustaches may still be seen in many photographs of the 1900s and early 1910s (Ch 4 Figs. 2 & 35, Ch 5 Figs. 18-21 and Ch 6 Figs. 7 & 29-31). During and after the war growing numbers of men abandoned the moustache so that by the later 1910s this feature mainly applies to the middle-aged and elderly (Ch 4 Fig. 36 and Ch 5 Figs. 24 & 25). The beard, which gave an air of dignity and authority to Victorian men for over 40 years, is less common in 20th century photographs, although a neatly trimmed beard was often retained, along with a moustache, by some conservative and older men (Ch 4 Fig. 24 & Ch 5 Figs. 21, 23 & 25). Headwear of this period includes the bowler hat, still worn for formal business wear and by the working classes for special occasions (Ch 5 Fig. 22) and a relatively new style of hat - the working man's cloth cap with a small peak. In the early 1900s the cap was round and neat, fitting the head closely (Ch 6 Fig. 18), but over time it grew larger, becoming broader and flatter by the turn of the decade (Ch 6 Fig. 31) For summer wear, the straw boater was very fashionable (Ch 2 Fig. 34 and Ch 6 Fig. 31), while for casual wear broad-brimmed hats with dented crowns were also popular (Ch 6 Figs. 29 & 30). Stylish felt hats were evolving rapidly at this time and by the 1910s new tall-crowned styles such as the 'Homburg', popularised by King Edward VII, were becoming a common sight (Ch 6 Fig. 31).

1920s

In photographs of the 1920s men are still wearing a slender, three-piece lounge suit, the continuing narrow cut being the main feature which distinguishes this decade from later eras. Usually the 1920s jacket has long lapels and the traditional watch chain may still be seen, looped across the waistcoat front (Ch 2 Fig. 41, Ch 5 Figs. 26 & 28). During the 1920s trousers appear narrow and are often worn with creases and turn-ups: made very short, to the ankle, they may reveal either old-fashioned laced boots or lower-cut shoes, most younger men wearing shoes by the 1920s - the more modern and comfortable style of footwear (Ch 2 Fig. 41, Ch 4 Fig. 37 and Ch 5 Fig. 26-29). Various types of neckwear appear in 1920s photographs, usually reflecting the age, status and personal taste of the wearer: older and more conservative men may occasionally wear a high standing or winged collar, perhaps even with a bow tie, as before the war (Ch 2 Fig. 41 and Ch 6 Fig. 44), although by far the most usual style is today's combination of turned down collar and knotted tie, well established by now: some collars still have a starched appearance in the 1920s (Ch 2 Fig. 41, Ch 4 Fig. 37, Ch 5 Fig. 27 and Ch 6 Fig. 44) but increasingly the softer, un-starched, pointed collar is seen, identifiable from the crease in the points (Ch 5 Figs. 26 & 29 and Ch 6 Fig. 33. Because most family photographs of the 1920s are snapshots taken outside, a wider variety of garments begin to crop up by this decade, such as bathing suits (Ch 6 Fig. 35) and the protective overcoats, duster coats and mackintoshes worn for motoring in open-topped vehicles (Ch 6 Figs. 34 & 37). Young men are generally clean shaven by the 1920s, as are many more men of advanced years, although some favoured a neat moustache, popular styles including the 'toothbrush' moustache later associated with Hitler (Ch 2 Fig. 41, Ch 4 Fig. 37, Ch 5 Figs. 27-28 and Ch 6 Fig. 37). Beards are uncommon by the 1920s but may still be worn by older men (Ch 6 Fig. 44). Headwear of this decade is very diverse, continuing earlier trends: the bowler is worn less and less for ordinary wear - usually only by the conservative and older men (Ch 6 Figs. 37 &

44) while the cloth cap is still popular (Ch 2 Fig.41 and Ch 6 Fig.s 34, 37 & 44). Meanwhile stylish, semi-casual felt hats such as the homburg, fedora and more modern trilby are becoming increasingly fashionable (Ch 2 Fig. 41, Ch 5 Fig. 27 and Ch 6 Figs. 33, 37 & 44)

1930s

The cut of the male suit changed radically during the 1930s: some ultra-fashionable young men had been wearing wide 'Oxford bags' in the late 1920s and the new loose style of trouser was gradually taken up by others, becoming very clear in photographs of the 1930s. During this decade there was also a pronounced fashion for pin-striped suiting materials. Lounge jackets appear significantly wider, shorter and altogether boxy in cut, made with broad padded shoulders and sharp lapels, the suit trousers very wide and often featuring prominent creases and turn-ups (Ch 2 Fig. 48 and Ch 5 Figs. 30, 31 & 33), even older men choosing a more comfortable fit (Ch 2 Fig. 46). Men's dress in general became considerably more relaxed during this decade, as reflected especially in casual snapshots: 1930s photographs may show, for the first time, the lounge suit being worn without a waistcoat or knitted sleeveless pullovers replacing the suit waistcoat, while young men even discarded ties, spreading their shirt collars wide over their shoulders (Ch 2 Fig. 48). Sportswear was also developing and open-necked sports shirts and shorts began to be worn for outdoor leisure activities like walking, camping and cycling (Ch 6 Fig. 45). Older men may still sport a moustache during the 1930s (Ch 2 Figs. 46 & 48), although beards are very rare, being seen as distinctly old-fashioned. A hat was, though, still obligatory when at work and out in public: the cloth cap was still preferred by the working classes (Ch 6 Fig. 22), while the bowler presented a more conservative or formal business style, as it would until at least the 1960s (Ch 2 Fig. 46). For casual wear and ordinary weddings the trilby and fedora hats were the most popular styles (Ch 2 Fig. 48 and Ch 5 Fig. 30).

1940s

The Second World War (1939-45) dominates photographs of the 1940s and many men, naturally, appear wearing military uniform of one description or another (Ch 2 Fig. 49, Ch 4 Fig. 17 and Ch 5 Figs. 34, 36 & 37). Few men acquired new clothing during the war and in the period of rationing which followed, while de-mob suits were often shapeless and lacking in style, so when civilian suits are worn in 1940s photographs they are either loose and baggy or appear similar to the sharp, broadly cut suits of the 1930s (Ch 2 Fig. 50, Ch 4 Fig. 22, Ch 5 Figs. 35 & 37 and Ch 6 Figs. 13 and 41). Special features which may identify photographs of this decade are the trend for checked sports jackets and the growing popularity of knitted vests and waistcoats and boldly-patterned ties (Ch 2 Fig. 50, Ch 4 Fig. 40 and Ch 6 Fig. 41), while even striped or checked shirts may be seen (Ch 4 Fig. 3). Men appear less often wearing hats, although a smart trilby might be worn for a special occasion (Ch 4 Fig. 3). Facial hair also more or less died out altogether after the war, the toothbrush moustache of the 1920s and 1930s no longer fashionable because of its associations with Hitler. After the war, a short back and side haircut remained fashionable but younger men sometimes grew their front hair slightly longer, sweeping it back from the forehead over the top of the head (Ch 2 Fig. 50, Ch 4 Fig. 40 and Ch 6 Figs. 41 & 49). The open-necked sports shirts, lightweight jackets and shorts worn for sports are similar to those of the 1930s (Ch 6 Fig. 47) while swimwear has become more modern in appearance, men's bathing trunks now worn without the upper vest section (Ch 6 Fig. 46).

(3) Dating children's dress 1840s - 1940s

Babies
Babies were rarely photographed on their own in the early decades of photography, partly because the longer exposure time was difficult to deal with, although they do appear in photographs more frequently from the 1860s onwards. Until at least the 1st World War, male and female babies are usually clothed alike in photographs, in robes and petticoats, and unfortunately in many cases there is no way of telling their gender, unless their identity is already known, as in Ch 6 Fig.s 28 & 30, or unless the baby is holding a doll – a toy usually reserved for girls (Ch 4 Fig.35). Except when fashionably-dressed adults also appear in the picture, 19th century baby photographs may also be difficult to date from visual clues alone, in which case other dating methods may prove most helpful - determining the time frame of the card mount and establishing photographer details. Very long white gowns and occasionally sack-like *porte bebe* contraptions were worn specifically for christening photographs, which may help to identify the infant in question (Ch 4 Fig. 1).

Moving into the 20th century, long dresses were still worn for boys' and girls' christening and baptism photographs (Ch 4 Figs. 2 & 3). When outdoors, babies and infants generally had their heads protected from the sun in caps and bonnets (Ch 6 Fig.s 28 & 30). During the Edwardian era, 'best' baby wear often comprised white frilled or flounced smock-like garments and, for outside in public, wide, circular 'halo' bonnets – the final exaggerated expression of ornate, impractical dress for small children. Conversely it is also during the early-1900s and, especially, in the 1910s that studio photographs sometimes portray semi-naked babies draped in blankets or wearing brief vest-like garments - a new vogue at the time which rules out any possibility of such photographs having an earlier date. From the later 1910s onwards, especially during the 1920s and 1930s, snapshots may depict older babies wearing knitted leggings and little matinee jackets, while baby dresses are noticeably simpler in style and shorter than in earlier eras (Ch 4 Fig. 38). In general, although it can be hard to recognise styles of baby wear and to accurately date baby photographs, once an approximate time frame for the picture has been determined, the age of the baby or infant (much easier to judge than adults' ages) will often provide a close date and in many cases a firm identity.

Girls

1840s - 1880

Photographs of the 1840s and early 1850s being rare, children are more likely to crop up in family photographs from the mid-1850s onwards. Victorian girls wore a shorter, un-corseted version of women's dress and a youthful hairstyle, their clothing echoing prevailing fashions. Gradually their appearance assumed more adult features as they grew older, until they came 'of age' at somewhere between fifteen and eighteen years, after which time they dressed as women. Between the 1840s and late 1870s, essentially girls' garments were styled with a close fitting bodice and full, gathered skirts (Ch 2 Figs. 3, 6 & 13, Ch 4 Figs. 4, 26 & 31 and Ch 6 Figs. 1 & 2). Throughout this era, typically little girls' dresses featured slit, boat-like necklines and short, puffed sleeves decorated with ribbon trimmings, their knee-length skirts revealing short white stockings (socks) and either leather boots or bar shoes (Ch 2 Figs. 6 (left) & 13 and Ch 4 Figs. 4 & 26). Slightly older girls sometimes wore white drawers or *pantalettes* for modesty or longer white stockings (Ch 2 Figs. 3 & 6 (right) and Ch 4 Fig. 31).

Photographic evidence shows that girls aged around ten or eleven and upwards wore longer skirts, their hemlines mid-low calf-length (Ch 2 Fig. 3 (right) & Ch 6 Fig. 2). Certain stylistic features can often narrow the date range of girls' dress: for example in photographs of c.1855-60 girls above infant age tend to wear very full, layered skirts, their bodices arranged in gathered folds or V-shaped arrangements and made with wide three-quarter length sleeves - styles which mirror women's fashions of that era (Ch 2 Fig. 6 (right), Ch 4 Fig. 31 and Ch 6 Fig. 1); similarly, girls' dresses of the late 1860s and early 1870s generally follow the flounced, layered style worn by women at the time, but without the adult bustle (Ch 6 Fig. 2). Hairstyles also offer a guide as girls' hair was often dressed in ringlets during the 1840s and the 1850s (Ch 2 Fig. 3 and Ch 6 Fig. 1), while during the 1860s and 1870s older girls, at least, wore their hair closer to women's styles of those decades (Ch 2 Fig. 6 and Ch 6 Fig. 2).

1880s & 1890s

In around 1880, girls' styles caught up with the elongated, slender shape that had defined women's clothing for several years. Photographs of the 1880s and turn of the decade show that dresses are significantly slimmer in shape, the sleeves close-fitting or slightly puffed, and skirts are narrower, sometimes pleated (Ch 2 Fig. 23, Ch 4 Fig. 23 and Ch 5 Fig. 13). Other clues which may signify the 1880s and early 1890s are dark velvet and plush (cotton velvet) materials - both fashionable fabrics at the time (Ch 2 Fig. 26 and Ch 4 Fig. 23). Hairstyles have also changed to reflect adult styles, short or longer haircuts often featuring short fringes by the late 1880s and early 1890s (Ch 2 Fig. 26, Ch 4 Figs. 23 & 33 and Ch 5 Fig. 13). By around 1890 we also notice that dresses are being secured at the waist with a fabric sash or wide ribbon (Ch 2 Fig. 26 and Ch 4 Fig. 23). Little girls generally wore sashes throughout the 1890s (Ch 4 Figs. 33 & 34), although for slightly older girls a new type of garment was being worn by the early-mid 1890s - the smock dress, made with a flat yoke at the chest, onto which the length of the fabric was gathered, then left to fall freely. The loose smock dress with full sleeves, easily recognised in photographs, dominated girls' styles for the rest of the 1890s (Ch 4 Figs. 33 & 34 and Ch 5 Fig. 16).

Early 1900s
The smock dress remained fashionable in the new century, being the mainstay of the young girl's wardrobe during the early 1900s: a white smock, worn alone, could be ornamented with frills and flounces for 'best' (Ch 4 Fig. 35 and Ch 5 Figs. 19 & 21) while plain, dark or coloured smocks were more practical for everyday and school wear, often being worn beneath a protective pinafore dress (Ch 4 Fig. 12). In Edwardian photographs slightly older girls are often seen dressed in a modified smock style, the dress caught in at the waist creating a more 'grown up' effect (Ch 5 Figs. 19 (front left) & 21 (right)). At the beginning of the 1900s little girls' hair often looks rather short, although some girls were wearing prominent bows and ribbons in their hair, beginning a trend that was to last for many years (Ch 4 Figs. 12 & 35). The hair was grown longer as the decade advanced, often being waved or styled into curls or ringlets: hair bows were often worn on one side of the head and, following women's fashion, wide-brimmed hats were popular for special occasions (Ch 5 Figs. 19 & 21).

1910s
Following broader trends, the 1910s were a transitional decade for juvenile clothing. Echoing changing women's fashion, young girls' dresses became simpler in style, leaving behind some of their fussy ornamentation, and grew progressively shorter in length. Loose smock dresses may still appear in some photographs of the decade although they are noticeably shorter (Ch 6 Fig. 21). As the smock disappeared, slimmer fitting dresses became usual, these generally having a waist seam and sometimes featuring three-quarter length sleeves (Ch 4 Figs. 2 & 36) or prominent collars (Ch 5 Figs. 23 & 25). Thick woollen stockings were becoming

outdated for little girls and the shorter dresses, worn well above the knee, were usually teamed with white socks, revealing an expanse of bare leg and sometimes a glimpse of voluminous knickers (Ch 4 Fig. 36, Ch 5 Fig. 25 and Ch 6 Fig. 21). Older girls of the 1910s usually wore knee-length dresses, drawn in at the waist, or separate blouses and skirts, with long stockings (Ch 5 Figs. 24 & 25). For school wear a recognisable uniform was becoming established by the early 1910s, older schoolgirls often wearing a shirt-like blouse and tie with a plain skirt (Ch 6 Fig. 9). By the 1910s the large hair bow was a very prominent feature and offers a helpful dating clue (Ch 4 Fig. 36, Ch 5 Figs. 24 & 25 and Ch 6 Figs. 9, 21 & 32).

1920s-1940s
During the 1920s and early 1930s simple unshaped garments with short hemlines worn above the knee characterised the dress of young girls. These styles are usually easily identifiable in photographs, heavier fabrics being worn for winter (Ch 6 Fig. 33), while cotton sleeveless or short-sleeved shift-like styles with a dropped waistline were usual for summer (Ch 5 Fig. 29 and Ch 6 Fig. 36). The popular image of the female toddler in a short white dress, ankle socks, bar shoes and a cotton sunbonnet emerged around this time (Ch 2 Fig. 43), although such photographs may be difficult to date closely as the general style continued into the 1950s. Another identifying feature of the 1920s and early 1930s is the haircut worn by young girls - a short bob with a short fringe (Ch 5 Fig. 29 and Ch 6 Figs. 33 & 36). Older girls often wore their hair longer, secured with a bow behind the head, and generally wore slightly longer, more ladylike hemlines; 'best' dresses of the 1920s are styled similarly to women's garments of the decade, being loose-fitting with a low-slung fabric belt (Ch 4 Fig. 37), while gymslips, blouses and ties were well established as regulation uniform for school girls.

Photographs of the early-mid-1930s begin to show young girls wearing more elaborate, party style dresses, influenced by the clothing styles of famous personalities of the day - Shirley Temple and the royal princesses, Elizabeth and Margaret. Floral printed fabrics, frills, puffed sleeves and neat collars are all features which may be seen by this time and long hair is sometimes dressed in long plaits (Ch 4 Fig. 39). In general, girls' dresses appear more shaped by the late 1930s and 1940s, usually made with a seam at natural waist level, short puffed sleeves and sometimes featuring gathered and smocked yokes (Ch 5 Fig. 34). When outdoor jackets and coats of the 1920s-1940s are seen in photographs, they are smartly tailored and often featured velvet-faced collars and pocket flaps (Ch 6 Figs. 33 & 41).

Boys

1840s & 1850s

Just as Victorian girls were usually wearing adult dress by the age of sixteen or seventeen, boys of the era had generally progressed to men's suits with long trousers by their early-mid 'teens', or earlier in some cases, depending on their lifestyles - in particular whether and where they were working. The emphasis here is on recognising and dating the juvenile clothing worn by male infants and 'breeched' boys aged around three and upwards, before they progressed to 'grown-up' clothing (see Chapter 4 for more about breeching). Following early 19th century trends, as described in Chapter 1, in 1840s, 1850s and some 1860s photographs we see young boys wearing tunics and dresses with fitted bodices and full knee-length skirts, similar to women's and girls' garments. Sometimes wide trousers were worn underneath the dress or tunic, identifying the wearers firmly as boys (girls never wore trousers or shorts at that date); however sometimes no such garments are visible and this can make it very difficult to tell gender in mixed groups, although a prominent collar often distinguished the boys from the girls (Ch 6 Fig. 1 and see also Ch 1 Fig. 18).

1860s & 1870s
The knee-length belted tunic or dress, worn with trousers, still appears in photographs of the early 1860s (Ch 2 Fig. 6). However during this decade major developments occurred as a modified version of the adult male suit was introduced for young boys. Typically the new style featured a short waist- or hip-length jacket, worn over a shirt, and teamed with short trousers (knickerbockers) that were either gathered or left open just below the knee. Variations on the basic knickerbockers suit dominate photographs of small boys for several decades from the 1860s through to the First World War, although stylistic elements usually narrow the date considerably. During the 1860s and 1870s a popular version was the *zouave* outfit comprising a short bolero jacket with sloping, rounded front edges that was fastened only at the neck, this being worn with matching or contrasting knickerbockers: this distinctive outfit was so-called due to the jacket's supposed resemblance to the picturesque uniforms worn by the Algerian Zouave troops who served in the Crimean War (1854-6) and again in the Franco-Austrian War (1859) (Ch 4 Fig. 10 and Ch 5 Fig. 2). However throughout the 1860s and early 1870s - still early an early period in the evolution of the youthful suit - photographs may demonstrate a variety of jacket and knickerbockers combinations (Ch 2 Fig. 13, Ch 5 Fig. 4 and Ch 6 Fig. 25).

1880s & 1890s
By the later 1870s and early 1880s boys' dress was, on the one hand becoming plainer and more uniform, echoing the growing sobriety of menswear at the time.

Photographs may, for example, show young boys wearing a complete miniature version of the adult lounge suit, characterised by a small lounge jacket with neat collar and fashionable handkerchief pocket (Ch 4 Fig. 11). Conversely, during the 1880s the picturesque sailor suit also came into vogue, and this style of outfit appears frequently from mid-decade onwards: when boys are fully 'dressed up' the sailor suit presents an authentic imitation of regular naval uniform, complete with the sailor's wide-collared blouse, lanyard and cap (Ch 2 Fig. 24), while simpler, everyday versions combine open-ended shorts or gathered knickerbockers with a striped, wide-collared blouse over the sailor's white vest (Ch 6 Fig 4). The new sailor style was so popular that a skirted version was also worn by tiny boys who had not yet been breeched (Ch 2 Fig. 23) and sailor-inspired suits continued to be worn both for 'best' and more ordinary wear throughout the 1890s. Other loose, blouse-style shirts, worn without a jacket, also appear as holiday and play wear in open-air photographs of the 1890s (Ch 4 Fig. 34 & Ch 6 Fig. 5). Meanwhile, smarter types of knickerbockers suits were also evolving during the 1890s and becoming more varied in their styling: for example the distinctive Norfolk jacket (traditionally worn by men for country and sporting pursuits), characterised by a fabric belt and vertical stitched down pleats, entered the young boy's wardrobe (Ch 4 Fig. 15 (left)). By mid-decade smart jackets either featured a wide, frilled white collar (Ch 2 Fig. 30) or a prominent starched white collar, now termed the Eton collar (Ch 4 Figs. 15 & 34 and Ch 5 Fig. 14). The buttoned lounge jacket with lapels also remained popular and, by late-decade it was being worn by school age boys with a round peaked cap (Ch 4 Fig. 34) - early signs of an emerging school uniform.

1900s & 1910s
As with girls' clothing, boys' wear of the Edwardian era continued along late-Victorian lines. Elementary school photographs of the early-1900s demonstrate the wide range of young boys' garments in common use - jackets and blouses made with varying collars in the sailor, wide frilled and stiff Eton styles, these upper garments worn usually with knee-length or longer knickerbockers and teamed with black woollen stockings - or occasionally shorter socks - and sturdy leather boots (Ch 4 Fig. 12). Photographs of this decade always feature these sorts of styles for boys and also show how garments were made in various winter and summer weight fabrics to suit the season (Ch 5 Figs. 19 & 21). Again, amateur snapshots depicting more relaxed situations may show boys casually-dressed without their jackets and collars (Ch 6 Fig. 29).

Formal knickerbockers suits, made with various jacket and collar styles and worn with thick stockings and boots continued into the 1910s, particularly for special occasions. Sailor suits - a picturesque choice - were sometimes worn for weddings (Ch 5 Fig. 23), although sailor styles were on the decline and disappeared from fashion completely in the years following WW1. A growing trend, first glimpsed in the Edwardian era and often noticed in photographs by the early-1910s, is for briefer, light-weight outfits for very small boys comprising a broad-collared, blouse-like tunic top (usually, though not always belted), worn with above-the-knee shorts and short socks and shoes (Ch 2 Fig. 38, Ch 4 Fig. 2 and Ch 6 Fig. 21); the shorter shorts and move away from traditional long black stockings and heavy boots are unmistakably 'modern' features which aid dating of photographs from the 1910s (Ch 6 Fig.9). Progressive ideas about children's needs and growing emphasis on the benefits of practical play clothes also inspired the popularity of the stretchy knitted jersey at around the same time. This was not strictly a new garment, jerseys being already worn by sportsmen, fishermen and other men engaged in strenuous physical activity, but the soft, comfortable jersey made with a small collar is rarely seen on small boys before the later Edwardian period and 1910s (Ch 6 Fig.9).

1920s-1940s
In the post war years versions of the tunic or blouse and shorts suit remained popular for little boys (Ch 6 Fig. 11 and Ch 4 Fig. 37), while the knitted jersey with a small collar became a mainstay of young boys' wardrobes: worn throughout the 1920s and 1930s for general play and for elementary school (where regulation uniform was not required), sometimes the jersey incorporated a knitted or other tie (Ch 6 Fig. 11). For older boys, school uniform consisting of flannel shorts, shirt and tie, jacket or blazer and cap was well established by the 1920s and we see this regulation uniform in school and associated group photographs throughout the 1920s, 1930s and 1940s. Precise dating of these images can be difficult, although the tendency for boys (and men) to discard their ties during the 1930s often identifies photographs of this decade (Ch 6 Fig. 38). The short-sleeved, open-collared sports shirt having become acceptable wear for men during the 1930s, boys were also photographed wearing that casual style of shirt in the 1930s and 1940s (Ch 4 Fig. 39). Throughout the 1920s-1940s, elements of school uniform and everyday day clothing were interchangeable, so in photographs of these decades, young school-age boys often wear collared shirts and grey shorts, with or without ties and with or without tailored jackets or blazers (Ch 2 Fig. 48, Ch 4 Fig. 37 and Ch 6 Figs. 33, 36 & 38). During the 1930s and 1940s a range of hand-knitted garments became popular, so sweaters and sleeveless pullovers knitted in Fair Isle and other patterned stitches may also occur in photographs of those years (Ch 4 Fig. 40).

Evaluating the visual image

The preceding pages have focused on analysing photographic images. Visual clues are all-important and hopefully readers will feel more confident about identifying and dating some of the key elements in their pictures. However, we all tend to see things

147

slightly differently and some researchers may feel unsure about accurately dating a photograph from its setting and the fashions worn by the subjects. If in doubt, there are professional photograph specialists who can assist with dating and analysis (see Web Resources). Otherwise familiarity is the key: it always helps to look at as many pictures as possible, to train the eye and develop a feel for the pictorial features and effects that were characteristic of different eras. While a selection of typical family photographs are reproduced in this book, there are many other examples in existence that are relevant and may, in some cases, offer very close comparisons for readers' own photographs. In the Bibliography are listed books that feature 19th and early 20th century photographs and browsing through some of these, as well as visiting the recommended photographic websites should help to build confidence and aid recognition of the characteristics that recur over and again in family photographs. Always remember that a photograph, whatever its date, presents a dateable pictorial record of a real person, or people, at a specific point in time: if the image is complete and genuine (hasn't been cut about, or edited using modern digital technology) it cannot possibly give false information. When the visual clues are successfully identified and the evidence combined with the other dating methods - format, style of mount and photographer's dates - a photograph cannot fail to fit in to a time frame that is accurate and meaningful for research purposes.

Photographic copies and memorial portraits

There is one type of photograph that, if and when it crops up, may seem to present conflicting information - the photographic reprint. Occasionally the estimated age of a photographic mount and/or the operational dates of the named photographer do not concur with the appearance of the image. Signs that an earlier photograph has been printed onto a later mount (it cannot be the other way around) may threaten to throw the dating process into confusion, but consider that the current photograph could in fact be a re-print of an older portrait. Copies of photographs could in theory be made any time, either from the original negative (if still available) or directly from a photograph; the latter tended to result in a poorer quality image, and so a faint picture may also be a sign of a reprint. In practise, the most common type of copy or reprint is the memorial portrait, produced after the death of the subject of the photograph. Copies of their earlier portraits were ordered by a close relative so that family members could each have a picture by which to remember the deceased. Naturally these memorial portraits followed the format which was current at the time of the reprint: for example an original daguerreotype photograph from the 1840s or an ambrotype photograph from the 1850s could be copied and printed in the 1890s onto a cabinet card, as in Ch 2 Fig. 51. Even a hand-painted miniature portrait from the pre-photography era could be reproduced later in the 19th century as a card-mounted photograph: very occasionally such an example may occur in the picture collections of families with prosperous ancestors. A photographic reprint of an earlier painted portrait is usually easily recognisable from the flat, 'painted' quality of the image, while accurate dating of the dress details should confirm whether the picture pre-dates the invention of photography (Ch 2 Fig. 52). Using a card mount for reprints enabled copies to be conveniently sent to relatives, and these could also, if desired, be placed in a photograph album. Some memorial portraits bear a helpful handwritten inscription on the back stating the name and date of death of the subject.

Picturing the face

One of the great benefits of old family photographs (as opposed to artworks) is that they offer an accurate depiction of ancestors and relatives, demonstrating what they actually looked like at the time they were captured by the camera. The name of the forebear(s) pictured in a photograph may already be known, or presumed, although, as discussed in Chapter 2, it is often close dating that helps to confirm or suggest identity where this is uncertain. In many collections there will also survive two or more images of the same person spanning a period of time, as seen for example in Ch 2 Figs. 34, 38 & 41 and in Ch 4 Figs. 6, 14 & 20: sometimes photographs are easily matched, while at other times it may be difficult to tell exactly who is who in different photographs, especially if they were taken many years apart and subjects have aged beyond recognition. Judging likeness and age in old black and white photographs is notoriously tricky: as humans we all have a natural ability to recognise and distinguish between different faces but levels of observation do seem to vary from person to person and our opinions about facial features and other physical characteristics don't always coincide with those of other viewers. We may also notice that, confusingly, the same person can *look* different, even in portraits of similar date, while another consideration is that images of varying quality may also create differing impressions of the same person. Such issues can sometimes cloud our perception and make identification of old photographs seem a difficult task: unfortunately there are no real solutions to these problems, but we should be firmly guided by the photograph's date, try keep an open mind when identity is uncertain, ask for the opinions of other family members and attempt to find other supporting pictorial evidence. Patience, further research and careful judgement (perhaps involving an element of informed guesswork) may help some uncertainties to become clearer over time.

Facial recognition technology

In the mid-1960s automated face recognition first became a reality as scientists began work on programming computers to recognise human faces. Every face has numerous distinguishable landmarks or *nodal points* - the various peaks and valleys that make up facial features - and facial recognition software measures key nodal points such as the distance between the eyes, width of the nose, shapes of cheekbones and length of the jaw line, from either a live image or a clear photograph. The measurements are then combined to create a template of the face known as a *faceprint*, a biometric record that is as unique as other identifying physical characteristics such as fingerprints or retinal scans. Theoretically a faceprint can be checked against others in a database and, as with fingerprints, a match is assumed when a certain threshold of shared values in two faceprints has been reached.

Since the first experiments, technology has come a long way, processes have been refined and now, in the 21st century, facial recognition is a significant area of research in computer vision and image analysis. In recent years the subject and its applications have attracted growing public interest and free software is readily available online. Several of the websites popularly used for photograph hosting and management (see also Chapter 7) have introduced facial identification tools to enhance their existing features. A genealogy website offering such a function is MyHeritage, which uses Family Tree Builder software that can also be downloaded free of charge and used as an independent programme. Outside the family history arena, other sites providing face detection and tagging features include Google's Picasa, a free photo editing system that also identifies similar faces in photos, using the same technology for its photo sharing website, Picasa Web Albums. Similarly, for Mac computer users Apple iPhoto 'Faces' employs face detection and recognition software. The social networking site Facebook, which hosts millions of members' photographs, has also followed suit with its own 'Photo Tagger'. The operation of these different systems may vary slightly; for example some have to be instructed which picture folders to monitor, while others are launched automatically. Essentially they all scan the photographs that have been uploaded, or which they have found on the computer drive, detecting the faces in pictures and automatically grouping them into 'people' folders or albums by matching faces that look similar. These can then be labelled or 'tagged' by the user if identity is known, a process which may then prompt the system to suggest further face matches from amongst the photographs in the database.

Some family historians are already trialling programmes such as these in the hope that they may aid identification of family photographs, but at present are experiencing a variable success rate. This is chiefly because the accuracy of using a flat, two-dimensional photograph to identify another 2-D photograph from an image database depends upon the pictures showing faces photographed in similar lighting conditions, looking almost directly at the camera and making similar facial expressions. When the technology is applied to old family photographs, variations in these criteria (for example faces turned at different angles) typically produce inconsistent results, failure to recognise some faces or erroneous matching of faces belonging to different people. Acknowledging the limitations of 2D models, the most up to date facial recognition systems operational today now involve three-dimensional technology, which is said to be far more accurate, but 3D software is not, at time of writing, widely available to the public. In conclusion, it has to be said that, despite the claims of some systems to help users recognise and identify unknown individuals within their own photograph collections, they may not spot facial resemblances that aren't already obvious to the naked eye and, of course, they cannot name faces until one of the matched faces has been assigned a name by the user. Undoubtedly face detection and face tagging tools are helpful when managing numerous family photographs as they enable convenient organisation of images into albums according to the people in them; however today's popular systems currently lack the sophisticated recognition features that might help to resolve some of the problems commonly faced by family picture researchers. Facial recognition is a complex and rapidly-evolving area of technology whose practical application isn't yet perfect, but hopefully more advanced and effective programmes will become available in the future.

Note: The above section on facial recognition technology derives from the author's article in *Practical Family History* magazine, December 2010.

FOUR

CHAPTER FOUR

*Picturing the family and
special occasions*

Getting the most out of family photographs means not only dating them accurately and identifying their subjects, but also interpreting them effectively - considering *why* they may have been taken and how they reflected the family's life at the time. Traditionally artworks were often commissioned to mark an important occasion, as shown in Chapter 1, and when photography became the new portrait medium professional photographers embraced those themes which were already popular, extending their repertoire further over time. Photographic opportunities were, necessarily, limited to the natural range of human experience, but during the 19th and early 20th centuries many rites of passage, successes and other important events might prompt a visit to the photographer for a commemorative portrait - christenings, birthdays, breechings, coming of age, career achievements, engagements, weddings, anniversaries, retirements and even death itself. It was not necessary - or usual - for a photographer to be present at the actual event; rather, participants visited their local studio on the day, or around the time of the occasion, dressed in their best, or the most appropriate clothing. The resulting images were, of course, removed from reality but they had an important function in that they symbolised the significance of the occasion within the family. Besides triggering personal memories for many years afterwards, special pictures shown to relatives and friends enhanced the family's reputation, demonstrating visibly their good fortune, success, respectability and social status, and also testified to their correct observance of social ritual. Certain Victorian and Edwardian customs are no longer recognised in western society, especially boys' breechings and extended public mourning following the death of a loved one, but these were major stages of life as understood by our forebears. Family gatherings bringing together relatives - important social events - could also inspire celebratory photographs, as might the birth of a baby representing a new generation of the family. Such were the traditions and experiences which guided the actions and shaped the lives of earlier generations and those captured on camera offer today's researchers a pictorial record signifying some of the most meaningful events from a family's past.

Understanding that special occasions often inspired the studio portraits of previous eras can shed new light on today's inherited family photographs. Their original purpose may take some working out from what appear to be standard images of forebears posing in a conventional studio setting, but there may be visual clues that can help, once we know what to look out for. For example some traditions entailed the wearing of special clothing or materials, such as mourning dress - unfamiliar to us today, but the details are generally identifiable in photographs. Equally, by the late 19th century it was common for men to wear a white tie or bow tie for a photograph marking a significant occasion. Floral devices also appear from time to time - bodice corsages, *boutonnieres* (buttonholes), posies and garlands; again these imply an important event, perhaps a coming of age, birthday, engagement - or even a wedding in the days before special bridal wear was customary (see Chapter 5). Fresh flowers may sometimes have been brought along by customers for the photograph sitting, although it is likely that studios could also provide 'props' of this nature. In some cases a photograph offers no obvious evidence of significant circumstances, but if the identity of the subject is already known or suspected, close dating of the portrait very often reveals that the family member in question would have been celebrating a special birthday or anniversary at around that time. By the same token, positively identifying an occasion can often help with closer dating, or identification where the name of the subject has not yet been established.

By the 20th century personal and family events and gatherings were increasingly recorded in amateur snapshots, although a professional studio photograph - still considered a superior picture - was often favoured for the most important commemorative portraits. This chapter looks at the various social customs and family occasions that were observed and documented throughout the period covered by the book, explaining how these may be recognised in surviving photographs. The sequence of images below provides pictorial examples that are representative of the special family photographs to be found in today's collections.

Christening

One of the most important events experienced by families is the birth of a new baby. In the past this was also a regular occurrence in many households, until the early

20th century when smaller families became more usual. The high infant mortality rate in previous eras led most parents to have their babies christened or baptised when young - usually between four and six weeks old. The ceremony might take place in church, although sometimes the clergyman visited the family at home. Despite the frequency of family christenings and baptisms amongst earlier generations, relatively few Victorian and Edwardian photographs recording these events seem to survive. However, tiny babies were very difficult to photograph in a studio, especially using the slower *collodion* process of the 1850s-1870s, as they could not be expected to keep still and maintain composure throughout the period of the exposure. Being too young to sit up unaided, babies also had to be held by an adult or, if they were to be portrayed alone, propped up on a couch or chair and tied in place with sashes and scarves. If this nerve-wracking experience did not deter clients from taking their newly-christened babies to be photographed in the studio, then probably many families simply could not afford to commission a professional photograph every time a new baby arrived. 20th century amateur snapshots of babies' christenings survive in greater numbers, these being a cheaper and more convenient method of capturing the occasion; they are often imperfect portraits, but they provide an important record of a new baby's first public appearance.

Christening photographs are usually distinguishable from other pictures of infants by the very young appearance of the baby and, especially, by his or her clothing. Special christening gowns, first introduced in around the mid-18th century, were usually white by the Victorian period, symbolising purity and innocence, and these continued into the 20th century. They were very long, covering the baby's feet by several inches, and were made of muslin or the finest fabric that a family could afford (Figs. 2 & 3). Since the cost of a christening gown was determined by the quality of its material and the nature and complexity of its decoration, a portrait of a baby in a costly gown embellished with exquisite lace or embroidery was a visual expression of a family's solvency and social status. Often such garments had a powerful family association, perhaps having been made at home, and passed down the generations, although by the early 20th century clothing companies and mail order firms were advertising 'Christening Robes' in their catalogues, prices ranging from around 5 shillings to nearly £3. Boys and girls were dressed alike, so it can be impossible to tell the gender of an unidentified baby at the time of its christening, unless there are other helpful clues. An alternative form of christening attire by the later 19th century was the *porte-bebe,* a sac or pocket-like arrangement comprising a coverlet attached to a pillow on three sides, into which the baby was placed and could rest comfortably, thereby reducing the likelihood of infantile upsets at the ceremony and for any photographs taken in the studio (Fig. 1). An ornate cap or bonnet and, sometimes, an elaborate cape or cloak completed the formal christening outfit.

Birthday

Although lively young children were not the easiest subjects for photographers to capture, some photographers actively developed this potentially lucrative line of work. Doting parents from affluent backgrounds might visit the studio every year around the time of a son or daughter's birthday, until the age of 21, to record their children's growth and development. Some commercial photographers astutely produced 'Baby's Album' encouraging the collection and display of regular annual pictures of children throughout their childhood and adolescence. An array of toys and novelties were kept in photographers' studios for the purpose of attracting young children's attention during the sitting and some birthday photographs of infants show them holding dolls or teddy bears or standing by prams or rocking horses, accessories which had also featured prominently in earlier paintings of children. For ordinary working families, commemorating a child's birthday in a photograph might be a rare event (Fig. 4) or it could be conveniently combined with another family celebration at the same time (Fig. 10). Sometimes the occasion was deferred altogether until much later - the more auspicious 21st birthday portrait when a son or daughter officially became an adult. Many a photograph was taken to mark the 21st birthday although surviving examples are not necessarily obvious and the young adult in the picture may simply be wearing elaborate or fashionable clothing (Fig. 6): floral tokens offer more of a clue, since these generally signify a special occasion, young men perhaps sporting a flower buttonhole, and young women wearing a floral corsage on their bodice or holding a posy or basket of flowers (Fig. 5). It is also worth looking out for items of jewellery in photographs that were perhaps presented as a special 21st birthday gift - these heirlooms may even have survived within the family (Fig. 6).

Older family members also celebrated birthdays in the past, as now, and it was not uncommon for elderly ancestors and relatives to commemorate landmark birthdays with a professional photograph to demonstrate their good health and longevity. Sometimes the occasion of such portraits may have been recorded, or remembered within the family (Figs. 8 & 9), but otherwise we have to judge whether a well-dressed mature ancestor or relative in a single portrait may have been celebrating a special birthday. Identifying such occasions is easier when the subject of a picture and his or her birth and death dates are known, as an accurate date-range for the image will indicate whether it coincided with a significant birthday, as suggested in Fig. 7.

Breeching

After christening and early birthdays, the next important event in a little boy's life was his 'breeching' - a rite of passage no longer recognised today but a significant family and social ritual which historically marked a son's transition from infancy into boyhood. Small children of both sexes wore baby dresses in the 19th and early 20th centuries but at some point between the age of three and six (usually at four or five) boys cast aside their androgynous baby robes and were ceremoniously dressed in their first pair of short trousers. In recognition of their new status, lucky boys might be given pennies by relatives and neighbours, and in some families the occasion was recorded in a professional photograph. Surviving breeching portraits are sometimes annotated on the back with the age of the boy and the date (Fig. 11), but they may in any case usually be identified from the appearance of the subject - a young boy of relevant age posing either on his own, or perhaps with a sibling celebrating a birthday at around the same time (Fig. 10). Photographic evidence suggests that double occasion portraits depicting small children was quite common: no doubt these were more convenient and cost-effective for the family than two separate visits to the studio.

Breeching portraits typically show the young son proudly wearing his new set of 'grown up' clothes - garments made in the style fashionable for young boys at the time. For example in the 1860s and 1870s a boy may be seen adopting the newly-introduced knickerbockers suit, which often took the form of the *zouave* ensemble (see Chapter 3) - a short bolero-style jacket with sloping front edges and open or gathered 'shorts' or knickerbockers (Fig. 10). By the later 1870s and 1880s, following trends towards greater sobriety and uniformity in male dress, a more conventional miniature lounge suit was popular for small boys at the time of their breeching, as seen in Fig. 11.

School, college and work

School was a regular routine for many children by the mid-late Victorian era and some families may be fortunate in possessing old school photographs of relatives or ancestors, either taken at elementary (primary) school or secondary school, or perhaps at an independent establishment if they were educated privately. Professional photographers were sometimes employed to photograph pupils at schools and academies in the early photographic era, certain studios building their reputations on academic portraiture, such as Hills & Saunders (established 1852) and Gilman & Soame (1856). However official school photography for the wider population developed later in the century, after the passing of the 1870 Elementary Education Act, which led to larger numbers of children from ordinary backgrounds attending school. Regular photographer visits to local day schools were also encouraged by technical advances during the 1880s - the introduction of more convenient dry photographic plates which facilitated work away from the studio. In view of these factors, most of the school photographs that have been passed down through families will date from the 1880s onwards, pictures treasured by proud parents in the past, in the same way that many of today's parents support the continuing tradition of the annual school photograph.

From the 19th century until the Second World War, usually school children were photographed in their class groups - or, less commonly, two classes grouped together - the children carefully positioned so that each small face was visible. Typically in early photographs the children are lined up in rows outside in the playground, the group flanked on one side by the head teacher, and on the other by their class teacher (Fig. 12), although views taken inside the schoolroom became more popular from the Edwardian period onwards. In group photographs sometimes a slate was positioned in the middle of the picture stating the year, school and class - details originally intended to help the photographer when printing and sorting, although they are a great bonus for today's family historians. However if a particular photograph is unmarked and is proving difficult to date and identify, further investigation may be needed. It may, for example, be worth trying to track down further copies from the school (if it is known, and still exists), as it may have kept amongst its pupil records named and dated copies of official photographs; alternatively it could be worth contacting the local record office for the relevant district. Accurate dating always helps when trying to find out more about a picture and it is possible to estimate the approximate date of many state run school photographs from the style of dress worn by the children, especially elementary school pupils who, even in the early 20th century (when a recognisable uniform developed for older children) often wore their ordinary garments to school. Children were simply told to 'come clean' for the photographer's visit, and judging from surviving pictures, most of them made an effort to dress up in decent clothes for the occasion (Fig. 12).

Some photographs of youthful ancestors and relatives taken in a photographer's studio may also celebrate academic attendance and achievement. When children left school - often at eleven or twelve in the Victorian era - or attained a recognised standard of education, it was common for them to be presented with a certificate and sometimes this was recorded in a special portrait (possibly Fig. 15). Surviving photographs suggest that by the late 19th century recipients of educational awards or certificates might hire an academic cap ('mortarboard') and gown for a commemorative photograph, even at the tender age of thirteen. Higher education and, especially, university, was a privilege enjoyed by only a small minority for much of the period covered by this book, but within those social classes often a special photograph would be taken to mark the beginning of a son or daughter's first term at university or later, upon graduation (Fig. 16). Other young people might pose for a photograph to mark further stages of education, for example attendance at technical college, or embarkation on a special training course (Fig. 15), while completion of vocational training and apprenticeships were also occasions deemed worthy of a photograph. At times of war new recruits into the army, navy, royal flying corps or air force and associated services were often photographed in uniform to demonstrate satisfactory completion of their military training, show off their smart and professional appearance and express their anticipation of their forthcoming role (Fig. 17). Commencement of a new career, promotion, or a notable success at work might also prompt a visit to the studio (Fig. 18), and where special occupational dress or uniform was required this was self-consciously modelled in the picture.

Coming of age

For girls, there was no equivalent of young boys' breeching, since female children were already wearing skirts, but as they grew older their hemlines steadily lengthened from knee, to calf, to ankle and clothing became progressively more 'grown up' in its style and construction. Finally at some point between the age of fifteen and eighteen - usually at sixteen or seventeen - a girl came 'of age' and was regarded as having entered womanhood. This important rite of passage was symbolised by the adoption of full adult dress - a firmly fitted corset, floor length skirts and the putting up of long hair into a neat bun or *chignon*. In some families such occasions were also marked by a special photograph, as seen in Figs. 13 & 14.

Engagement and betrothal

Becoming engaged or betrothed was an important episode in young people's lives, the length of the engagement depending upon family circumstances and other factors, including the age of the couple. In many families apparently the engagement period was brief and led on swiftly to the marriage ceremony, especially at times of war, or if the woman was already pregnant - as seems to have been quite often the case. More formal or leisurely engagements typically lasted between six months and two years: where an engagement was recognised as a distinct event in its own right it was sometimes marked by a special photograph, following a long portrait tradition dating back to the Tudor era when an engagement often cemented an important dynastic alliance. A 19th or early 20th century couple celebrating their commitment to marry could be pictured together in the photographer's studio, or they might choose to be portrayed in separate companion photographs which were then exchanged between them; however in many cases it seems to have been the young lady who was most keen to demonstrate her new status in a portrait, a copy of which might then be given as a token to her fiancé. A formal engagement usually entailed the presentation of a ring from the prospective bridegroom to his intended - a custom which under Roman law expressed his provision of security for the completion of the bargain. The ring was therefore highly symbolic, a very clear sign of the engaged or betrothed state, and accordingly in photographs of newly-engaged females, the young woman is generally carefully positioned so as to display the glittering new ring on the third finger of her left hand (Figs. 19 & 20).

Marriage

Marriages are always very special family occasions and visual images depicting or symbolising weddings have existed since the earliest days of portraiture. All family historians will possess wedding pictures amongst their collections: some may be of 19th century date, although the marriage portraits of ordinary Victorian ancestors often go unidentified because the visual clues which we generally associate with weddings - special white bridal wear, flowers and bridesmaids - are generally absent (Fig. 21). By the 20th century many more weddings were elaborate 'white weddings', more recognisable to the modern eye, yet the occasions - and the photographs in which they were recorded - varied enormously, reflecting different family's circumstances and the times in which they lived (Fig. 22). Because marriages are such significant events and wedding photographs are so numerous and diverse, this genre of family pictures is dealt with separately in Chapter 5.

Wedding anniversary

The celebration of wedding anniversaries can be traced back at least to the Middle Ages in Central Europe, when a husband might crown his wife with a silver wreath after 25 years of marriage, or a gold one after 50 years - an old Germanic practice perhaps rooted in a belief in the connection between certain luck-bringing substances with a specific number of years. In the following centuries, milestone 25th (silver) and 50th (golden) wedding anniversaries remained important, but it was only much later, during the 19th century, that the ritual and celebration surrounding the 'anniversary wedding' were redefined and popularised, as were many other social customs at that time. It was probably the Victorian predilection for classifying and categorising that inspired the development of the 'traditional' listing of prescribed gifts for particular anniversaries: for example in 1875 appeared the first known reference to a 5th wedding anniversary being symbolised by wood, and in 1897 Queen Victoria appropriated the diamond for her jubilee year, to mark 60 years of rule. Printed and online sources on the subject vary but together they suggest that by the early 20th century around nine principal wedding anniversaries were officially recognised - 1st, 5th, 10th, 15th, 20th, 25th, 50th, 60th and 75th. Photographic evidence supports a growing trend for the celebration of ever more anniversaries, which may in some families have included all 5- and 10-year anniversaries by the late Victorian and Edwardian eras.

With wedding anniversaries being celebrated frequently in the past, it is likely that many of today's photograph collections will include portrayals of ancestors or later relatives who were celebrating a special anniversary. Some images will show the couple depicted on their own, while in others they are surrounded by other family members. By the late 19th century, when larger group photographs became popular in general, parents, children (and grandchildren where relevant) often gathered in the studio to celebrate a landmark anniversary, the anniversary couple prominently positioned in the group (Fig. 23). Sometimes there is a strong oral tradition identifying photographs of such events, while at other times it is again the accurate dating of a likely image which may suggest an anniversary occasion, as in the case of Fig. 24.

Mourning

Families in the past being generally much larger and the average life expectancy lower than today, most of our ancestors experienced the personal trauma of bereavement and mourned the passing of loved ones of all ages on many occasions during their lifetimes. Extravagant mourning customs date back many centuries in Europe but, like various other social rituals, public mourning became more pronounced and widespread during the 19th century. By the 1850s ostentatious funerals and the wearing of special mourning attire were well established in Britain, especially amongst the middle and upper echelons of society, and the mourning industry had developed to the extent that British undertakers and specialist outfitters were cashing in on a booming trade. Following the death of Prince Albert in 1861, Queen Victoria adopted a sombre public image and continued to dress in black and half-mourning colours for the rest of her life, appearing to her subjects as the ideal Christian widow. It was, then, under royal influence that the growing cult of mourning gained mass appeal in Victorian Britain, and throughout its overseas colonies.

The observance of lengthy mourning following the death of a relative or a major public figure was at its height from around the 1860s until the 1890s, declining slightly by the end of the century. However mourning continued to be observed within some families well into the Edwardian era and throughout the First World War when, it has been claimed, the streets were full of black-clad women, although by the 1910s the strictest rules governing mourning had relaxed considerably. After the war, public mourning was practised less often, except amongst royalty, the aristocracy and within some upper class families, and, conversely, some poorer communities, eventually becoming one of many vanishing social customs that had underpinned and symbolised the old world. However for 50 or more years, the importance of visibly mourning the deceased was entrenched in the lives of many of our forebears - men, women and children. Essentially the nature and length of mourning was dictated by the relationship of the mourner to the deceased. Mourning conduct and attire were governed by labyrinthine and ever-changing 'rules', advice being promulgated in the etiquette manuals and domestic handbooks that proliferated from the mid-19th century onwards. Over time the regulations became more numerous and intricate and the mourning periods longer, the tendency for different sources to vary in their specifications adding to the complexity of the whole business (for more detailed information see *Mourning Dress* by Lou Taylor, listed in the Bibliography). In its heyday some critics (including Charles Dickens) condemned the huge pressure under which the requirement to wear special mourning clothing placed impoverished families, as well as the excessive luxury and display that it encouraged amongst the wealthier classes. Clearly only the better off could afford to follow recommendations down to every last detail, but many people of humble background adopted elements of mourning as far as they could within their means, for to be seen following social etiquette correctly was important to most respectable families.

A formal portrait representing the bereaved decked out in suitable mourning attire was a significant aspect of the ritual. Paintings fulfilled this requirement in the pre-photography era but by the mid-19th century studio photographs were being taken to mark mourning occasions, ancestors in mourning sometimes being noticed in early daguerreotypes and ambrotypes (Ch 2 Fig. 5). From the 1860s onwards mourning was a common theme of cartes de visite and cabinet prints, so many researchers will discover mourning photographs in their archives: these take all forms, ranging from single portraits, through double portraits to larger family groups. Mourning affected everyone - men, women and children - so people of both sexes and all ages may appear in mourning pictures, although female mourning portraits are most common. Women carried the heaviest burden, especially widows who were officially supposed to mourn their husbands for two and a half years, although in practise many older widows never wore colours again but dressed in sombre black for their remaining years. Since mourning dress basically followed current fashions, all mourning photographs can be dated from the basic style of garments and hairstyles in much the same way as any other family pictures. Pinpointing the occasion relies upon recognising the subtler details of clothing that signified mourning - sartorial elements that were not associated with any other circumstances: these may be quite obvious in some photographs while sometimes they are more difficult to positively identify.

Essentially black garments were worn for early stages of mourning, small amounts of white sometimes being introduced, for example in a collar or cuffs. As seen in several photographs in this book, dark materials were sometimes used in ordinary fashionable dress, and black was definitely favoured by older ladies, so in some cases it may not be entirely clear whether a forebear is in mourning or not. One helpful feature to bear in mind is that traditionally nothing about dress was to shine or gleam, so shimmering silks were put aside and matt black materials such as *bombazine* (worsted and silk material) and *paramatta* (worsted and cotton) were worn instead. Although the precise quality of different fabrics may not always be evident in photographs, sometimes materials with a very dull, matt appearance can be discerned and in most cases they are a good indication of mourning attire, as seen in Figs. 26 & 27. Even more obvious to the naked eye is black *crape* (crimped, dull silk gauze) - a fabric recognisable from its distinctive textured quality: crape could be used to cover whole garments in early stages of mourning, although in practise it was often reduced to panels and trimmings (Figs. 29 & 30). Mourning specifications also extended to ornaments and accessories, so heavy jewellery of jet or cheaper black glass ('French jet') often replaced brooches, lockets and other trinkets of gold and coloured stones (Fig. 27). Further indications of female mourning may include black clothing worn with a special headdress - headwear that could take many forms such as a black hat and veil (Fig. 25), a modest black bonnet tied under the chin (Title Picture) or a cap made with crape or dull black fabric 'falls' - the trailing streamers sometimes worn by widows (Fig. 28). Mourning for men was less complex and by the Victorian era was usually represented by a black suit worn with a black tie (Figs. 26 & 29), although sometimes a watch chain fashioned from a dull black metal instead of gold, or a black armband may also be present. The children of a household were also put into mourning dress if, for example, they had lost a parent or sibling and where a child is clothed in black in a photograph this is very likely to indicate mourning as usually children were not dressed in this colour (Fig. 26 (right)). In some circles it was thought inappropriate for the very young to wear black, so instead infants were often dressed in white garments with black trimmings (Fig. 26 (left)).

Identifying the mourning photographs in a collection reveals visual records of some of the most poignant moments in a family's experiences and may also help with wider picture research. Once a mourning portrait has been identified, it is generally possible to connect it to within a year or so of a recorded death in the family, this being most easily established if the subject or subjects are already known since they were most likely to have been mourning a close relative. Similarly, once the approximate time frame for a mourning photograph has been determined from the style of dress, the occasion can often pinpoint the date of the picture to within a year or two. A closely dated mourning photograph may even assist with identifying a forebear who has not yet been named, as the occasion will narrow down the possibilities.

Family groups

Group paintings representing several members of the same family were a popular subject for artists from the earliest times - portraits of parents with their offspring, extended family groups, or the children of a household - pictures which, over time, reflected shifting ideas about the significance of family and contemporary experiences of domestic life. By the time photography offered an alternative portrait medium in the mid-19th century there was a growing emphasis on the importance of family life - hearth and home representing (in theory at least) a secure and comfortable retreat from the toil and routine of work and the accelerating pace of life in the outside world. Middle class Victorian values are expressed in family group photographs of the 19th century, a sense of traditional family hierarchy conveyed by a patriarchal father dominating the group, or the shared joys of parenthood evoked in pictures of father and mother together, surrounded by their children (Figs. 31, 33 & 34). The popularity of formal family group photographs continued well into the 20th century, carefully-posed studio representations of domestic stability and unity (Figs. 35-40).

Following artistic tradition, early photographers often charged higher prices for portraits composed of several figures. In the 1850s and early 1860s, photographing large groups of people was considered a complex operation, a technical feat and test of the photographer's skill and judgement, and so most family group photographs dating from the early decades of photography were restricted to relatively small numbers of people. A mid-Victorian household might be photographed by a professional photographer outside their home, as seen in Ch 6 Figs. 1 & 2, but it was more usual for clients to visit a local photographer's studio for a family group picture (Figs. 31 & 32). With the widespread use of faster dry photographic plates by the 1880s it became easier to successfully capture greater numbers of people, and this is noticed especially by the 1890s, when large group photographs become common. The extended family gathering, either photographed indoors in the studio, or outdoors, was a popular theme by the late Victorian and Edwardian eras (Figs. 34 & 35 and Ch 6 Fig. 6). Within the genre of family group photographs a special type of picture may also crop up in a collection - the portrait depicting successive generations of the family. Examples may occur in a 19th or 20th century context, the occasion often prompted by the birth of a new baby representing the next generation: as soon as he or she was old enough to visit the studio, attended by father, grandfather (and great grandfather, if he was still alive), or mother, grandmother and great grandmother, a celebratory photograph followed, demonstrating the healthy progression of men or women in the family - the successful continuation of the male or female line (Fig. 38).

Fig. 1 Christening carte de visite, c.1887-90.
This Victorian photograph from the album depicted in Ch 2 Fig. 54 shows a baby around the time of her christening, propped up on a couch next to a canine companion. Dogs occasionally appear in 19th century studio photographs, although they are more common by the early 20th century. Nothing is known about this infant but she is probably a girl, judging from the towering white ribbon-trimmed bonnet which mirrors fashionable women's headwear of the late-1880s. She is bundled up in a *porte-bebe*, a comfortable contrivance popular for late-Victorian christenings, and also wears a decorative cape for this special occasion.

Fig. 2 Baptism studio photograph, late 1911 or early 1912
This studio photograph of uncertain format shows a middle-class family posing in their best clothing to commemorate the baptism of their baby boy, born in October 1911. He wears a traditional christening gown, which is typically very long and is ornamented around the hem with bands of cutwork, a popular form of decoration for baby wear. Unfortunately he died of meningitis in 1913 when only eighteen months old, making this photograph particularly special to the family

Fig. 3 Christening snapshot, London, September 1946
Amateur snapshots often captured 20th century family christenings and this informal photograph was taken outside Westminster Cathedral in September 1946, where the baby girl seen here was christened. She was the first grandchild of the then High Commissioner for Ireland, who holds her proudly in this picture. She wears a fine white christening gown embellished with delicate tucks and a crocheted shawl.

T. F. FARTHING   IPSWICH

Fig. 4 3rd or 4th Birthday carte de visite, c. 1870s
This studio portrait belongs to a collection of family photographs from a Victorian album dated 1863
(see Ch 2 Fig. 53). The style of the little girl's clothing and the padded velvet chair together suggest a
date range in the late 1860s or 1870s. She is thought to be one of several children born to the family
between 1870 and 1889 - most likely the first daughter, born in August 1870, or the second, born in
December 1873. The fact that she appears in this photograph alone, without her parents, suggests that
she was celebrating a personal occasion – perhaps her third or fourth birthday.

Fig. 5 21st Birthday Cabinet Print, c.1887-9

Although nothing is known about this young woman, judging from her appearance the photograph may well have been taken to mark her 21st birthday. She is dressed in the fashionable style of the late-1880s, characterised by an extremely tight-fitting bodice with pointed centre-front and shortened sleeves, and a skirt whose fullness suggests the later stages of the bustle or the residual padding about the hips that followed its collapse. The dark velvet or plush and satin fabric combination in the one outfit was a common feature of late-1880s dress. Signs that she was celebrating a special occasion are the floral corsage on her bodice and the basket of flowers.

Fig. 6 21st Birthday cabinet print, 1895

This studio portrait represents a relative born in 1874. Although the popular late-Victorian head and shoulders oval vignette composition offers only a limited view of her appearance, the very full puffed sleeves confirm a date in the mid-1890s, strongly suggesting that this photograph was taken in 1895, to mark her 21st birthday. The ribbons on her bodice, easily removed, add a decorative effect for this special occasion, while her brooch, which still survives within the family, may well have been a 21st birthday present.

Fig. 7 70th birthday ambrotype, c.1858

This undated ambrotype depicts an elderly lady who, like many women from the Luton area was a straw plaiter throughout her working life - as were both her mother and daughter. She wears a matron's modest frilled cap and her clothing is largely concealed by a shawl and apron, making it difficult to date very closely, but her appearance, combined with the simple studio setting, suggest a date of c.1855-60. The time frame suggests that she may well have sat for this portrait in 1858, to mark the occasion of her 70th birthday. She was the first of 7 successive generations of females in the family to be portrayed in a photograph.

Fig. 8 60th Birthday Portrait, dated 1889

This head and shoulders oval vignette composition - popular between the end of the 1880s and early 1900s - is a splendid portrait of an elderly lady who visited the photographer's studio in 1889 to commemorate her 60th birthday. She is very well-dressed in a manner befitting her age, the occasion and also her social status as the wife of a successful master boot maker and owner of a shoe shop in Woodbridge, Suffolk. She wears elaborate outdoor clothing comprising possibly a dolman (a short, cape-like coat worn during the 1880s) and a towering bonnet of fashionable black lace and white velvet, tied under her chin with a black silk ribbon.

Fig. 9 70th Birthday studio photograph, dated 1934
Although amateur snapshots were more popular than professional photographs by the inter-war years, this lady chose a formal studio portrait to commemorate her 70th birthday in March 1934. Her hair is stylishly waved and bobbed in typical early-1930s manner and she is smartly dressed in a fine white blouse decorated with a brooch (perhaps a birthday present), a long cardigan with fashionable scalloped edging and a skirt secured with a bold buckled belt. Although married, she ran her own tobacconist and sweet shop for many years and was rather a grand lady, who her descendants recall did not 'do' housework, but employed others to clean, wash and iron for her family.

Fig. 10 Breeching and birthday carte de visite 1876/7
These children from a working-class family may well have visited the studio together to mark the boy's breeching and possibly the girl's birthday – an economical double portrait for a joint celebration. He looks to be a suitable age for breeching and here wears the popular *zouave* ensemble that was first introduced for small boys during the 1860s. This distinctive outfit comprised a short bolero-style jacket with rounded edges, waistcoat and knickerbockers that were either gathered below the knee or left open, as here. His sister wears the full-skirted style of frock that remained fashionable for young girls until the end of the 1870s.

LOVELL   WHITEHAVEN.

Fig. 11 Breeching carte de visite dated 1880
The handwritten note on the reverse of this photograph confirms that this little boy, born in March 1876, was aged four when he visited the photographer's studio. This was a common age for boys' breeching and here he wears a miniature version of a man's lounge suit, comprising a lounge jacket, matching waistcoat and shorts or knickerbockers ending just below the knee, although we cannot see their hem. His jacket, fashionably edged with silk braid binding, is tailored in the narrow style of the period and even features a handkerchief in the breast pocket: a little bowler hat completes his new outfit.

Fig. 12 Elementary school photograph, 1903/4

This official school photograph, taken in 1903 or 1904 in Kent, shows a large class of elementary school children aged around five, with their teacher and probably the headmistress. Uniform was not required at that level, so the children are wearing everyday dress typical of the Edwardian era, although they had probably been told to 'come clean' that day for the photograph. The girls all wear smock dresses - usual for young girls from the mid-1890s until the 1910s - many of them protected by a clean white pinafore. The boys wear knickerbockers suits, the jackets showing the popularity of many different collar styles at this date - the very wide frilled variety, the Eton collar and versions of the sailor collar. Black woollen stockings or shorter socks, worn with laced leather boots, also confirm a very early 20th century date.

Fig. 13 Coming of age carte de visite, c.1864

Like many portraits of children and young people, this carte de visite had the subject's name and age written on the back. This ancestor, born in 1849, was only fifteen when she posed for her photograph, but is already wearing full adult dress, suggesting that the portrait was taken to commemorate her 'coming of age' - the point at which she put her hair up and lowered her skirts to the floor. Her fine silk outfit with fashionable geometric trimming certainly suggests a special occasion, while the full shape of her crinoline skirt supports a likely year of 1864, as indicated by her age.

Fig. 14 Coming of age carte de visite, c.1890-92

This photograph shows the same relative (centre) who appears in Fig. 6 and was born in 1874. Her companions here are not recognisable as family members and, since they all seem to be of similar age, the three young women were probably friends. A close date range of c.1890-2 can be deduced from their fashionable tight-fitting bodices and plain panelled skirts, in particular the vertical puffs at their shoulders - an early sign of the 'leg-o'-mutton' sleeve. In 1890-92 the known subject would have been aged between sixteen and eighteen, the stage of life at which Victorian girls commonly progressed to full adult dress. This would have been a suitable event for young female friends to celebrate together, their garland of leaves or flowers (possibly a studio prop) suggesting that this photograph did indeed mark a special occasion.

Fig. 15 Brothers' celebration photograph, c.1896-8

These three brothers from a working-class family apparently visited the studio together to mark important stages in their young lives. The oldest, born in September 1881, wears naval uniform, and to judge from his cap tally, was about to join the Admiralty-run boy seaman training establishment known as *HMS Boscawen*. Internet research reveals that in the late-19th century it accepted boys between the ages of 15 and 16 ½, so this offers a date-range of late 1896 - early 1898 for the photograph. The middle boy, aged 13 or 14, wears a white tie, suggesting a special occasion for him also - perhaps his first wearing of long trousers as part of a 'grown-up' suit. The youngest, aged 10 or 11, wears a smaller boy's suit comprising a Norfolk jacket and knickerbockers. In the 1890s children could leave school at the age of 11, so this brother, who may be holding a certificate, had quite possibly just completed his education.

Fig. 16 University carte de visite, c.1897-9

Initially this photograph was a mystery, except that the head and shoulders vignette composition indicated a likely 1890s date, while the Oxford location suggested that the subject may have been a student. The three feathers embossed on the black mount narrowed the date to at least 1893 as online research into the photographers (operating today as Gilman & Soame) revealed this to be the year of their Prince of Wales appointment. Aided by the estimated date range, the subject was identified as an ancestor born in 1879 and recorded on the 1901 census as a student. The white tie and formal frock coat seen here imply a special occasion, while his youthful appearance suggests that he was still aged in his 'teens'. It seems likely, then, that this photograph marked his entry into Oxford University, probably some time between 1897 and 1899.

Fig. 17 Second World War Studio portrait, early 1940

This photograph depicts the author's father, who at 22 signed up for military service in 1939 and served throughout WW2 with the Royal Engineers. Were his regiment not known, it would not be obvious from his new army uniform, which bears no cap badge, shoulder title or insignia. An early war date is, though, confirmed by the style of his battledress blouse, which is standard 1937 Pattern, featuring pocket flaps and pleats and covered buttons (economy battledress, introduced during 1940, had no pleats or button coverings), so this photograph was probably taken early in 1940 after he had passed through basic training. This was a popular subject for a professional wartime portrait, a visual record of successful completion of the first stage of military duties, expressing glowing health, confidence and anticipation before the true horrors of war became a reality.

Fig. 18 Achievement ambrotype, c.1855-9

This fine ambrotype, protected in its original folding case, was sent from Australia to England in the later 1850s - a photograph for the family at home demonstrating a new life overseas, achievement and financial success. The ancestor portrayed, aged here in his 30s, was a struggling agricultural labourer until he emigrated with his wife to Australia in 1852 to seek his fortune prospecting for gold (discovered there in 1851). By 1855 the couple were making a good living as miners, able to afford to send £10 home to each of their mothers, and his photograph probably dates from that time or soon afterwards. His pale-coloured linen sack (or *sacque*), a relatively casual coat worn during the 1840s and 1850s in summer and, especially, in hot climates, follows the narrow tailored style of the era and is teamed here with formal waistcoat and necktie. His beard, grown under the chin, is the early type worn in the later 1850s.

Fig. 19 Engagement carte de visite, c.1880-83

This studio photograph of an unknown young woman is dateable to the 1880s from the studio setting, especially the presence of the bark-covered fence. The style of her fashionable outfit comprising long cuirass bodice and narrow gathered and pleated skirt confirms a date early in the decade. She wears a rose corsage on her bodice and holds a small posy of flowers, features strongly suggesting that she visited the photographer to mark a special occasion. Careful positioning reveals her left hand, where we see a single band, possibly set with gem stones, displayed on her engagement and wedding ring finger, implying that the picture marked her engagement. Her matching bracelets may also have been presents from her fiancé.

U. H. Jacob

BROADWAY STUDIO
SANDGATE.

Fig. 20 Engagement Cabinet print, 1896/7

The same relative pictured in Figs. 6 & 14, this young lady visited the photographer again one or two years after her 21st birthday to mark the occasion of her engagement. For this important portrait she wears a stylish costume whose shape demonstrates the hour-glass silhouette that was evolving by the late-1890s. Her bodice features interesting double-puffed sleeves - an unusual version of the late *gigot* or leg-o'-mutton style - while her gold bar brooch is another item of jewellery still owned by the family. Her outfit is teamed with fashionable outdoor accessories and her engagement ring is seen clearly on the ring finger of her left hand. She married in December 1897.

Fig. 21 Wedding carte de visite, c.1864-6

This is a typical mid-Victorian marriage portrait depicting a young, newly-wedded couple who visited the photographer's studio after the church ceremony. Although they are unidentified, the close circa date derives from a combination of the photographer's operational dates and the style of clothing. In the absence of any other obvious visual clues suggesting a wedding, the main feature identifying the occasion is their close positioning in this characteristic composition - one figure seated and the other standing. Most ordinary working ancestors simply wore their best clothing on their wedding day at this time, 'white' weddings being the preserve of the wealthy. The groom is well-dressed in a formal frock coat with matching waistcoat and trousers and the bride wears a good silk gown in the full style of the mid 1860s.

Fig. 22 Wedding scene, June 1946

This airy outdoor wedding scene contrasts strikingly with the sombre Victorian studio portrait seen in Fig. 21, illustrating just how far weddings and their representations evolved in 80 years. During the early 20th century the custom for brides to wear special white bridal gowns slowly became established and it became usual for bridesmaids in matching outfits to attend, as seen in this London wedding photograph from 1946. There is no mistaking the occasion here, although even 'traditional' white weddings followed different conventions and modes of bridal wear evolved over time. Were the year of this wedding not known, a 1940s date would be evident from the style of the dresses and the short veils worn by the bridesmaids.

Fig. 23 Wedding Anniversary carte de visite, 1890

Although unmarked, this group portrait is thought to date from 1890, a date well supported by the style of the lady's outfit, especially her close-fitting, front buttoning bodice with narrow sleeves and fashionable velvet panels and cuffs. In September 1890 this couple (the bridal couple seen in Ch 5 Fig. 1) celebrated their 25th wedding anniversary, so this was probably the event that inspired the photograph. Often a whole family was included in anniversary photographs and here the mother and father are surrounded by their four surviving children - sons aged 16 and 11 and daughters aged 10 and 8. Everyone is well-dressed for this memento of an important occasion.

Fig. 24 Studio anniversary photograph, c.1908

Several undated photographs of this London working-class couple and their relatives survive in the Victorian album illustrated in Ch 2 Fig. 53, these two ancestors also being seen in Fig. 26 below. Because elderly forebears tended to dress rather conservatively, it may be difficult to date their clothing very closely and here the stylistic clues merely suggest a late-Edwardian date. By this time women usually wore a separate blouse and skirt, as seen here, older ladies often favouring black garments. The man wears a conservative winged collar with a typically plain, dark lounge suit. The couple married in 1868, so it seems quite possible that this formal studio photograph was taken to mark their 40th wedding anniversary in 1908.

Fig. 25 Mourning carte de visite, c.1866

This unmarked photograph depicting the same ancestor seen in Fig. 13 was not fully understood until her appearance was recently analysed. Her stylish outdoor ensemble comprising a short jacket and vast crinoline skirt with a pronounced backward sweep was dated to around the mid-1860s, a time frame also indicated by her hair, drawn off her face in a fairly high chignon. Her fine, sombre garments are fashioned from black or dark-coloured silk and velvet - fabrics not officially recommended for mourning, especially later in the century, but seemingly acceptable for a girl of seventeen in the 1860s: certainly her fashionable hat, draped with a black veil suggested that bereavement was the occasion that had prompted the photograph. Family records, consulted again, revealed that her older sister died in 1866, a year which perfectly fits the visual evidence.

Fig. 26 Mourning carte de visite, c.1875

This subdued family group portrait depicting the same couple as in Fig. 24 above, with two of their children, represents a much earlier and more troubled stage of their lives. Although initially undated and unidentified, close scrutiny of the subjects and dating of their dress indicated that the photograph was taken early in 1875, specifically to record the family in mourning following the tragic death of their 2-year old son in December 1874. Deep mourning is evidenced by the mother's outfit, a dress made in the style of the early 1870s from dull black fabric, with only a hint of white at the cuffs. Victorian men wore little obvious mourning attire, but the father, a carter by trade, wears a black tie with a black lounge suit. Their oldest daughter, aged about 4 ½, wears a new black frock, while the dress of the little girl, aged about 15 months, follows the latest recommendations for infants in mourning - a white frock trimmed with black ribbon. Another son born later, in 1876, was named after his deceased brother; 8 of the 9 children born to this family between 1870 and 1889 survived.

H.LENTHALL
PHOTOGRAPHER

222,
Regent Street,
LONDON

Fig. 27 Mourning carte de visite, c.1869-75
This unmarked and unidentified photograph is dateable from the layered style of the woman's fashionable clothing and from her high-piled hairstyle to the period c.1869-75. The most striking feature of the picture is her wearing of mourning dress, as seen distinctly from the very dull quality of her black dress fabric - probably *bombazine* or a cheaper *bombazet* or *paramatta*. She also wears prominent mourning jewellery - black beads, brooch and possibly the cross pendant - which may be made of jet or of inexpensive black glass, known as 'French jet'.

Fig. 28 Mourning studio photograph, c.1880s
This photograph is mounted as a circular medallion on a square black mount of a non-standard size, the black frame or border occurring from time to time in connection with mourning portraits. The young lady, reputedly an ancestor born in 1873, is clearly wearing mourning attire, judging from her black cap with its long black veil or falls hanging down behind. Her deep circular white collar was a fashionable feature of the 1880s, making her no older than sixteen here - or perhaps her identity is incorrect.

Fig. 29 Mourning cabinet print, c.1897/8

This unmarked studio portrait is closely dateable to the later 1890s from the style of the lady's outfit, especially the shape of her 'leg-o'-mutton' sleeves. The decoration of her dress demonstrates that she is in mourning, the textured crape bands trimming her cuffs, bodice and shoulder epaulettes and also forming a belt at her waist. Her husband, a prosperous Liverpool butcher and freemason, is also wearing a black tie, which is often the only obvious sign of mourning in men. Research confirmed that the couple's six year old daughter died in September 1897, so evidently here they were formally marking the sad event with a visit to the photographer.

JAS.R.MᶜKIE   LIVERPOOL.

Fig. 30 Mourning cabinet print, c.1897/8
This ancestor was the sister of the lady portrayed in Fig. 29 and is very stylishly dressed for a woman aged in her mid-40s. Although it appears rather different in some respects, her outfit also dates to the same period as the previous photograph, judging from the shapely hourglass silhouette and the style of her sleeves. The large areas of crape fabric on her bodice suggest that she is in mourning here for the same child - her little niece, who had died in September 1897. Mourning dress was expected to look fashionable as well as subdued, and here the crape material has been cleverly used to form the puff of the late-1890s sleeve, as well as the central bodice panel.

Fig. 31 Family group ambrotype, c.1857-60

This photograph originates from Ireland - probably the Limerick area - and was taken in the photographer's studio, as far as it is possible to tell from the rather blank background. Having lost its original frame or case, the fragile image on glass has been broken but it remains a fine early family portrait, the late-1850s date judged from the fashion clues. The father, standing masterfully at the back of the group, wears the narrow frock coat of the era, with a contrasting chequered waistcoat. The mother is well-dressed in a shining silk gown featuring the fashionable flared *pagoda* sleeves of the 1850s and handsome black jewellery. The daughters look picturesque in matching dresses, their bodices displaying the characteristic V-shape and wide sleeves of the 1850s and full skirts accentuated with flounces. As was common, the image has been retouched to bring a faint blush to cheeks and pick out the girls' bright neck ribbons.

Fig. 32 Family group ambrotype or late daguerreotype, c.1860-5
The format of this one-off framed photograph has not been positively identified by the owner, but it is
either an ambrotype, or a late daguerreotype protected by a layer of glass. Judging age accurately in
photographs can be difficult, so it is unclear whether the members of this family group are a brother and
four sisters, or the three older sisters and their mother. Everyone is well-dressed for this photograph in
keeping with their middle class status, the style of the ladies' clothing dating the picture to the early
1860s. They all wear wide crinoline skirts with fashionable short jackets, topped by contemporary hats
including the feathered 'pork pie' hat (front, and back left), in vogue in the late 1850s and early 1860s,
when the hair was still worn in a low chignon. Their male relative is stylishly dressed in a lounging
jacket and an early form of the bowler hat, characterised at this date by its low crown.

Fig. 33 Family group cabinet print, c.1891-3

This photograph was displayed in the 1886 photograph album depicted in Ch 2 Fig. 54. Unfortunately nothing is known about this family group, or even the name of the studio, since the back of the card is blank. However, the mother's outfit closely dates the image to c.1891-3, the best dating clue being the well-defined vertical puff at the shoulder of her blouse or bodice - an early phase of the 'leg-'o-mutton' shape. Her husband wears the elegant morning coat that was often teamed with slim-fitting, pin-striped trousers in the 1880s and 1890s. Their two daughters both wear their hair in short fringes, fashionable for girls in the 1880s and 1890s. The older daughter's dress is an early version of the smock, soon to become the principal style for girls, while the dress and pinafore of the youngest daughter are caught at the waist by a sash, also a common feature of the 1890s.

Fig. 34 Family group professional photograph, c.1896-8

Large group photographs taken outside are a notable feature of the 1890s, these portraits being well-suited to large family gatherings, as shown by this undated photograph of a couple with their nine children. As usual in mixed groups, the lady's outfit offers the best dating clues: the shape of her sleeves suggest a date of c.1896-8, years when the 'leg-o'-mutton' sleeve may still appear full, but the puff was starting to retreat up the arm. This date range is supported by the appearance of the eldest son in his military uniform, for he had joined the Royal Marines in 1895. His next two brothers both wear lounge jackets and round caps, an embryonic school boys' style which was soon to evolve into a recognisable uniform, while a younger brother (right) wears the usual young boys' knickerbockers suit with the fashionable Eton collar. Two sisters wear smart smock dresses, introduced in the 1890s for younger girls, and the 'baby' - a daughter of around three - wears the usual dress and sash combination.

Fig. 35 Family group studio portrait, 1905

The Edwardians loved large family gatherings and here an extended family group posed in a studio in 1905, everyone dressed up for the photograph. The ladies look formal in their decorative, high-necked blouses, the wide lace collars a fashion feature often seen around mid-decade. The men mainly wear the turned-down starched shirt collar that was rapidly becoming established as the norm, although one still favours the more formal standing collar. They have all adopted the 'modern' clean shaven look, except for the slightly older man, who retains a prominent moustache. The little boy at the back wears the belted tunic and shorts beginning to be worn by small boys during this decade, his vast collar reflecting the continuing popularity of the sailor style. The girls all wear the loose smock dresses introduced in the 1890s, these 'best' versions very elaborate, in keeping with contemporary taste. One girl is wearing the huge hair bow which became a familiar sight as girls grew their hair longer.

199

Fig. 36 Family group studio portrait, c.1919

This formal studio portrait shows how families generally became smaller as the 20th century advanced, although this is a particularly modest example as there was only the one child, born in 1914, whose birth year helps to closely date the image. Her father, a dock worker for most of his life and aged 40 or 41 here, is conservatively dressed in a smart lounge suit and starched collar and bow tie, his toothbrush moustache a style characteristic of the 1910s-1930s and worn mainly by mature men. His wife wears a good day dress of fine fabric, its prominent collar a major fashion feature of the later 1910s and early 1920s. Their daughter wears the latest modes for small girls - a short white dress, much simpler in form and detail than earlier styles, made, typically, with three-quarter length sleeves and worn with 'modern' white socks. The enormous bow in her hair is a feature often noticed in photographs of the 1910s.

Fig. 37 Family group studio portrait, 1923

This photograph was presented as a folding card and inside was written 'Christmas 1923', several copies being sent to different branches of the family in both England and Australia. The family are the same one featured in the 1911/12 baptism photograph (Fig. 2) but, having lost the baby, have since acquired three more children, making six in all. The mother has kept abreast of changing fashions and looks smart and well-groomed, her hemline still firmly calf-length in 1923. The adult daughter is very fashionably dressed in the new round-necked style of dress, her neckline decorated with a string of beads - a new fashion accessory, while the younger girls, of school age, wear 'best' matching dresses secured with a low sash. The older son wears an adult three-piece lounge suit, his very short, narrow trousers worn with sharp creases and turn-ups typical of this decade. The younger son's jacket and shorts, worn with long socks, are reminiscent of school wear.

Fig. 38 Four generations of the family studio portrait, c.1925
This photograph, taken c.1925, reflects the enduring popularity of group portraits depicting several generations of either females or males within a family, a theme that celebrated birth, parenthood, longevity and the continuation of the family line. The four generations of women captured here are great grandmother (left), born in 1849 (also pictured in Figs. 24 & 26), grandmother (right), born in 1878, mother (centre back) born in 1901, and her baby daughter, born in 1925. The two younger women wear loose, round-necked, calf-length dresses typical of the mid-1920s, with long strings of pearls, while their older relative prefers a traditional floor-length black outfit, an outmoded style that many elderly ladies retained well into the 20th century.

Fig. 39 Family group studio portrait, c.1933-7

The composition of this undated studio portrait is typical of inter-war photographs, when the camera moved in closer and heads were often angled against a skillfully-lit backdrop. The mother's fashionable appearance suggests a date around the mid-1930s, her hair waved and bobbed in early-mid decade style and her dress fabric printed with bold motifs in late *Art deco* style. Her daughter's appearance shows the growing taste for elaborate 'best' and party wear for girls by the mid-1930s, her hair dressed with prominent ribbons and her highly-patterned dress made with puffed sleeves and a rounded collar. The son wears a casual style of short-sleeved shirt with a collar, similar to the new sports shirt becoming fashionable for men at that time.

Fig. 40 Family group studio portrait, 1948 or 1949

The son in this professional photograph was born in 1945, so a date of 1948 or 1949 seems likely. His appearance is typical of this decade, when little boys often looked rather formal in shirts and ties, his patterned fair isle-style knitted waistcoat demonstrating the early-mid-20th century fashion for hand-knitted garments. His father also wears a knitted woollen waistcoat, his checked sports jacket and patterned tie again characteristic of the era. The mother wears the curled or rolled neck-length hairstyle fashionable during the war and afterwards, until c.1950/51, when shorter hair returned. Her full-skirted dress is influenced by the 'New Look', introduced in 1947.

FIVE

CHAPTER FIVE

*Family Wedding
Photographs*

M arriage has been one of the most common themes within family portraiture for centuries and every picture archive will include images of past weddings - special occasions that have influenced the course of every family's history. Original artworks portraying prosperous ancestors at the time of their betrothal or marriage have been passed down in some families (see Chapter 1), while surviving wedding photographs are plentiful, some being preserved in special wedding albums. This chapter looks at the unique significance of wedding photographs to the family historian, offers help with recognising early wedding pictures where the occasion may not be obvious and generally highlights the main features to look out for in wedding photographs of different eras. Changing social customs and bridal traditions underlie family wedding photographs: dress is especially significant and costume dating clues are emphasised as styles of bridal wear and the clothing of fashionably-dressed bridesmaids and guests offer the best method of dating, and ultimately identifying, unfamiliar wedding scenes. Finally there are suggestions as to how to find complementary newspaper reports of weddings, as written details can complement and explain further the pictorial details seen in photographs. The photographic sequence at the end of the chapter illustrates a wide variety of family weddings from the 1860s to 1950 - life-changing events experienced by affluent and poorer ancestors and relatives alike.

The significance of family wedding photographs

All family historians appreciate the significance of discovering and recording forebears' weddings when drawing up the family tree and reconstructing the past, paired names and dates deriving from one of the principal genealogical sources - the national marriage indexes. Surviving wedding pictures add another, more tangible dimension to this key aspect of historical research, for when a photograph can be connected directly with an entry in the marriage index, it provides a clear visual expression of the recorded fact. Old photographs often help to illuminate genealogical research, bringing life and colour to the printed details, and pictorial and documentary evidence combines most effectively when we are able to see in a surviving wedding photograph a view of the very event registered in the official records.

Family wedding photographs may portray ancestors and relatives from all walks of life, span different time periods and show various geographical locations, so as a genre they are extraordinarily varied and full of interesting detail. Larger wedding group scenes show how bygone weddings, as today, brought diverse relatives together for the occasion and so, helpfully, they often depict many faces from the past all in the one picture. This can assist identification of unknown family members who appear in other photographs and may also help with making vital connections between individuals. In addition a wedding photograph may offer the only known picture of more elusive forebears who otherwise seem to have evaded the lens of the camera.

Wedding pictures are uniquely emotive images which often inspire profound personal attachments and sentiments. There is a powerful sense of occasion attached to weddings and, whatever our individual views on marriage or religious convictions may be, most of us regard wedding photographs as special mementoes. They may act as a reminder of a joyful event personally attended in the past, while older examples show ancestors at what we like to believe was a happy, optimistic stage of their lives. Standard poses and fixed expressions convey little of the private thoughts or feelings of the participants, yet wedding pictures embody some of the most potent human emotions, understood by all generations. They are also the mask behind which lie the real-life family dramas which often surrounded these momentous occasions, and which are relived in the stories traditionally handed down through families - tales of romance, pregnant brides, borrowed dresses, torn veils, lost rings, missing bridegrooms or uninvited guests.

Identifying mystery wedding photographs

Because inherited wedding pictures tend to enjoy a special status within families, many are well-documented or can be firmly identified. It may seem surprising that any picture as important as a wedding photograph could possibly have gone unrecorded but the fact is that some examples have been passed down unlabelled and are now unfamiliar to today's generation. In some cases there is confusion over whose marriages they represent, especially if an ancestor or relative married more than once, or if there were several weddings in a family within a short space of time. Such cases highlight the importance of making careful records of such events; meanwhile, when trying to solve the problem of 'mystery' weddings from the past, the first step, as always, is to establish a close and accurate date range for the picture. Once a firm time frame has been determined for an unidentified wedding scene, it should in most cases be possible to link it to a recorded family marriage, assuming that the marriage details were entered in the register and copied into the indexes correctly. However if a connection is proving difficult to make, it could be that the photograph depicts more distant relatives, suggesting that the net might be cast wider when searching by name. It is also worth considering that a wedding photograph kept by forebears may not have been a souvenir of a family marriage at all, but a memento of a friend's, neighbour's or work colleague's wedding that they attended as guests.

Recognising early wedding photographs

Most private collections feature a number of wedding photographs but family historians may have inherited even more of these pictures than they realise. Although we know that photographs often marked a special occasion in the lives of past family members and that we should always consider *why* a particular photograph may have been taken (see Chapter 4), we may still easily overlook a Victorian or Edwardian marriage picture; this can even apply in cases where the names of the subjects portrayed are known, because early wedding images do not always fit in with our modern ideas about what they should look like. Nowadays we usually expect to see an elaborate setting, perhaps a white bridal gown, flowers, bridesmaids and other special accoutrements, yet many 19th and early 20th century wedding photographs display few, or none, of these identifying elements and simply appear as ordinary studio portraits of fashionably-dressed subjects. Recognising these precious pictures amongst a larger collection of family photographs becomes easier once we understand something of earlier pictorial conventions and past wedding customs.

Before the advent of photography and during the 1840s, when the new medium was in its infancy, it was common for prosperous ancestors to commission companion marriage paintings - individual portraits (often miniatures) of the betrothed or newly-married man and wife that were executed at the same time and afterwards hung side by side on the wall (see Ch 1 Figs. 11, 13 & 14). This tradition lingered on into the photographic era, so early daguerreotype and ambrotype photographs may well portray a bride and groom separately, and even later card-mounted cartes de visite and cabinet prints occasionally follow this earlier format. In such cases, with luck both wedding photographs will have been passed down together, the images usually easy to pair from their complementary frames or card mounts, identical photographer's details (where present) and, naturally, dress details confirming a comparable time period; sometimes, however, the paired pictures may have become disconnected over time, as was possibly the case with Fig. 7 - an isolated photograph of a bride.

The introduction of the carte de visite in the early-1860s brought photography to the masses and photographic evidence suggests that by mid-decade significant numbers of newly-weds - including brides and grooms from working class backgrounds - were recording their special day with a photograph. Since only wealthy Victorian families could afford to employ a professional photographer to attend the actual wedding, it became customary for a bridal couple to visit a local photographer at a convenient time after the ceremony. Generally no special setting was used to suggest the occasion, simply a conventional studio backdrop and furniture, and - unless the bride and groom had chosen separate portraits - they posed for a photograph together in the one picture. They might both stand side by side, as in Fig. 1, although the usual convention was for one to be seated, the other standing, as seen in Figs. 3, 5, 6, 9-12 & 15: sometimes it was the man, not the woman, who was seated, especially if he was tall, as the main concern was to fit the two heads comfortably into the limited field of focus. Generally the bride's wedding ring was prominently displayed so this feature can offer a helpful clue, although a tiny band may not be clear in faded or imperfect photographs, so apparent lack of a ring should not be a reason for discounting a possible wedding photograph. A simple, one-off photograph was all that most ordinary Victorian couples could afford: nor could they meet the expense of special white bridal attire which could not be worn again, hence the wearing of 'best' day dress, as seen in any other formal portrait.

Understanding that a photograph of a fashionably-dressed, often young couple in a standard studio setting is quite likely to be a wedding picture, can lead to many more such discoveries in family collections. The following sections expand this theme and explain more about past wedding practises by charting the evolution of the familiar 'white' wedding and demonstrating more specifically the features to look out for in wedding photographs of different decades.

The development of 'white' weddings

The special white gown and veil that have been popular with recent generations of brides developed only slowly, over many years. For centuries a fashionable coloured dress was the norm, often made in pale blue or pink - soft, fresh colours deemed appropriate to youth, although a preference for white (that is, ivory or cream) was developing amongst the upper classes by the late 18th century, becoming more pronounced in the Regency period. In 1840 Queen Victoria married her cousin Prince Albert of Saxe-Coburg, the event being depicted in a painting by Sir George Hayter and disseminated to a wider public through engraved copies. Departing from the heavy state robes worn by previous monarchs, she wore a creamy-white Spitalfields silk satin gown with a deep flounce of exquisite Honiton lace, which resembled evening dress of the period, on her head a circlet of orange blossom with a lace veil, and a long satin train ornamented with sprays of orange blossom, its reported six yards of material carried by twelve white-clad attendants. Flower-trimmed white bridal dresses with veils were worn again by the queen's children on their wedding days, lavish occasions that were well-publicised in photographs during the late 1850s and 1860s. It was then, under royal influence, that from the mid-19th century onwards an ornate white bridal gown and veil became fashionable for aristocratic and upper class weddings: this was the ideal to which all brides aspired, even if it was unattainable in practise. By this time the wearing of white had also become firmly linked to connotations of innocence, purity and inferred virginity, contemporary fashion plates and ladies' magazines actively promoting idealised images of demure, feminine brides wearing frothy white dresses and veils.

All the trappings associated with a formal 'white' wedding also came together around the same time. Bridal flowers made a fashionable comeback - both real blooms and artificial flowers: wreaths for the head, corsages on dresses, bridal bouquets and flower baskets. Typical Victorian choices were lily of the valley, stephanotis, rosebuds, myrtle, orange blossom and leaves, jasmine leaves and asparagus fern, many of which remained popular in the 20th century. For centuries cakes had been baked for wedding feasts, although elaborate tiered and encrusted confections of white sugar paste were another Victorian invention: cake decorations included flowers, ribbon favours and good luck charms and a tradition evolved for the top layer to be reserved for the christening of the first child. The 16th and 17th century practice of strewing dining tables with flowers was also revived in the 1870s, when wedding breakfasts began to feature elaborate table settings festooned with a formal tracery of flowers and greenery. Such extravagant weddings were costly affairs, however, and although embraced by wealthy ancestors, for many more years they were beyond the means of most working families.

Traditionally the expense of weddings was borne by the bride's parents and although respectable families made every effort to rise to the occasion, the heads of ordinary Victorian households could seldom afford to provide their daughters with an elaborate outfit just for the one day, stylish clothes for a bevy of bridesmaids and all the other accoutrements of a 'white' wedding. For brides from ordinary families the most practical and economical outfit was a fashionable day dress - a new purchase or simply a 'best' coloured dress - which could be worn again many times in the future. Surviving wedding garments in museum and private collections demonstrate the variety of colours worn in the 19th century, from the bright purples and magentas of the 1860s, following the invention of artificial dyes, to deep russets and browns in vogue during the 1870s and 1880s, while muted greys and mauves were chosen by brides in mourning at the time of their marriage. Coloured dresses made in the prevailing style might be teamed either with fashionable hats or with veils - the latter often treasured items handed down through the family (fulfilling the convention for brides to wear 'something old'). As the 19th century advanced more festive elements crept into weddings and wedding dress, and the full complement of bridal wear, flowers and bridesmaids grew increasingly popular amongst the middle classes, yet it was not until the early 20th century that 'white' weddings became common throughout society. By the 1920s white bridal wear was more affordable and the white wedding was less of a status symbol than previously: since then many brides have worn white and weddings have often been extravagant events, although there have always been exceptions, due to the exigencies of war, financial position, personal preference and considerations of age or status.

The extraordinary variety of bridal styles adopted by earlier generations from different social and occupational backgrounds, in all areas of the country and abroad, is seen in the diverse array of family wedding photographs surviving today, which depict ancestors and later relatives posing in photographer's studios, fields, back yards, the grounds of villas and country houses, pub gardens and outside churches. Looking closely at wedding photographs from the 1860s through to the 1940s in the following sections illustrates how these important events were represented at different times and should help researchers to date, identify and understand more about their own family wedding pictures.

The 1860s & 1870s
The earliest known photograph of a bride wearing a special white wedding dress is a daguerreotype taken by a Boston photographer in 1854, while the first known photograph to include bridesmaids is that depicting the marriage of Queen Victoria's eldest daughter, Princess Vicky, to Crown Prince Frederick in 1858, so family historians are very unlikely to discover photographs displaying such features until after those dates. The earliest photograph demonstrating bridal wear that this author has seen is an ambrotype of 1860, in which the bride wears a plain white dress without headwear (not featured). Photographs of impressive white weddings begin to occur in some family collections from the later 1860s onwards, outdoor scenes depicting elaborately-dressed bridal party and guests gathered in the elegant grounds of the bride's family home (Figs. 2, 4 & 8). Wedding group photographs such as these were taken outside using the more portable apparatus of the wet collodian process, but nonetheless the outdoor photographer of the late 1860s and

1870s had to bring a complete darkroom with him to the venue - often a handcart covered with a black tent into which he placed his upper half so that he could work in the dark, producing instant negatives; the photographic prints, providing different views of the occasion, were produced later, back at his studio.

Prosperous ancestors' white weddings of the 1860s show the bride and several bridesmaids all wearing extravagant white silk or muslin dresses with orange blossom wreaths and lace or tulle veils (Figs. 2 & 4). Since her attendants often carried neat, round posy bouquets similar to that of the bride at this time it can be difficult at first glance to identify who is actually getting married (Fig. 4). By late decade a pronounced backward sweep to the skirts of bride's and bridesmaids' dresses is usually evident - a helpful stylistic clue seen best in Fig. 2. Meanwhile the bride's father, the groom, his best man and groomsmen or ushers - who were often as numerous as the bridesmaids - are depicted wearing dark (blue, claret, green or black) knee length frock coats with paler trousers, their outfits completed by a top hat, although hats were often removed for photographs (Figs. 2 & 4). This formal mode of male wedding attire continued to be worn for significant weddings into the 1870s (Fig. 8).

Lower down the social scale, more modest 1860s wedding photographs taken in a studio generally depict only the bridal couple, the bride dressed in a fashionable coloured daytime outfit made of silk, or the best fabric that she could afford. In photographs of early-mid decade the wide crinoline skirt is the fashionable style (Fig. 1 and Ch 4 Fig. 21); after c.1865 the skirt fullness is concentrated increasingly at the back and by c.1869 the silhouette has changed noticeably, the skirt becoming layered and the back draped up behind (Fig. 3). Grooms of the decade are portrayed wearing either a traditional frock coat (Fig. 3 and Ch 4 Fig. 21) or a loose lounging jacket, usually teamed with contrasting trousers (Fig. 1). As the casual lounge suit gained wider acceptance, it became the customary 'best' outfit for working class men, worn for Church, weddings and other social events. By the 1870s all three pieces of the suit were usually dark in colour and presented a more uniform appearance, as seen in wedding photographs of the decade (Figs. 5 & 6).

Following the style that was evolving by c.1869, brides' dresses of the early 1870s are layered and draped over a bustle: the bustle projection, which offers a clear dating clue, may not always be very apparent, especially when a bride is seated, but her layered and flounced skirt, elaborate bodice, high-piled hairstyle and complementary accessories will show the general look of the period (Figs. 5 & 6). After the mid-1870s, following another major fashion shift with the introduction of the new, elongated *cuirass* bodice, narrow one-piece 'princess' dresses with a train came into vogue (Figs. 7 & 8). White bridal dresses of this period were often made of a rich creamy satin, and since a trained *toilette* was customary for both formal daywear and for evening wear in the late 1870s, such wedding dresses might be altered and worn to dinner parties and other genteel social occasions afterwards, in keeping with contemporary etiquette. For formal and semi-formal weddings brides of the era generally wore veils (Figs. 7 & 8), but by now any bridesmaids were more likely to wear fashionable hats instead of veils: bridesmaids' headwear and the style of their garments often help with dating group wedding photographs, as in Fig. 8.

The 1880s

Most family wedding pictures surviving from the 1880s will, as in earlier decades, portray a respectably-dressed couple in the photographer's studio, for large group photographs taken outdoors were still the preserve of more prosperous ancestors at this time. Since bridal outfits followed current fashion, early in the decade the elongated *cuirass* line was still in vogue, presenting a narrow, sheath-like silhouette (Fig. 9). The long skirt train of the late 1870s having become outmoded c.1880, in full-length views it can be seen how brides' hemlines of the early 1880s were worn well off the floor, often being ornamented with tiers of kilt-pleating (Fig. 9). A significant shift in style occurred c.1883/4, when the bodice shortened and the bustle began to re-form, so projecting drapery at the back of skirts is evident once more in wedding pictures by mid-decade, remaining fashionable until around 1889 (Figs. 11 & 12). Photographic evidence also reveals that by the 1880s brides from various social backgrounds were beginning to adopt special accessories suited to the occasion - if not a veil, then perhaps a white hat and decorative ribbon trimmings worn as a sash or girdle (Figs. 10 & 12). By the end of the decade a growing interest in bridal flowers also becomes apparent, especially amongst the middle classes - for example a formal bouquet and/or a corsage for the bodice, as seen in Fig. 12. This trend, which helps us to recognise wedding photographs from this period onwards, may have evolved partly to compensate for the tendency by the late 1880s, for some better-off brides to abandon special white bridal wear in favour of fashionable coloured outfits on their wedding day. This development, noted in the fashion press at the time, was put down to a major change in canonical hours which occurred in 1886: until then marriage services had always taken place before noon, but afterwards weddings were often conducted in the afternoon, making it possible for brides to marry in fashionable afternoon ensembles - sufficiently formal to double-up as a going-away outfit after the festivities.

Throughout the 1880s many working-class bridegrooms and male wedding guests continued to wear the lounge suit, although following the general move away from the stately mid-Victorian frock coat towards the stylish morning coat for business and semi-formal wear, sometimes ordinary grooms wore a dark morning coat as part of a matching suit, these garments easily identified from their distinctive sloping front edges and neat, high lapels (Figs. 9-11). Like the lounge jacket, the morning coat of this era was slender in cut and was usually worn with the bowler hat (Figs. 9 & 10). By the end of the decade the formal frock coat was making a comeback in some circles but it was, by then, a closer-fitting garment, only worn in sombre black with dark, narrow trousers (Fig. 12). During this decade, echoing subtle developments in bridal attire, some bridegrooms wore a white tie as a sign of the occasion (Figs. 10 & 12); when partnering a bride carrying or wearing flowers, grooms might also sport a flower buttonhole or *boutonniere* (Fig. 12) - features which again draw attention to the occasion depicted in the photograph.

The 1890s

The 1890s witnessed a sharp rise in the number of large group wedding scenes - not only those representing elite weddings, but also those of the expanding middle classes. While modest studio portraits marking working class weddings typically portray only bride and groom, as in earlier decades (Fig. 15), more elaborate indoor photographs were beginning to picture entire wedding parties comprising several people (Fig. 13). By the mid-late 1890s many more photographs of even larger wedding groups were being taken outdoors, this trend reflecting a general growth in outdoor photography at that time and establishing a pattern for wedding pictures of the future (Figs. 14 & 16). Extended group wedding photographs inevitably offer family historians a more detailed and accurate impression of ancestors' weddings and convey a greater sense of occasion: for example they show that, by the 1890s, middle-class brides might have several attendants (once the preserve of the wealthy) comprising both adult bridesmaids and young flower girls dressed in white, carrying baskets of flowers (Figs. 13 & 16) - a tradition which was to continue well into the 20th century.

1890s wedding scenes also testify to the continuing popularity of fashionable daywear for brides, even within comfortably-off families: this may have been a continuation of late-1880s developments, although formal dress of the 1890s in any case produced a very ornate effect, well-suited to a special occasion. By mid decade photographs demonstrate boldly-coloured silk dress fabrics, vast puffed 'leg-o'-mutton' sleeves and a taste for elaborate lace and frills on bodices (Fig. 14). Equally, headwear was becoming increasingly decorative as hat brims grew wider by the year and crowns were piled with flowers, ribbons, bows, feathers and, sometimes, entire stuffed birds, this perhaps explaining why many 1890s brides chose fashionable hats instead of veils (Figs. 14 & 16). The custom for both bride and bridesmaids to wear corsages and carry bouquets also became more established during the 1890s, so many family wedding photographs from this decade are more easily recognisable, even if a special white bridal gown is absent. Grooms and best men from the lower classes generally wore their 'Sunday best' lounge suit (Fig. 15) while in large groups a mixture of male styles is evident, expressing the varying social status of different participants (Figs. 14 & 16): for example working men who employed others generally considered themselves a cut above the rest and for weddings dressed as gentlemen in either the newly-revived formal, silk-faced black frock coat or an elegant morning coat, with plain or striped grey trousers. A white knotted tie or bow tie - the 'correct' wear with evening dress - also became habitual for weddings and other special occasions during the 1890s.

The early-1900s

While some weddings of the new century were recorded in a studio photograph (Figs. 17 & 18), the outdoor wedding group photograph became increasingly popular - thus a great many Edwardian and later wedding photographs are posed in the open air, whether the location be a garden, the narrow yard of a terraced house or perhaps the sprawling grounds of a country pub or hotel (Figs. 19-21). Outside settings offered more scope for a professional (or amateur) photographer to take various shots of the bridal party and guests, and so several different photographs of a particular wedding are more likely to survive from around this time onwards.

Large group photographs lend Edwardian weddings a sense of grandeur, even though many were essentially relatively low-key affairs, as reflected in their setting. An appearance of luxury was accentuated by the exuberant style of Edwardian women's clothing and accessories, especially the vast hats of the era, and the vogue for extravagant floral bouquets with trailing greenery (Figs. 18-21). Fashion turned its back on the strong colours, heavy silks and stiff frills of the previous decade, ushering in soft pastel shades and lightweight fabrics such as chiffon and lace, well-suited to weddings. Bridal styles in fact varied widely during the early-1900s, as demonstrated in surviving photographs of the decade. For both formal and some humbler weddings a special 'white' (cream or ivory) bridal dress was becoming popular, the style of this era usually showing a high neckline and full sleeves: these were worn with a short veil, held well back on the head with a wreath of flowers (Figs. 18-20). However further down the social scale other combinations of dress and headwear remained common, possibilities including a veil or a stylish hat worn with a fashionable coloured dress (Fig. 17) or a white hat teamed with a smart white blouse and skirt (Fig. 21) - a choice which expressed the growing taste for white attire as the decade advanced, even if a special gown and veil were beyond reach. Bridesmaids, present at many weddings by this time, were dressed alike, or in different coloured dresses which complemented the bride's outfit, while the role of flower girl was often performed by younger sisters or nieces of bride or groom, as seen in Figs. 19 & 21. Late-Victorian conventions surrounding male wedding attire continued, the hiring of formal morning suits also becoming common by now (for example, Moss Bros, established in 1851, first opened its men's hire department in

1897). Alternatively men with a military background might wear a uniform for weddings (Figs. 19 & 21), uniforms being set to feature more frequently in wedding photographs throughout the following decades.

The 1910s

Studio wedding photographs may survive for the 1910s, these being a common choice of the First World War years (1914-18), when weddings were often simple affairs, perhaps organised at short notice to fit around the groom's departure for war, a brief period of leave, or following his return home. Otherwise outdoor wedding pictures predominate during this decade, some examples representing amateur 'snapshots', others evidently the work of a professional photographer, hired for the occasion. Photographs of the 1910s demonstrate that flowers and bridesmaids were an established feature of most weddings, although the social status of a family may still be judged generally from the size of the party, the location or setting, the elegance - or otherwise - of the participants, and the scale of the floral arrangements.

Early-1910s photographs reveal the narrower, sleeker lines of post-Edwardian female fashion, brides wearing either special bridal attire or formal daywear, the vogue for sweeping feather-trimmed hats and exotic boas and stoles lending an exotic air to regular garments. Stylish dresses draped asymmetrically or layered, tunic-style, with or without trains, were worn for weddings before the war (Figs. 22 & 23), but from around mid-decade onwards fashion favoured more functional tailored suits or blouses and skirts, often in white (Figs. 24 & 25). Skirts were being worn wider and shorter by 1915, and the display of the lower leg inspired the wearing of white stockings and dainty white shoes, especially for summer weddings (Figs. 24 & 25). Fashionable headwear was also much plainer by the later 1910s, many young women still wearing wide-brimmed hats but with less decoration by this date, while older female guests may be seen in modest fitted hats with smaller brims or brimless tocques (Fig. 25). Up until the outbreak of war in 1914, established convention prevailed for men: within the upper classes a conservative black frock coat was still considered 'correct' wear for weddings, although the sloping morning coat was usually favoured by successful businessmen and others of middling status (Fig. 23). Ordinary working men and many forward-looking men, especially the younger generation, wore their best lounge suits (Figs. 22, 24 & 25), a modern knotted tie in a plain colour often replacing the formal white tie or bow tie which had been popular for late-Victorian and Edwardian weddings. During and immediately after the war it was customary for grooms from all social backgrounds serving with the armed forces to proudly wear military uniform on their wedding day, as seen in Figs. 24 & 25.

The 1920s

Post-war wedding photographs include the occasional studio portrait, but the preference for outdoor scenes was well established by now. By the late 1920s views of bridal couples leaving the church were beginning to be taken - a new trend which became more pronounced in the following decades. Two important royal weddings were widely reported to the public in the early 1920s - the marriage of King George V and Queen Mary's daughter, Princess Mary, to Viscount Lascelles in 1922, and that of their second son, Prince Albert, Duke of York, to Lady Elizabeth Bowes-Lyon in 1923. These lavish occasions and the fairytale royal bridal gowns of ivory and silver inspired a new generation of brides and revived the sense of romance which had been absent from weddings during the war. Many 1920s brides chose cream or ivory, as seen in photographs, although pastel colours were also fashionable, especially soft blues, blush pink or peach, fine surviving wedding dresses being made of silk and chiffon and embellished with embroidery, lace, pearls and beading. In style most 1920s bridal and bridesmaids' dresses emulated the royal bridesmaids' afternoon length outfits, rather than the royal brides' long, trained gowns. Since fashionable hemlines fell and rose again throughout the decade, bridal wear followed these shifts, usually ending somewhere between mid- and low-calf length in the early-mid 1920s (Figs. 26-28), until c.1926, when they rose dramatically to just below the knee, and there they stayed until around 1930 (Fig. 29). The fluctuating hemlines of this decade and the 1930s offer a useful guide for closer dating of unknown weddings of the inter-war era.

There were no set rules about headwear although bridal dresses were often teamed with net veils, the headdresses worn characteristically low over the forehead (Figs. 26, 27 & 29); often 1920s and 1930s veils and headdresses were put away and passed down to daughters in the 1940s and 1950s. Alternatively a fashionable hat could be worn by brides and/or bridesmaids, formal hats generally having wide brims in the early-mid 1920s (Fig. 28) until c.1925/6 when the narrow cloche hat pulled down over the forehead came into vogue. Bridesmaids sometimes wore bandeau-like headdresses in the later 1920s, and there was a significant fashion at the time for young flower girls to wear distinctive wired headdresses like Dutch caps (Fig. 29). Upper- and middle-class bridegrooms generally favoured a dark morning coat and grey trousers, these remaining a formal option for weddings throughout the 20th century. The average working man, meanwhile, wore a smart lounge suit, the trousers generally very short and narrow in the 1920s and made with sharp creases and turn-ups (Figs. 26-29). The modern knotted tie was almost universally worn, coloured silk ties, plain or patterned, being popular throughout the next few decades. For headwear, stylish felt homburg and trilby hats were beginning to take over from the more traditional bowler hat (Fig. 27).

The 1930s

As before, a sprinkling of studio photographs characterise 1930s wedding pictures (Fig. 30) although outdoor photographs are more common, including photographs taken against the backdrop of the church (Fig. 33). Significant changes in bridal styles also occurred as wedding dresses acquired a new sense of glamour under the influence of Hollywood films. Graceful dresses of plain silk, satin or artificial silk (rayon) fabric sometimes incorporated panels or trimmings of silver lamé and were expertly bias-cut to achieve the soft, figure-hugging drape demanded by fashion. They could either be day length - hemlines having plunged again to calf-length in the early 1930s - or evening length, sweeping the floor, with a long train (Figs. 32 & 33). The medieval style, inspired by historical epics at the cinema, was popular with brides, as expressed in slender gowns made with narrow sleeves which often ended in points, and rounded 'Juliet' caps to which a long veil was attached (Figs. 30 & 32). White Madonna and arum lilies became especially popular for bouquets during this decade, simple, sophisticated blooms which reinforced the 'medieval' look and complemented other elegant bridal wear (Fig. 30). There was also an alternative bridal vogue for summery 'garden party' dresses in flower-print georgette, chiffon or rayon fabrics, which often had a matching jacket or 'coatee'. These were teamed with wide-brimmed hats rather than veils and, being versatile outfits, were often worn again. By the late-1930s, though, long trained gowns in a cold white satin, sometimes woven in a damask-like flower pattern ('bridal satin'), had largely replaced the soft ivories and creams of earlier decades, and such wedding dresses were 'special', not intended to be worn again for any other occasion.

1930s Bridesmaids generally wore pastel-coloured plain or floral-sprigged dresses extending to the floor or made slightly shorter, in afternoon length (Figs. 30 & 31). The style of their headwear, gloves and other fashionable detailing such as necklines and sleeve shapes can offer helpful dating clues. From around mid-decade the shoulders of garments worn for weddings became squarer and padded, following the style of fashionable dress (Figs. 32 & 33). Both brides and bridesmaids of the mid-late 1930s are often distinguished by their diadem or tiara-like headdresses, following the trend set by Princess Marina of Greece when she married the Duke of Kent in 1934 (Figs. 31 & 33). The average bridegroom wore a good lounge suit, now made in the wide, boxy style of the 1930s-1950s (Figs. 30-32), his jacket typically double-breasted with sharp lapels, and matching trousers worn full with knife-edge creases. For the middle and upper classes a formal morning suit remained usual, a dark tailed coat worn with pin-striped grey trousers (Fig. 33).

The 1940s - 1950

Weddings of this decade were dominated by the 2nd World War (1939-45) although church wedding ceremonies went on more or less as usual and it was during the 1940s that many more photographs were taken in the church doorway (Figs. 34, 35 & 37), or even occasionally inside the church. At the beginning of the decade white weddings were still common (Fig. 34): despite - or perhaps because of - the war and the growing uniformity of civilian dress, brides wanted their wedding day to be special, a dazzling occasion to treasure in times of escalating hardship. Often bridal dresses from the late-1930s were loaned to wartime brides by friends or relatives, or, after clothes rationing began in 1941, families might pool together their coupons to buy a new white dress or the material to make one, a few dresses being expertly fashioned from parachute silk. Wartime and post-war bridal gowns and bridesmaids' dresses had their own distinctive style, generally featuring fashionable padded shoulders and either puffed or tight-fitting sleeves, subtle details such as rounded collars or ruching of the bodice fabric adding extra interest (Figs. 34, 35, 37 & Ch 4 Fig. 22). Cloth shortages dictated that new wedding gowns were made with narrow or slightly flared skirts without trains. Veils, however, were often long and were generally worn well back on the head with tiara-style or halo-like, tall framed headdresses (Figs. 34, 35, 37 & Ch 4 Fig. 22). Bridesmaids of the 1940s also wore veils, theirs shoulder-length versions - a distinctive feature which helps to identify weddings of this decade (Figs. 34, 35, 37 & Ch 4 Fig. 22). Also noticed often in 1940s and 1950s wedding photographs is the custom of presenting the bride with a lucky boot, horseshoe or heart, as seen in Figs. 34 & 38.

As more men joined the armed services, military uniform became the accepted mode of wedding attire for bridegrooms, as it had been during the First World War (Figs. 34 & 36). More women also entered the services as the war advanced, often meeting and marrying fellow servicemen, so that both bride and groom might both marry in uniform. Throughout the decade ordinary civilian grooms wore the generously-cut three-piece lounge suit which had been fashionable before the war, the jacket single- or double-breasted and featuring sharp lapels (Figs. 35, 37, 38 and Ch 4 Fig. 22). Civilian brides and their families did not always have the resources for a white wedding during the war, or the time to organise one: as a result many wartime brides were married in a slim-fitting, knee-length utility-style suit or dress, a floral spray, glamourous hairstyle and a stylish tilted hat being the only concessions to the occasion (Fig. 36). For several years following the end of hostilities in 1945, as Britain was gripped by economic depression, regular tailored daytime outfits remained a common bridal choice, as seen in a many photographs of the later 1940s and turn of the decade (Fig. 38).

Newspaper Wedding Reports

Important weddings in the past often drew large crowds of onlookers along the route to the church and to the reception, so these were, in part, public, as well as family events. From the 18th century onwards, society weddings received further publicity when reports of the event appeared soon afterwards in the local - or national - newspaper. A published newspaper account of a prosperous ancestor's wedding offers a fascinating and detailed record of the occasion and may include all or some of the following information: names and addresses of the bridal couple and their parents, the number and names of the principal guests, the name and location of the church, the name of the clergyman conducting the service, the music selected, the method of transport used by the bridal couple, the location of the reception venue and how it was decorated, descriptions of the clothing worn by the bride, bridesmaids and female guests, the wedding gifts given to the main parties and details of the honeymoon destination.

Early newspaper notices from the pre-photography era provide a valuable contemporary eye-witness account of family weddings for which no picture survives and about which perhaps little is otherwise known. Later newspaper reports may coincide neatly with surviving photographs, offering precise information which complements and enhances the evidence contained in the visual image, as mentioned with respect to Figs. 4, 8, 16, 20 & 23). By the 1880s and 1890s some ordinary weddings were being reported in the press, while published accounts of elite marriages might even be accompanied by head and shoulders illustrations of the bride and groom. Relatively few daily and weekly newspapers contained photographs until the 1940s, but following the end of the 2nd World War in 1945, almost every British regional newspaper began to publicise news of local weddings, showing photographs of the bride and groom in their wedding attire.

The British Library holds copies of all UK daily, UK national daily and Sunday newspapers from 1801 to the present, and most UK and Irish regional and local newspapers, some dating from the early-18th century. Researchers can currently consult these in the reading rooms at Colindale in North London, although the British Library has also made some of its collection of local and national papers available online: see their website to check whether the relevant area is covered - http://newspapers.bl.uk/blcs . For researchers with Scottish ancestors, Ancestry (www.ancestry.co.uk) has limited digitised sequences of *The Scotsman, The Edinburgh Weekly Journal, The Dunfermline Journal* and some other Scottish, English, European and North American titles, whose pages may be viewed with an Ancestry subscription. Ireland's entire collection of newspapers from the 1700s to the present day, both national and regional, is being digitised by the Irish

Newspaper Archives. Searching for reports of births, marriages and deaths is free, but subscription is required for complete access (www.irishnewsarchive.com). Remember that the local library, archive or record office for the district where an ancestor's wedding took place may also keep copies of historical newspapers published in that area.

Victoria & Albert Museum wedding database

Finally, on the subject of wedding pictures, mention should be made of the interesting and very helpful Victoria & Albert Museum database of wedding photographs, which can be found at www.vam.ac.uk/things-to-do/wedding-fashion/home. Covering firmly-dated wedding images from all cultures dating from the early 1840s right up until the present day, this visual sequence aims to help researchers date any unidentified wedding pictures, while visitors to the site are also invited to upload their own dated and named family photographs - so the online collection is constantly growing. This project has been undertaken in advance of a forthcoming exhibition of Wedding Dresses at the Victoria & Albert Museum, London, currently scheduled for 2013. It is understood that there will also be a small book produced in conjunction with the exhibition, as well as a series of talks and workshops. Look out nearer the time for more details of the exhibition and associated events on the V & A website - www.vam.ac.uk.

Fig. 1 Carte de visite studio photograph, Stepney, East London, September 1865
This is a typical studio portrait of a modest 1860s wedding, offering no special signs of the occasion. The couple married at the Parish Church in Stepney, London and the photographer's address on the reverse is also given as Stepney, so they probably visited the studio soon after the wedding ceremony. The groom, born in 1838, in Sebergham, Cumberland, wears a loose lounging jacket with a matching waistcoat and the contrasting trousers which were usual during this decade. The bride, born in 1844, in Saint Mary, Hampshire, wears a fashionable daytime costume comprising matching bodice, bolero-like *zouave* jacket and bell-shaped skirt supported by the vast crinoline frame of the early-mid 1860s. The couple emigrated in 1870, to Jersey City, USA, where the husband worked as an engineering blacksmith in New York.

Fig. 2 Outdoor wedding scene, Hampstead, North London, September 1868

Outdoor wedding group photographs were beginning to be taken in the late 1860s and depict prosperous ancestors' formal white weddings featuring special white bridal wear, veiled bridesmaids, flowers and well-dressed guests. This elegant reception followed a ceremony at St. Saviour's Church, South Hampstead, the setting the garden of a substantial villa in Camden Town, the home of the bride's uncle (her guardian), who may be the gentleman standing centre-left with his wife. He was the leading bookbinder of the day, his patrons including the royal family and many well-known collectors. Towards the right, the bride, aged 21, carries a bouquet and next to her the groom, aged 27, wears a dark frock coat and carries a top hat. He too came from an affluent background, his father having been a wine merchant and his widowed mother - perhaps the seated lady towards the left - a landowner. He also entered the wine and spirit importation business and later became a successful wine merchant. Following their marriage, the couple lived in Islington but later moved to a large house in Maldon, Essex, where he became a JP and County Councillor.

Fig. 3 Carte de visite studio photograph, Islington, North London 1869

The first of two wedding photographs dating from 1869, this simple portrait, taken in a studio, is very different to the following example. The couple, originally from Essex, were both aged 40 - an unusually advanced age for first marriage - although they are well-dressed in smart and stylish clothing for their wedding. The groom, recorded as a Dock Master on the 1871 census, wears a formal frock coat with matching waistcoat and trousers. The bride's fashionable silk dress, probably in a bold colour deriving from one of the new aniline dyes, reflects the fashion for layered and draped skirts by the end of the 1860s. The abundant fringing trimming her outfit was also a feature of the new style.

Fig. 4 Outdoor wedding scene, Hawkhurst, Kent, October 1869
Another early outdoor wedding group, this photograph depicts a marriage which took place in Hawkhurst, Kent, the venue here the bride's family home. Seen as a child in an earlier crayon portrait (Ch 1 Fig. 17), she was the daughter of a prosperous civil engineer who built many of the railways in Yorkshire. The groom, a clerk at the Admiralty, came from a Hertfordshire family who had earlier been successful coach masters in Bond Street and had aristocratic connections. The social status of the families is reflected in this picture showing the bride wearing special white bridal attire and attended by eight bridesmaids, all decked in veils and carrying flowers, according to 1860s custom. As would be expected at an extravagant wedding of this date, the groom and groomsmen wear formal dark frock coats, pale trousers and prominent floral buttonholes or *boutonnieres*. The event caused quite a stir in the locality and was reported nationally in *The Times* newspaper on 23rd October. The notice vividly evokes the sense of occasion and describes the festivities which included decorative displays of floral arches, flags, banners, and gas-lighted stars. Details of the clothing reveal that the bride wore an expensive white *poult de soie* gown, a Brussells lace flounce and veil and orange blossom and myrtle wreath.

Fig. 5 Carte de visite studio photograph, Wimborne, Dorset, December 1873
This modest photograph commemorates a mid-Victorian working-class wedding. Before their marriage, the 22 year-old bride, from Cerne Abbas in Dorset, had already given birth to a daughter in the Cerne Workhouse. For her wedding she wears a good daytime outfit in the fashionable style of the early-mid 1870s, with draped up overskirt and bustle, her neat feather-trimmed hat on her knee. She may also be wearing a floral corsage on her bodice for the occasion. The groom, also 22, was born in Wimborne, Dorset, the son of an agricultural labourer. He wears the three-piece lounge suit which was established by the 1870s as accepted wedding attire for working men, all the suit pieces matching by this date. After their marriage the couple lived in London where he, being a carpenter and wheelwright by trade, sought work on the extensive house building sites there, although they later returned to Dorset.

CHARLES PHOTO.   BIRMINGHAM.

Fig. 6 Carte de visite studio photograph, Birmingham, c.1875
This is one of two different engagement or wedding photographs of similar date, portraying the same couple: in the other (not shown) the fiancée or bride looks upset and is clearly pregnant. The couple married in late 1874 in Alcester, Warwickshire and she had a child in early 1875. This may be the later of the two photographs as she is smiling, has clearly acquired her ring and can wear well-fitting clothes again. Her outfit is made in the layered style of c.1870-75, with a modest bustle behind the skirt. Her white jabot and pendant or locket on a black ribbon were fashionable accessories and her hair, dressed into a high chignon with long tresses left to hang loose, was a style in vogue during those years. The groom wears the usual working man's three-piece lounge suit, his 'four-in-hand' tie popular during the 1870s. Unfortunately the bride died around two years later, in 1877, following the birth of their second child.

20, MANNINGHAM LANE   BRADFORD.

PERMANENT CHROMOTYPE.

Fig. 7 Cabinet studio photograph, Bradford, West Yorkshire, 1878

This single studio photograph of a bride was perhaps originally paired with another photograph of the groom. The bride, aged about 21, was the daughter of a joiner and builder, a successful tradesman who employed 14 men in 1871. She married a carpenter/joiner who may have been one of her father's employees. Her wedding costume combines a bridal veil and floral sprigs - special bridal features - with a fine coloured daytime outfit, a combination which appears to have reflected her family's middling sort of financial position. Her stylish silk dress is trained and follows the fashionable, narrow 'princess' line of the late-1870s. The flowers were probably removed afterwards so that she could re-use the dress.

Fig. 8 Outdoor wedding scene, Deal, Kent, August 1878
This outdoor photograph, also dating from 1878, portrays a more elaborate wedding scene, set amongst the flower beds in the garden of the family villa in Deal, Kent. The striking setting reflects the profession of the bride's father, a nursery man, seeds man and florist who hailed from a family of successful and well-known gardeners. He and his wife sit on the bride's left, while the groom's parents, members of an established Sandwich family, are seated to his right. The older ladies look rather 'matronly' in their shawls and bonnets but this was clearly a stylish wedding, as demonstrated by the bride's special attire and her five fashionably-dressed bridesmaids. The groom, groomsmen and fathers are equally well-dressed in the dark frock coats and light-coloured trousers which were *de rigeur* for formal weddings of the era. A report published in the local newspaper, the *Deal, Walmer and Sandwich Mercury,* on 24th August 1878, confirms the importance of the occasion. It highlights the 'spacious marquee on the lawn at the rear of the house' - seen on the left of the picture - in which 46 guests enjoyed the wedding breakfast. We also learn that the bride wore a white silk 'princess' robe, her bridal train embellished with costly Honiton lace and orange blossom, while the bridesmaids wore cream cashmere trimmed with pale blue satin, their hats made in the fashionable 'beefeater' style.

E.IRELAND.   MANCHESTER

Fig. 9 Carte de visite studio photograph, Manchester, c. 1881

This studio photograph portrays a book keeper and the daughter of a canal boatman from Hulme, Manchester, who married at the Primitive Methodist Church, Higher Ardwick, in June 1884. It could possibly be their marriage portrait, although the young woman's very narrow, sheath-like outfit indicates a slightly earlier date than 1884. She is dressed in outdoor wear, her round plush hat or tocque and slender coat, fashionably ornamented with an embossed design, being typical of c.1881-3. This suggests that the photograph was probably taken to commemorate their engagement, which may well have occurred in 1881. In that year the bride-to-be suffered a serious knife attack by her step-brother who, for uncertain reasons, was opposed to her marriage. Luckily she survived and the wedding went ahead three years later.

Fig. 10 Studio photograph, Howick Township, Huron County, Ontario, Canada, June 1884
This Ontario-born couple both came from protestant Irish immigrant families, Howick being a rural area
only settled for about 30 years by the time of their marriage. The studio setting indicates that these
farmers had a modest wedding although clearly they are dressed up here for the photograph. The bride
wears a fashionable daytime outfit comprising a tight-fitting bodice and matching skirt with kilt-pleated
hemline, typical of the early 1880s, her striking white sash, white feathered hat and earrings special
accessories in keeping with the occasion. The groom appears to be wearing a morning coat, fashionable
for semi-formal wear by that time, with dark waistcoat and trousers, his bowler hat resting on the table.
His formal white necktie was an accessory being adopted by many grooms by the 1880s. Born in 1851,
he was 11 years older than the bride and died after 11 years of marriage, leaving her to raise 5 children
alone on the farm.

Fig. 11 Studio photograph, Bow, London, September 1885

There is nothing about this studio photograph to suggest that the couple were newly-weds, but their identity is certain and the image accords well with their recorded marriage of 13th September 1885 in Bow, East London. The groom, the son of a boot and shoemaker from Bow, was only 18 and worked as a commercial clerk to a glass manufacturer. His smart suit is cut in the narrow style of the 1880s, his stylish morning coat much in vogue at the time - a genteel garment which reflected his occupational status, or perhaps his ambitions! The bride was also a clerk, the daughter of a widowed dressmaker who possibly made the fashionable outfit seen here - a tight-fitting bodice and matching skirt draped up over the usual bustle of c.1884-9. Initially the couple lived in Bow, next door to the bride's family, but after the husband became a commercial traveller, they moved upmarket to Muswell Hill in North London.

Billinghurst & Smith   JERSEY &
                                          WEYMOUTH.

Fig. 12 Studio photograph of unknown wedding, c.1887-9

Nothing is known about this unidentified bridal couple but the photograph is very closely dateable to c.1887-9 from the bride's appearance, a date-range which also accords well with the photographers' operational dates. Her sumptuous velvet costume comprising a close-fitting lapelled bodice with shortened sleeves and skirt draped up into a bustle behind would have been the height of fashion in the late-1880s, as also her extraordinary towering gable hat which may include organic material, much in vogue at the time. Her satin sash reflects the growing popularity of such bridal accessories during the 1880s, while the evident quality of her outfit and her corsage and bridal bouquet suggest that her family enjoyed a comfortable financial position. The groom is also immaculately-dressed in a formal frock coat bearing a *boutonniere* and a formal white tie, his silk top hat and gloves both genteel accessories.

234

Fig. 13 Studio photograph, Bermondsey, Surrey (now London), September 1890
This photograph reflects the growing trend for group wedding scenes by the 1890s, although the group is unusually large for a studio portrait of 1890. It commemorates a marriage at St James' Church, Bermondsey (then in Surrey) and portrays the bride (21), groom (24) and seven bridesmaids, all thought to be the groom's sisters. The bride and two adult bridesmaids wear coloured dresses, as was fashionable following the shift to afternoon weddings after 1886, while the large number of her attendants and prolific blooms used for bouquets, flower baskets, corsages and wreaths reflect the families' comfortable financial status. Both fathers were successful tradesmen, the groom's father being a Southwark brush maker who supplied the army with brushes for uniforms. The bride's father was more prosperous, running a shop in Bermondsey and various other businesses pertaining to the upkeep of horses; he also kept horses for hire, including a pair of greys for weddings and carriage horses for special events, so quite possibly he provided the transport for his daughter's wedding. The groom was a self-employed brush maker and corn merchant.

Fig. 14 Outdoor wedding scene, Maidenhead, Berkshire, June 1895

Large outdoor wedding scenes became more common during the 1890s and it is thought that photographs of this 1895 wedding were taken by the bride's older brother's professional photography studio. She was living with him in Maidenhead when she married, aged 31, and he probably gave her away in marriage as neither of their parents was alive: he stands behind her here in the back row. Their father had been a London silversmith and their mother came from a family of farmer-landowners from Bedfordshire and this was evidently a substantial wedding, judging from the well-dressed bridal party and guests and attractive setting. The bride and other women wear elaborate dresses featuring the vast 'leg-o'-mutton' sleeves of the mid 1890s with fashionable hats: one of her sisters was a milliner and two others dressmakers, so they may have made some of the outfits. Several men wear morning coats or stately frock coats and white ties, indicative of a formal wedding. The groom (37), whose mother sits beside him, reputedly inherited land on the death of his father, another Bedfordshire farmer. The couple raised their family on a farm in Stevington, Beds.

Fig. 15 Studio photograph, Tividale, Staffordshire, July 1897
This is a very modest wedding photograph compared with the larger scenes that were becoming more common by the mid-late 1890s. The bride and groom both wear respectable everyday clothing, she in a smart dress featuring the wide 'leg-o'-mutton' sleeves which were most fashionable in 1895 and 1896 and he in the customary working man's 'best' three-piece lounge suit. Unusually for this date, there are no special signs that this photograph commemorated the couple's marriage; it may well have been a very low-key wedding as the bride's father, a carpenter, had died ten years previously. In the 1891 census she was based in Redditch, helping her maternal aunt and uncle - a police inspector - with their young family. Two doors away lived a widowed police constable; they met and married when she was aged 26, he 44, and spent 30 years together until his death in 1927.

Fig. 16 Wedding group, Merstham, Surrey, August 1899

This wedding group photograph was taken in the garden of the bride's mother's home in Merstham, Surrey, following a service at St. Katharine's, Merstham parish church. The bride's father having died some years earlier, she was given away by her brother, a local blacksmith, standing here second from right. Many 1890s brides wore elaborate day wear, and the style of her narrow-sleeved dress and wide-brimmed, high-piled hat typify the fashions of the turn of the century. In the 1891 census, the bride was running her own dressmaking business so perhaps she made her own wedding outfit and those of her two adult bridesmaids, one of whom was her sister, and who are dressed identically. Their large bouquets with trailing greenery are comparable in shape and size to that of the bride, as often seen in photographs of the 1890s and early 1900s. Some men wear formal frock coats and carry top hats and all of them, including the groom, born in Somerset, wear white ties and floral buttonholes. Two years later, in the 1901 census, he was recorded as running a drapery business while his wife was a costermonger, employing staff. A modest report of the wedding was published in a local newspaper.

Fig. 17 Studio photograph, Barrow-in-Furness, Cumbria June 1900

Everyone is elaborately dressed in this wedding photograph from 1900, although the studio setting suggests a modest occasion. The bride (24) was a domestic servant, the daughter of an iron filler from the Barrow iron works and a cotton factory worker, although her mother had died fourteen years before the wedding. The groom, 11 years her senior, was a carter born in Cartmel, Lancashire but living in Accrington. He and his best man wear formal white ties and floral buttonholes with their lounge jackets, the usual male wedding accessories of the era. The bride and her bridesmaids all wear fashionable coloured dresses with narrow-sleeved, decorative bodices and sweeping skirts. Their ornate, plate-like hats, piled high with feathers and bows, the bride's impressive bouquet and the bridesmaids' posies and floral corsages all add to the picturesque scene.

Fig. 18 Studio photograph, Wimborne, Dorset, January 1902

This photograph was taken in a Bournemouth studio following a service at the parish church in Wimborne. The 25-year old groom, having lost both parents in the 1890s, had been earning a living doing various jobs and at the time of his marriage was a butcher in Weymouth. The bride, aged about 22, was the daughter of a Wimborne farm carter: prior to her marriage she worked as a live-in cook and domestic servant to a miller. She or her family had evidently saved hard for her wedding, for here she wears special bridal wear. Her white dress with full sleeves has a flounced, trained hemline which exemplifies the Edwardian 'frou frou' effect of layers of swishing frills and flounces, while her veil attaches to a floral wreath worn, typically for this date, far back on her head. The groom wears the usual working man's lounge suit with the white tie and floral buttonhole customary for late-Victorian and Edwardian weddings, his white gloves being another special accessory. In 1903 the couple became licensees of the World's End Inn in Almer, Dorset, which they continued to run for 28 years.

Fig. 19 Outdoor wedding scene, Norwood, London, November 1905

This wedding took place at All Saints Church, Norwood, London, between a 29 year-old member of the Royal Horse Artillery who originated from Dover and a bride about whom little is known. She wears a wedding veil to complement her white dress, and a corsage of flowers on her bodice, features which distinguish her from the adult bridesmaid, whose vast trailing bouquet equals her own in size. The bride's parents (possibly the couple seated to her left) were evidently in a position to provide a formal white wedding with several attendants. Two young flower girls in the front row, thought to be the groom's nieces, wear white frocks and fashionable halo bonnets and carry baskets of flowers. The groom and his best man both wear their RHA uniforms for the wedding, according to tradition. He was posted to South Africa only a month after their marriage, and afterwards to India; there is no mention of his wife accompanying him when he served abroad and the couple had no children.

Fig. 20 Outdoor wedding scene, Merstham, Surrey, June 1907

This was one of several photographs taken in the grounds of a public house in Merstham, Surrey - the venue for the wedding reception following a service at the parish church of St. Katharine's. The bride's father, seated far right, was long established in Merstham as a farrier and blacksmith (also the brother of the bride seen in Fig. 16). The groom, 39, who ran a successful and well-known local building firm, was a respected community member, a parish councillor and bowls club secretary. Predictably this middle-class wedding was a formal occasion, as reflected in the impressive scene and the attire of the bride (22), her attendants and guests. Her three bridesmaids - her cousins and the bridegroom's niece - wear matching outfits and carry the large trailing bouquets characteristic of the Edwardian era. Some male guests wear traditional frock coats, while the groom wears a smart but more contemporary morning coat and grey pin-striped trousers. This important event was recorded in the Surrey Mirror in a lengthy newspaper report. It describes the bride's white silk gown, orange blossom wreath and bouquet of white roses and lilies as well as the bridesmaids' pale blue dresses and white hats trimmed with pink roses which echoed the pink roses in their bouquets - colours and textures which cannot be discerned from a century-old black and white photograph. We also learn who made the dresses and the cake, who provided the flowers, what 'numerous and handsome' gifts were received, and that the couple honeymooned in Bournemouth.

Fig. 21 Outdoor wedding scene, Pembroke Dock, Pembroke, April 1908

This photograph, following a wedding service at Pembroke Church, was taken in the back garden of the bride's older sister's home in Pembroke Dock, where the brother-in-law served in the forces. Their father, a greengrocer, had died when she was just 3, her mother - the elderly seated lady here - remarrying and having 8 children in all (one of whom is the groom in Fig. 19). This was clearly a modest wedding: the bride wears a fashionable daytime outfit, suitable for spring and summer wear, although a bouquet was customary for all brides by the Edwardian era. It was also fashionable to have young flower girls carrying baskets, as we see here, the two older bridesmaids here having attended the bride's brother's 1905 wedding as flower girls (Fig. 19). The bride, aged 29, was in service until her marriage and the groom, 27, was a farmer, like his parents, who are positioned next to him here. He had commoners' rights in the New Forest and the couple spent their married life in Burley, Hampshire, until he had a fatal fall from a hay cart aged 49.

Fig. 22 Outdoor wedding scene, South Moor, Co. Durham, December 1912

This wedding photograph shows the bridal couple and close family members posing in front of a painted backdrop, like those used in studios, here pinned to the brick wall of the house. Both bride and groom came from poor working families and had experienced turbulent childhoods: in 1901 the bride's mother had left their crowded terraced miners' house, taking with her three children. The bride's father, a miner and grower of prize vegetables, stands here at the back, left, and next to him is one of her sisters; the other sister, front left, was bridesmaid. The groom's alcoholic father had died in 1897 and, his mother unable to care for her children, the five boys were taken into care by Dr Barnado's. The groom and one brother were then sent to Canada and returned home c.1905. At the time of his marriage he was a stone worker but later became a coal hewer at the Holmside and South Moor Collieries. He and other men here wear their 'Sunday best' lounge suits and bowler hats with white ties and prominently displayed watch chains for the occasion. The young women all wear fashionable layered dresses with floral corsages and wide, feathered hats but this was a very modest wedding: there is not even the usual bouquet.

Fig. 23 Outdoor wedding scene, Hawkhurst, Kent, April 1913

This elegant scene set in the garden of the bride's family home depicts a prosperous wedding of 1913 which contrasts strikingly with the wedding of just a few months earlier seen in Fig. 22. This bride, aged 43, was the eldest daughter of the bridal couple in Fig. 4, her parents seated here in the front row to the right. Little is known about the groom, the son of a deceased local vicar, although he is thought to have been a sheep farmer in New Zealand prior to marriage. The guests all look very stylish, the ladies wearing the slender dresses or suits fashionable in the pre-war era, set off with slanting feathered hats and elaborate fur or feather boas. A newspaper report in the *Kent & Sussex Post* dated 26th April described the occasion, including the bride's outfit of 'silver-grey chiffon velvet, with court train draped with Brussells lace veil (worn by her mother on her wedding day)' and her grey hat, trimmed with silk to match her gown and a grey shaded ostrich plume. The groom wears the dark morning coat and grey trousers usual for formal weddings of the time and the male guests are all well-dressed: a London tailor's receipt survives for a relative who had travelled back from South America and ordered a new suit for the occasion.

Fig. 24 Outdoor wedding scene Walthamstow, London, July 1915

This couple married at St. Stephen's Church, Walthamstow and the location of the photograph is probably the garden of the groom's parents' home in Walthamstow. His father, seated in the centre with his mother, was a solicitor's clerk. The bride's parents were both deceased but her father had been a corn dealer in Hendon, where the groom worked at the aerodrome as a pilot. The groom appears here in his wartime uniform as a lieutenant in the Royal Flying Corps; he ended the war as a major. The bride, like many wartime brides, does not wear a special gown and veil, but a stylish afternoon outfit comprising a white blouse, skirt and fine overdress with frilled collar, with a fashionable hat, all suitable for a summer wedding. Some onlookers at the back are unidentified but otherwise everyone in the photograph was from the groom's family, including his five sisters and cousin, and his brother-in-law, the best man.

Fig. 25 Outdoor wedding scene, Reigate, Surrey, September 1918

The bride and groom here were second cousins, a fairly common situation in the past when relatives often remained in close touch with, or lived amongst family. The groom was born in London but when his father died in 1909 his family moved to Surrey where they were supported by his uncle. He fought in the First World War and was awarded the Military Cross in 1917 while serving with the 5th Pioneer Battalion of the South Wales Borderers. Here as a bridegroom, aged 22, he wears his military uniform, as usual for wartime weddings; he must have married while on leave in September 1918 for his discharge as a lieutenant from the army only occurred in 1919. The bride, also 22, wears a fashionable suit tailored from white fabric, as was common during this decade, and a broad-brimmed white hat. The guests have also dressed up for the occasion, the women's wide-lapelled suits and various styles of hats characteristic of the late 1910s.

Fig. 26 Outdoor wedding scene, Hook with Warsash, Hampshire, March 1922
This bride, born in 1901, and groom, born in 1902, both worked on a country estate, he as a tractor driver
for the farm, which supplied London markets with fruit, she as a domestic in the house. This photograph
was taken after their wedding at St Mary's church in Hook, outside a row of cottages built for
agricultural workers on the estate. Their fathers were both carters on local farms. The bride wears a
stylish calf-length white bridal dress, with white stockings and shoes decorated with bows, all features
fashionable in the early 1920s. Her net veil is also typical of the decade, embroidered - like her dress -
with floral motifs and worn low over her forehead. The groom and male guests wear the usual working
men's lounge suit, very narrow in cut at this time. Many of their shirt collars show clearly the distinctive
fold made by the collar bar often worn beneath the tie to hold down the points of the modern soft, un-
starched collars then becoming fashionable.

Fig. 27 Outdoor wedding scene, Croydon, Surrey, 1923
This is one of several different views of a family wedding that took place in the Croydon area in 1923, the setting here the garden of the bride's home. Seen as a girl of fourteen in Ch 2 Fig. 35, and later, in middle age, in Ch 6 Figs. 12 & 13, the bride (aged 30) was six years older than the groom and was also his first cousin. She wears special bridal wear, as was usual by the 1920s, her long calf-length dress confirming a date early in the decade. Her veiled headdress is worn low over her forehead in the manner characteristic of the late 1910s and 1920s. The groom, a plumber, looks very dapper in a narrowly-cut lounge suit, holding fashionable accessories - a felt homburg or trilby hat and white gloves.

Fig. 28 Studio photograph, Liverpool, March 1925

This wedding photograph, taken in a professional studio, is mounted on card printed with brief details of the photographer in the corner - a common feature by this time. The groom, an engineer, was marrying a 26-year woman who had an illegitimate son, aged six. The bride's father, standing at the back with her brother, worked as a police constable and a dock worker. The bride wears white but has chosen in preference to a bridal gown a fashionable day dress trimmed with swansdown, which almost matches her bridesmaid's outfit, and a hat rather than a veil. Their two dresses follow contemporary lines, being round-necked and loose in shape, the hemlines low calf-length, as was still usual in 1925, just before much shorter skirts came into vogue. Their bar shoes were the usual style by mid-decade. The men all wear lounge suits, the only special feature their flower buttonholes. The groom's very narrow trousers with creases and turn-ups are characteristic of this date.

Fig. 29 Outdoor wedding scene, Barking, Essex, June 1929

Little is known about this family wedding, except the date and location. It was evidently a low-key event, judging from the photograph, taken on the pavement in front of a ramshackle building. By the 1920s nearly all brides wore white, whatever their social background, bridal gowns and veils being much cheaper than in earlier decades, due to the mass production of economical clothing in the inter-war era. The bridal wear seen here is typical of the late 1920s, making this a good example of its time. Note the short hemlines of bride and adult bridesmaids, reflecting the fashion for knee-length dresses and skirts c.1926-30. The bride's headdress is worn low over her forehead in the manner characteristic of the decade, while the adult bridesmaids' bandeaus and the wired Dutch-style caps worn by the little flower girls are also both popular features of the period.

Fig. 30 Studio photograph, Hackney, London, September 1932
This wedding was originally scheduled for March 1932 but had to be postponed until September, following the death of the bride's father. The photograph was one of two - all that they could afford - taken at a studio in Hackney directly after the wedding. The youngest of eight children, the bride, aged 21, was given away by an older brother, who stands second from right next to their widowed mother. A professional dressmaker, the bride made her own elegant white wedding gown and veil, the style of which reflects the vogue for medieval-inspired bridal wear during the 1930s. She also made the bridesmaids' fashionable dresses with draped cowl necklines and puffed sleeves. The nattily-dressed groom, 22, who wears a sharp pin-striped suit and carries a trilby hat, was a carpenter who went on to be the foreman of a furniture factory. Both were keen gymnasts; they had first met at a local gymnastics club and they later became gymnastic instructors during the 1940s. They were married for an impressive 74 years.

Fig. 31 Outdoor wedding scene, Bromley-by-Bow, London July 1936

This wedding photograph, which followed a church service in nearby Poplar, the bride's local parish, was taken in the back garden of the groom's parents' house in Bromley-by-Bow, probably by his 13-year old brother. The groom, 25, worked as an assistant miller in a flour mill where his father was a miller. For the wedding both he and his best man, left, wear three-piece lounge suits tailored in the wide, boxy style of the decade, their jackets made with broad, flat lapels and their trousers featuring sharp creases. The bride, aged 21, worked at a firm of milliners. Her wedding dress demonstrates the fashionable padded shoulders of the mid-late 1930s, while her three bridesmaids - her niece and the groom's sister and cousin - are dressed in identical light floral-print 'garden party'-style dresses with puffed sleeves. They all wear the tiara-style wedding headdresses popularised by Princess Marina in 1934.

Fig. 32 Bridal couple, Merstham, Surrey, July 1937

This 1937 wedding photograph demonstrates the fashion for long, elegant bridal wear and trailing veils by the later 1930s - snow-white, floor length trained gowns which were 'special' outfits, not meant to be worn again. Historical influences were often present, seen here in the bride's close-fitting 'Juliet' cap headdress and the narrow, medieval-style sleeves extending over the hand in a point. The groom looks more ordinary in his lounge suit, tailored in the wide style of the time, although he wears smart white gloves and a buttonhole as wedding accessories. Aged 28, he had earlier worked for his father's building firm, a long-established business which unfortunately collapsed during the 1930s, after which he joined London Transport as a scheduling clerk. It was there that he met his future wife, the Reigate-born daughter of a coach builders' foreman. They married when she was 23 and had four children together, but sadly their relationship did not last and they divorced in the mid-1960s.

Fig. 33 Outdoor wedding scene, New Malden Surrey, September 1939
This wedding was held in the Parish Church at New Malden, in rather a hurry on the day before war was declared, although it appears to have been a stylish event. The bride wears a floor-length wedding dress, the long train arranged elegantly in true 1930s fashion. The groom, his best man and father-in-law wear the dark morning coats and pin-striped trousers expected of a formal wedding. The groom was an electrical engineer for the Air Ministry, the bride a university graduate and secretary. Her father (second from right), was a headmaster in Richmond, so hers was a middle-class upbringing, whereas her husband came from a working-class family. Their social differences are reflected in the two mothers' outfits, both suitable for middle-aged women in the late 1930s but clearly differing in their quality and fit.

Fig. 34 Church wedding scene, Wellington, Herefordshire, June 1942
This photograph is one of several views of a wartime wedding which took place at Wellington Parish Church in Herefordshire, a typical, if informal shot showing bride, groom and attendants in the church doorway. The bride (22), the daughter of a building manager, worked as a book keeper. She managed to acquire a white lace bridal gown for her special day and also wears the oval-framed headdress characteristic of the 1940s. Her bridesmaids are dressed in long outfits also, the adults having fashionable padded shoulders, white gloves and wearing the short bridesmaid veils that were usual during this decade. The groom, 23, wears army uniform, his jodhpurs, long leather boots and Sam Browne belt reflecting his role as a motorcycle despatch rider for the Royal Signals in Egypt. Guests hand the bride a heart and horseshoe, good luck tokens seen often in wedding photographs from the 1940s onwards.

Fig. 35 Wedding scene, London, October 1944

This is another wartime photograph demonstrating the increasing popularity of wedding groups posed outside the church doorway, the bridal couple seen here with three bridesmaids (the bride's older and two younger sisters) and both sets of parents. During the war the bride worked as a personal secretary at a company that stocked and supplied aircraft parts to the Air Ministry. She was the first of three daughters to be married between autumn 1944 and summer 1946, special occasions which had to be celebrated but must have stretched the resources of this ordinary London family at a difficult time. Her gown, in figured 'bridal satin' is narrow and made without a train, reflecting the wartime shortage of materials, while her tall framed headdress, worn with an unusually long veil for the era, is the fashionable style of the decade. The bridesmaids' dresses of pale blue crepe de chine feature the pronounced padded shoulders and puffed sleeves then in vogue, the short veils worn by the adults typical of 1940s weddings. Their mother, right, a court dressmaker by trade, is smartly attired in Utility-style clothing worn with a fox fur stole and jaunty hat.

Fig. 36 Bridal couple, Edmonton, North London, November 1944

Like many wartime weddings, this modest event was organised at short notice and followed straight on from the bride's sister's wedding in October 1944 (see Fig. 35). The bride, (the author's aunt), aged 20, had only known the groom, a Canadian serving with Bomber Command in England, for 5 months when he was ordered back home to join Tiger Force. They married just before his departure, the groom wearing his Royal Canadian Air Force uniform for the wedding. Having little time to prepare, the bride wore civilian clothes: a knee-length crepe de chine dress cut down from the long dress she had worn as a bridesmaid the previous month, a full-length beaver fur coat which her father bought her in preparation for the cold Canadian winter and a stylish pillbox hat. In December 1944 she left England for Canada, travelling by ship to Halifax, Nova Scotia, then across country by train to the groom's home in Penticton, British Columbia. Theirs was a long marriage, and she lives in Canada still, where her family extends to great grandchildren.

Fig. 37 Outdoor wedding scene, Liverpool, 1949

This photograph was taken some years after the war at a time of economic depression and clothes rationing in Britain. The bridegroom, wearing a smart double-breasted jacket and fashionable wide trousers, was a Mersey river pilot, a highly-skilled job. His best man was an RAF officer, as seen by his uniform, which displays his pilot's wings. Special floor-length bridal gowns and veils were becoming more common again after the war although the narrow dress worn by this 27-year old bride continues war time modes. Its plain satin fabric and wide, padded shoulders are also typical of the decade, as is her tall, halo-like headdress. The bridesmaids' different dresses suggest that they may not have been new garments but had perhaps been worn on previous occasions, or may have been hired. Their tiara-style headdresses are worn with short veils, as was usual in the 1940s.

Fig. 38 Studio photograph, Gosport, Hampshire, July 1950

This bridal couple, both aged 25, visited the photographer's studio for this photograph following their marriage at the Gosport Register Office. The groom was born in Newcastle upon Tyne, the son of a coal miner, but at the time was stationed at *HMS Dolphin*, Gosport, where he worked as a stoker/mechanic for the Royal Navy. Here he wears a lounge suit made in the loose style of the 1930s-1950s, a flower attached to his lapel in honour of the occasion. The bride is modestly dressed, as were some brides as late as 1950, clothes rationing being still in force. Her smart tailored suit is economical in cut, made with the wide, padded shoulders of the 1940s, her slender waist fashionably accentuated by a narrow belt. She carries no bouquet but wears a floral corsage and holds a lucky horseshoe and boot, good luck tokens especially popular in the 1940s and following decades.

SIX

CHAPTER SIX
Picturing the Occasion
- Home, Work and Play

Unlike formal studio portraits representing ancestors and relatives posing solemnly in a contrived indoor setting, photographs taken away from the studio show earlier generations in their own environments and provide a more authentic visual record of the past. Informal images surviving in today's collections portray past family members wearing everyday clothing, against a backdrop of solid buildings, amongst real objects, in natural surroundings. Diverse and informative, these fascinating pictures are of great documentary value and reveal a great deal about forebears' experiences and lives.

Early outdoor photographs crop up quite rarely in family collections, these usually having been taken by itinerant photographers or other professionals working away from the studio. By the late 19th century amateur photography was on the rise and after the First World War most photographs set in the open air, and even some indoor scenes, were casual 'snapshots' taken by family members or friends. Sometimes the prints were annotated by the photographer or collector with the date and details of the occasion, or they may be recognisable from familiar people and places. Unidentified images can usually be assigned a useful time frame from their visual details, especially styles of dress, and even 'mystery' photographs whose subjects and locations are unknown may contain clues offering leads for further investigation. This chapter includes some ideas and web addresses for investigating snapshots and other photographs taken in genuine settings, although the possibilities offered by the internet in particular are limitless and online research can result in many discoveries.

Every picture is unique and important to the family to whom it belongs but when looking at many images from different collections common themes emerge: views of homes once owned or rented by the family, places where they took holidays, favourite haunts in their locality, memorable outings, special events, leisure activities and ordinary domestic scenes, as well as the people they knew, beloved household pets, family vehicles and other treasured possessions. These subjects provide the framework for the photographs reproduced at the end of the chapter, which are organised chronologically within separate categories covering Families at Home, Working Lives, Holidays and Outings and, finally, Sports and Leisure Activities. A few of the selected examples are unusual and special pictures, worthy of publication, but many others are very typical of their day. These image sequences should provide a broad historical context and useful visual comparisons for readers' own informal photographs and family snapshots.

Professional outdoor photographs

The majority of 19th century portrait photographs surviving today were taken in the artificially-controlled setting of the photographer's studio but occasionally outdoor photographs of early date crop up in family collections. In many cases these are the work of professional photographers, for amateur snapshots of pre-20th century date are relatively uncommon. As explained in Chapter 2, by the mid-late 1850s many commercial photographers were adopting the wet collodion process, which was simpler than the daguerreotype method and had the significant advantage of being able to produce high-quality photography away from the studio, giving mid-Victorian photographers the freedom to travel with a camera. Nonetheless wet plate photography still involved tricky manipulations and specialised equipment, since the plates had to be prepared just before use and then exposed and developed swiftly before the solution dried; therefore outdoor photographers of the 1850s-1870s travelled to their locations with cumbersome processing facilities - mobile darkrooms of various descriptions including horse-drawn vans, handcart or wheelbarrow dark tents (if the venue was within walking distance) or collapsible darkrooms packed into substantial and heavy backpacks. Some photographers of this era toured the British Isles taking scenic views, or ventured overseas to picture exotic locations or record the progress of war. More relevant to genealogists, however, are those scenes depicting earlier generations of the family.

As discussed in Chapter 5, by the late 1860s professional photographers were hired occasionally to take photographs of prosperous ancestors' wedding receptions. Equally clients could request that a representative from a local studio visit them at home on other occasions: this often resulted in a group photograph of the family posing in the yard or garden outside the house, as shown in Figs. 1 & 2. During the

1850s and 1860s, when successfully photographing groups of several people presented a technical challenge, the benefits of an outdoor setting were more space and plenty of natural daylight which could reduce the exposure time, thereby minimising the likelihood of someone in the group moving and blurring the picture. Some studios at this time also sent photographers to picture members of the public at outdoor events such as important race meetings and other well-attended venues: an example of this type of photograph is Fig. 25, showing ancestors photographed at the 1866 camp of the National Rifle Association, an annual event held at Wimbledon Common. During the 1880s and 1890s there was a surge in professional outdoor photography following the introduction of dry photographic plates, which facilitated the taking of photographs away from the studio. This advanced certain areas of portraiture like school photography, as seen in Chapter 4, and led to many more private occasions such as weddings and other family gatherings being pictured in open-air group scenes by the late Victorian era (Figs. 6, Ch 4 Fig.34 and Ch 5 Fig.s 14 & 16).

Early outdoor photographs cropping up in family collections may alternatively have been taken by itinerant photographers who operated from no fixed premises but travelled around the countryside speculating for business. Even in the early 1840s a few daguerreotype photographers were already taking to the road in search of custom, journeying to smaller towns and areas not yet boasting a portrait studio where they were welcomed by the social elite - successful businessmen, the landed gentry, squirearchy and senior clergy. Travelling photographers continued to serve outlying communities, the villages and hamlets whose inhabitants made only infrequent trips into towns and cities and where their varied clientele included the local gentry, school teachers, shopkeepers, domestic servants and labourers: sitters might visit the photographer's mobile studio in person or else request that he attend them at home for a photograph in the garden or grounds of the house. This rural market gradually declined as the railway networks and road systems improved and suburban districts developed, linking areas more closely. However many Victorian itinerants remained in business by offering on the spot 'pavement portraits' of customers on the street, outside their places of work (Fig. 15) or on their front doorsteps. Some travelling photographers astutely positioned themselves temporarily at locations certain to attract business from the general public, for example at race meetings, fairs, the seaside (Ch 2 Fig. 21), public parks, commons, heaths and other local beauty spots (Fig. 26). Many inferior ambrotypes, produced using the wet collodion process, will be the work of travelling photographers, as will many tintypes from the late 1870s onwards - inexpensive 'instant' photographs which provided ordinary working people with a souvenir of an enjoyable day out (Ch 2 Fig. 21). By the later 19th century the commercially-minded operators who toured around with their brightly painted caravans, canvas booths and boxes on wheels touting for business, were regarded by the professional establishment as little better than showmen or entertainers who undermined the status of serious photography. However they brought photographic portraiture to a wider public and their photographs, taken away from the rigid confines of the studio, offer glimpses of the real world as experienced by earlier generations.

In the 20th century some professional photographers continued to earn their living photographing customers outdoors, especially the street photographers who snapped tourists and holiday makers strolling on the piers and promenades of popular seaside resorts (Ch 2 Fig. 49). Sometimes high street studios were called upon to send a photographer out to photograph clients in an outdoor setting, as seen in Ch 2 Fig. 46, while many weddings were attended by professional photographers, as they are today (see Chapter 5). However most informal and open air photographs of early-mid 20th century date and later will be amateur snapshots and these offer the most intimate and detailed views of the family.

Early amateur snapshots

In Chapter 2 it was noted how amateur photography developed from being a genteel pastime for the privileged leisured classes in the mid-19th century to a consuming hobby for middle-class 'snapshooters' during the 1880s, following major advances in photographic processes and equipment. It was at this time that the term 'snapshot', first coined c.1860, came into popular use to describe the spontaneous photographs being taken by the new wave of amateur photographers using the simpler types of camera then becoming available. Kodak's famous marketing slogan of 1888, 'You push the button, we'll do the rest', summed up the convenience of new cameras ready-loaded with film which, once finished, could be sent back to the factory for processing. Some serious amateurs preferred the traditional glass plate method and developed their own photographs, but for enthusiasts with little technical expertise the practise of photography was becoming much easier. That said, amateur photography was still a specialist interest in the 1880s and 1890s: owning a camera was not yet an option for everybody and it was to be some 30 or more years before the camera became a familiar household item. Researchers whose forebears enjoyed experimenting with photography at an early date, whether as a serious pastime or essentially for amusement, may be fortunate in finding amateur photographs dating from the late Victorian and Edwardian eras. Two family collections featured here include late 19th and very early 20th century snapshots which offer unusually casual portrayals of ancestors of these years dressed in their long skirts and restricting suits yet relaxing on their annual summer holidays, picnicking outdoors, visiting relatives abroad, making journeys and getting together with family and friends at home: Figs. 3, 4 & 27 were taken in

England and Argentina by a cattle rancher who first took up photography in the 1880s, his original glass plate negatives having been recently discovered by his great grandchildren; Figs. 5, 7 & 28-30 dating from the 1890s and beginning of the 1900s are the work of an under-manager in a Lancashire cotton mill, a working man of humble origins who managed to find time for various hobbies including photography. Other informal Edwardian snapshots featured here are Fig. 18 and Ch 2 Fig. 33.

Popular photography

By the early-1900s interest in amateur photography was gathering momentum. In 1900 the user-friendly Box Brownie camera, ready-loaded with film, was introduced and this inexpensive and popular model, which encouraged many ordinary people to try the new hobby of photography, was still going strong on the eve of the Second World War, selling at its original retail price of five shillings. By the 1910s more convenient models of cameras were also coming onto the market such as the Kodak Vest Pocket Camera, launched in 1912: it is said that during the First World War many a soldier took one of these folding cameras away with him, a massive increase in sales being recorded during 1915. Family collections generally reflect the surge in amateur photography that occurred in around the mid-1910s, many more snapshots surviving for this period onwards. Informal photographs of this decade may include family members in First World War military or other service uniforms (Fig. 19), but in most other cases they are low-key scenes depicting people relaxing in the garden at home, going about their daily business and enjoying local excursions (Title picture, Figs. 8-10, 20, 21, 31 & 32 and Ch 2 Figs. 38 & 39). These evocative images representing past lives at a time of transition, poised between the old and modern worlds, may seem familiar in some ways: their subjects are often relaxed and smiling, clothing appears more functional and recognisable, wheeled vehicles crop up more often and garden furniture looks similar in style to that used today, yet such scenes pictured around a century ago are within the living memory of only a very few.

Picturing the 1920s-1940s

Snapshots dating from after the war are most common in family picture collections, expressing the popularity of home photography by that era. Roll film photographs were generally taken outside as they relied on bright, natural light: photographers learnt to stand with their backs to the sun, so it may be noticed in many early 20th century snapshots that their subjects are squinting directly into the glare. Interior scenes of this era are relatively uncommon because of the difficulties of dealing with the dim lighting conditions indoors, Fig. 12 being a fairly rare example for its date. Flashbulbs and Photoflood lamps were introduced in the early 1930s, although some photography historians suggest that these were not widely used by amateurs until well into the 1950s, later than the period covered by this book. Either way, indoor photographs taken without the convenience of modern flash equipment generally involved using more hazardous lighting techniques such as burning magnesium ribbon in a holder, the magnesium powder flash lamp or various other individually-contrived lighting systems. Colour photographs may very occasionally crop up by the 1930s or 1940s, but colour photography was in its infancy and so the vast majority of family snapshots taken before the mid-20th century will be black and white images.

Informal photographs of the 1920s-1940s are very diverse in their subject matter, reflecting both the tendency for the new generation of photographers to enthusiastically snap all kinds of occasions and the more active and varied lives of family members living during those decades. Casual domestic scenes remained a common subject for the camera - photographs taken at home on the front doorstep or in the garden (Figs. 11, 13 & 14). Also popular were photographs recording daily life as an employee or employer, snapshots taken at work or outside the workplace - interesting images which, like earlier depictions of shops, work yards and other business premises, often display fascinating historical details (Figs. 22-24). Day trips and touring the countryside between the wars and after the Second World War offered a break from routine, motoring becoming a fashionable pursuit amongst the more affluent classes by the 1920s (Fig. 34). Many forebears in the armed forces and other services learned to drive vehicles during the Second World War, encouraging private vehicle ownership afterwards, so photographs of the late 1940s onwards reveal more ordinary relatives enjoying the freedom and mobility afforded by their own cars (Fig. 42). Snapshots taken on holiday reveal many families enjoying a summer break in Britain in the days before cheap package holidays abroad were available. Beach resorts were always a popular choice (Figs. 35 & 40), although the more fortunate could afford to visit relatives living abroad (Fig. 27). Some relatives had the opportunity to travel to more exotic locations through their work, as seen from time to time in photographs set in overseas locations (Fig. 39), while the war changed many lives, often instigating a new place of residence (Fig. 48).

Membership of church groups, social clubs and other work-related or special interest organisations was common in the interwar and post-Second World War eras and these associations often arranged outings for their members (Figs. 36, 37 & 41). A familiar sight in the English countryside in the 1920s and 1930s was the *charabanc,* a motor coach or bus, usually open-topped, with bench seats allowing for around 16 or more passengers, these vehicles often being hired for works and club excursions (Fig. 37). Many children of these decades joined the Scouts, Girl Guides or other youth organisations and members of such groups were often photographed attending events and training camps (Fig. 38). Physical exercise was, in general, high on the agenda. Participation in organised sports and other outdoor activities filled the leisure time of many people, as seen over and again in photographs of this era. Cycling, enjoyed by enthusiasts since the 1880s, became especially popular with the manufacture of relatively cheap bicycles in the 1920s, with many family snapshots of the 1930s and 1940s depicting earlier generations with their bicycles, or even tandems (Figs. 45 & 47): this was the heyday of the bicycle, now affordable for virtually everyone and still a safe and pleasurable pastime before there were many cars on the roads. Cycling was a common mode of transport, groups of friends and members of cycling clubs enjoying cycle tours and outings (Fig. 47) and bicycle racing becoming a competitive sport (Fig. 45). Swimming was another favourite pastime (Fig. 46), encouraged by the building of many public open-air swimming pools or lidos during the 1930s. Joining local sports clubs such as lawn bowls (Fig. 44), football and cricket clubs (Fig. 49) offered members a chance to play regular matches against other teams and enjoy an active social life centred on the clubhouse. Family photographs reveal that many other pursuits such as ice skating, golf, tennis (Fig. 43) and shooting (Fig. 48) were also enjoyed during during the first half of the 20th century.

20th century prints and albums

Many 20th century snapshots are contact prints which relate directly to the size of the film from which they derived. The first Box Brownie cameras, introduced in 1900, produced 5.7cm square prints, while the No.2 Brownie camera, launched in 1901, gave larger (5.7 x 8.3cm) snapshots - a size which remained popular for over 50 years. The 1912 Kodak Vest Pocket camera produced pictures of 6.4 x 4.2cms. Postcard prints were also common in the early 20th century, these usually measuring 8.3 x 14cms, while other larger prints became more common after the First World War, especially during the 1930s. The size of snapshots can therefore offer a broad guide to their date, although this is not a very precise method of dating, and the visual evidence will usually offer more accurate clues.

Old snapshots are often discovered loose in envelopes, boxes or tins (a conservator's nightmare), although some may have been passed down in their original albums. Early 20th century snapshot albums naturally survive in far greater numbers than the weighty, leather-bound Victorian bible-like albums seen in Chapter 2. Examples from the early 1900s - 1920s may be relatively small volumes, their pages typically formed of thick card with pre-cut apertures designed to take the neat snapshots of the era. By the 1930s and 1940s, larger albums were more common, the pages often thinner and left plain so that prints of various sizes could be arranged inside. As in the previous century, albums were frequently given as Christmas or birthday presents so there may be a helpful inscription and date inside the front cover, as in the case of Fig. 50 - a Kodak album dating from 1917. Earlier photographs could of course have been displayed in a new album, but in many cases the year of a dated album will suggest the earliest date for the snapshots displayed inside. As with any inherited photograph album, when removing photographs from a snapshot album it is important to replace them in their correct positions as the original sequence may be relevant, other photographs displayed on the same and adjacent pages often helping with identification of unknown images.

Analysing family snapshots

Sometimes helpful details such as names, dates and location are recorded on the backs of snapshots, or on the album pages - handwritten notes that are likely to be accurate since the author was often the photographer, a person in the picture or the family member who organised the album. Other photographs may be unmarked - baffling images of unfamiliar people or places which appear to give little away, yet patient research can eventually lead to accurate dating and clarification of many of these unidentified pictures. 20th century snapshots may be recognisable by someone else in the family, especially if they were taken within living memory, so it is always worth consulting relatives, especially older generations, for ideas or information as pictures often trigger recollections from the past; or perhaps another family member has a copy of the same, or a similar view that was annotated on the back. Other random snapshots, perhaps those of early origins, may be harder to date and identify: analysing these pictures requires careful study of the visual evidence and may well benefit from further investigations.

Dating the visual evidence

Without the card mount characteristics, photographer information or studio settings which aid the dating of professional photographs, the picture itself is generally all that is available when it comes to determining a time frame for family snapshots and other photographs posed in the open air. Much has been written about identifying and dating the different types of visual clues seen in outdoor photographs but it is usually the people in the picture who are of most interest to researchers and they wear clothes which can usually be dated far more accurately than buildings or any other features that may crop up in a picture. Vehicles can also offer a *post quem* date for a photograph, if they can be positively identified, so tips on researching and dating these are also included in this section.

In some amateur photographs, family members are 'dressed up' in smart, stylish garments, especially if the picture marked a special occasion and high-fashion outfits are generally the easiest to date, as explained in Chapter 3. However even regular clothing worn at home, at work and other everyday occasions broadly followed fashionable lines by the early 20th century, so the ordinary, practical dress often seen in snapshots may not in reality appear very different to that worn for formal studio portraits of comparable date. There are a few exceptions to this, for example between the 1900s and 1920s, special protective motoring coats and headgear may be worn in snapshots of forebears driving in open-topped vehicles (Fig. 34). From the 1920s onwards, and especially during the 1930s and 1940s, the clothing seen in holiday and weekend snapshots also becomes noticeably more varied, reflecting the gradual relaxation of etiquette surrounding dress in the post-WW1 era, in particular the growing acceptance of simpler garments for leisure wear that were more comfortable and often more revealing than earlier styles. New developments affected the design of swimming and bathing costumes (Figs. 35, 39 & 46), summer beachwear (Fig. 40) and casual sportswear for cycling (Figs. 45 & 47) and other outdoor pursuits such as walking, rambling and camping. Although not strictly mainstream fashion, these modes of dress can also be assigned to specific time periods with a fair degree of accuracy. The dress dating guide in Chapter 3 refers to the clothing worn in many of the snapshots reproduced in this chapter, while the individual image captions below also highlight the main dress clues in each picture - recognisable garments and hairstyles that are mirrored in many other family photographs of comparable date.

Occasionally ancestors or relatives were photographed outdoors wearing special occupational uniforms in the later 19th and early 20th centuries and with luck such pictures will be firmly dated or identified, as in the cases of Figs. 16 & 19. Undated photographs of family members dressed in civilian uniforms can sometimes be difficult to pin down closely as relatively little has been published about this category of dress, which tends to fall between the expertise of both fashion historians and military specialists. However the regulation garments provided for staff employed in the principal services - nursing, the fire brigade, the police force, the postal service and so on - evolved in stages over the years, gaining and shedding specific features which can, theoretically, be dated. Although useful resources on these subjects are fairly scarce, an internet search will reveal whether a booklet may have been produced about the relevant service uniform, or whether the official website of the organisation in question has a 'history' section including historic photographs or a timeline charting the development of their particular uniform.

Where vehicles appear in a photograph, these also provide visual evidence that can help with dating and perhaps with locating unidentified scenes. The website of the

Surrey Vintage Vehicle Society (SVVS) - www.svvs.org - displays thousands of historic images, which provide very useful comparative examples, while their 'Help' page offers free assistance in identifying cars, buses, vans, motorbikes and other private, commercial and agricultural vehicles in old photographs. SVVS experts may be able to identify the make and model of a vehicle in a family snapshot, suggesting its likely time frame, as was the case in Figs. 32, 34, 37 & 42. Where the registration plate is visible this can also confirm the year and county of registration, although it is important to be aware that the year of a car's registration does not necessarily give the exact year of the photograph - only its earliest possible date. Another useful website for researching family vehicles from the past is Old Classic Car - www.oldclassiccar.co.uk - which includes a Car Registration Numbers Index. In addition, certain car manufacturers have a 'Heritage' division within their organisation and sometimes employ an archivist who may be able to explain more about the cars seen in early family photographs.

Discovering more about family snapshots

It is very satisfying when the subject and date of a snapshot are established, whether this information was already provided in writing or has been judged by estimating the time frame and identifying the family members in the photograph. Yet there may still be more to discover about a photographic image from the past - perhaps its geographical location, or background details surrounding the occasion - aspects which may invest the scene with greater personal meaning, fitting the captured moment into the lives and experiences of the forebear(s) portrayed.

Unidentified views of rural landscapes, unspoilt areas of coastline and other natural or anonymous open-air environments can be notoriously difficult to locate precisely, as in the case of Figs. 33, 34, 37, 40 & 42, and their geographical setting may remain undiscovered unless further evidence comes to light about the occasion behind the photograph. Buildings in the background of a picture are often helpful and can in some cases reveal the location if they are identifiable or can be successfully researched. Public edifices and commercial properties in street scenes may not be instantly recognisable but where a name appears on a building it may be possible to find out more online, as in the case of Fig. 47, which was firmly located from the name of an incidental shop in the background of the picture. Private dwellings and other domestic buildings such as garages, sheds, greenhouses, studios, barns and stables, along with their gardens and grounds, may well be familiar if they relate to family homes remembered from childhood, or perhaps they can be recalled by other relatives. Some of the properties pictured in photographs will have remained in family hands for many years, as in the case of Figs. 2, 12-15 and 43, and may still be a family home (Fig. 8): far from being simply bricks and mortar, houses were integral to forebears' everyday lives - places of tremendous family significance that may inspire great personal attachment. Some residences were also combined with business premises, with home life and work routine being conducted under the same roof, as in the case of the public house depicted in Figs. 2 & 15 and the shop photographed in Fig. 23. Where sequential images of different dates survive, these provide an interesting visual history of the house and its development over time, showing the maturing of the garden, building extensions and other structural refurbishments reflecting the changing lives of the occupants.

Some houses pictured in 19th and early 20th century snapshots taken in eras before living memory may not be instantly recognisable today but where ancestors or relatives in the picture can be identified and an accurate date range has been determined, other records can be consulted to establish where those family members would have been living at the time of the photograph, as was the case with Figs. 3, 4 & 9. This is a reminder that investigating the homes pictured in family photographs also links closely with house history research - a subject about which much has been published and for which many helpful documents survive to aid those starting from scratch. Particularly useful are the 10-yearly census returns, which were already underway by the time of the earliest photographs, electoral registers and old directories that listed the head of the household. Maps, plans and land surveys are also invaluable tools when trying to locate an ancestral property, especially as a house name, street number or even the road may have changed over the years - see the Web Resources section. If the precise address of an old family home or rented property can be determined and its location is within travelling distance, it may be interesting to pay a personal visit to discover how much the building has changed over time. If it still exists and the present occupants are at home and amenable to discussion, it may transpire that they know something of the house's history and can add to the family information already accumulated.

Even when the essential facts surrounding a photograph - the date, identity of the person or people and perhaps the location - are already known, it can be interesting and rewarding to carry out a little detective work into the events or occasion behind the picture. Written details on the back of a print may provide leads for further research, as in the case of Fig. 45, where an online search turned up a museum website recording sporting events that tied in perfectly with the picture, giving it a firm context of both personal and wider historical interest. Features contained within the image itself may also offer possible avenues of inquiry, as was true of Fig. 40, which seemed rather baffling until specialist help was sought. Knowledge about the life and movements of family members may also suggest paths of exploration that can add interest and meaning to old snapshots in which they appear, as with Fig. 39, where an application for Royal Navy records produced a full itinerary of the young sailor's cruise in the year that he was photographed on a foreign beach. Photographs implying or indicating travel between countries can often be investigated further using ships' passenger lists, these records being used to aid firm dating of Figs. 3, 4, 9 & 27.

These and other examples featured in this chapter demonstrate how many of the documentary records used regularly by genealogists in their family history research can also help when it comes to understanding more about photographic images in the family picture collection. It is also worth remembering that the internet is a marvellous tool for random searches about virtually any subject. Many organisations named on, pictured in or connected with family photographs are still in existence today, or there may be modern incarnations of the same that perhaps operate museums, host informative websites or keep detailed records from the past that can be accessed by researchers, either via the internet, by written request or through a personal visit. In recent years many interesting independent and community websites have also been developed which may record local historical information or keep picture archives for the geographical areas in which ancestors and relatives lived and worked. Their holdings may even connect directly with family photographs, as was discovered when researching Fig. 22.

Family snapshots and other photographs depicting forebears in a natural setting are fascinating visual documents of both personal value and broader historical interest: they offer endless potential for further research, tell many ordinary and extraordinary stories and help us to picture in vivid detail how earlier generations of the family lived, worked and spent their leisure time, connecting us closely with our past.

FAMILIES AT HOME

Fig. 1 At home in Rattlesden, Suffolk, c.1857
This retouched and framed ambrotype was taken outside the family farmhouse, probably by a visiting photographer from a local studio. Photographing groups of several people was difficult in the early days of photography and the younger subjects here have clearly struggled to maintain their pose. A likely date of 1857 is suggested by the children's birth dates, supported by the fashion clues. The sons (left) aged around two and four, both wear the full-skirted tunics that were usual for small boys in the 1850s, while the daughters, aged about nine and twelve, wear youthful versions of women's clothing, a gathered bodice attached to a full skirt, their short hemlines ending below the knee. Their mother wears the wide pagoda sleeves of the decade and the married woman's cap usual in the mid-Victorian era. Her husband, a gentleman farmer, wears the formal, narrow frock coat of the 1840s and 1850s, his beard the early style, typical of the mid-late 1850s.

Fig. 2 Outside the back parlour of the Bath Arms, Minsterley, Shropshire, c.1872
This group photograph is set outside the back of the public house which was also the home of the family seen here, the mother having grown up there as the daughter of the previous publican. A relatively early outdoor photograph, it may have been taken either by an itinerant photographer or by a representative from a local studio. The birth dates of the four children suggest a date around 1872, assuming that the youngest daughter, right, is aged about nine and the son at the back around eighteen. The clothing styles support a date in the early 1870s, the most fashionably-dressed woman being the daughter at the back. Her younger sisters wear shorter, layered garments, youthful versions of adult dress.

Fig. 3 In the conservatory at 'Arreton', Bournemouth, c.1886-9
This beautiful image is one of two surviving snapshots taken in the conservatory of a family home in Bournemouth, its location confirmed by accurate dating of the scene and checking the address on relevant censuses. The tight bodices, draped skirt fronts and bustles of the ladies' dresses suggest a mid-late 1880s date: the older sisters also wear elaborate lace collars and caps - matronly accessories reserved for the middle-aged and elderly by this time. This photograph and others of similar date (see Fig. 4) were probably taken by their brother-in-law, who is thought to have been a keen early amateur photographer. Recently his original glass plates (negatives) for these photographs have been found - a rare discovery.

Fig. 4 In the family garden at 'Arreton', Bournemouth, c.1888
Featuring members of the same family seen in Fig. 3, along with four young siblings, this informal photograph was dated closely to the late 1880s from the appearance of the younger women, especially their *plastron* bodices and hairstyles. The name and location of this house, suggested by the census, was confirmed by another photograph showing the same grassy bank, marked 'Arreton'. As suspected it was the house with the conservatory again - the home of the children's grandparents, where one of the boys stayed while a pupil at Wimborne Grammar School. Their parents lived in the Argentine (see Fig. 27) but are known to have visited England in 1888; their father may well have taken this snapshot of the family in that year.

Fig. 5 Outside cottages in Garrs Lane, Grassington, Yorkshire, 1893

This is an amateur snapshot, although the image has been printed and mounted as a cabinet portrait, like many late 19th century professional photographs. It was one of a number of early family photographs taken by a Lancashire cotton mill worker who was also a keen photographer. His family and their relatives, pictured centre and right here, were staying in one of the cottages during their summer holiday in Yorkshire in 1893. Recent research has led to the discovery that the previously-unidentified lady and children seen outside their cottage on the left had cousins in Burnley, where the holiday makers lived - a connection which perhaps explains their stay here. The building was also located a few years ago but it has, predictably, been altered.

Fig. 6 Outside the farmhouse, Heath Farm, Homersfield, Suffolk, c.1895-7
This attractive photograph depicting a Suffolk farming family in front of their farmhouse was probably taken by a professional photographer, a blanket laid on the ground outside for the occasion. The elderly man in the centre - a widower - and his three sons standing in the back row were all farmers, the women here being two wives and four unmarried daughters, while the boy in the fashionable sailor suit is his grandson. The women's very wide, puffed 'leg-o'-mutton' sleeves immediately date this scene to around the mid-1890s and 1897 must be the latest year as the son standing back right died in January 1898. Another son, centre back, later moved to a new farm at Stoke Ash, Suffolk, where his grand daughter still farms today.

Fig. 7 A house probably in Brierfield, near Burnley, Lancs, 1901

This early Edwardian snapshot is presumed to have been taken by the same amateur photographer responsible for Figs. 5 & 28-30 and shows members of the same inter-related families. The bay-fronted residence has not yet been positively identified but it was the home of an ancestor, pictured here on the steps, who was a Borough Surveyor: his house was provided with the job and he and his family moved around several times within the area. The ladies' fashionable dresses and hairstyles confirm an early-1900s date, yet the scene picturing parents with their children in the garden is a timeless image.

Fig. 8 In the grounds of 'The Fisheries', Herts, c.1910

This early 20th century photograph depicts previous occupants of a riverside property which has been a family home for over 70 years. Once part of a country estate belonging to Lady Ella Russell (d.1936), sister of the Duke of Bedford, the cottage situated in these grounds was first rented by the parents of the present owner in 1938; she was born there in 1946 and later bought the cottage from the local council in the 1980s. She discovered this early photograph in a box of papers and photographs - an image dateable from dress to the turn of the 1900s and 1910s. Consulting the 1911 census revealed the residents at that time to be Lady Ella's 'Park Keeper', his wife and 19 year-old son, the property then being known as 'Fishing Cottage'. These details fit the photograph perfectly, demonstrating how dating followed by further research can bring a picture to life and give it a meaningful historical context.

Fig. 9 In the garden at 33 ('Livonia') Broomwater, Teddington, Middx, 1914
This snapshot is typical of casual family photographs taken at home during the 1910s, when amateur photography was growing more popular. These relatives were recorded at 33 'Livonia' Broomwater on the 1911 census, a house they rented before buying No.11 in the same road. The elderly gentleman, wearing his London Rowing Club cap, had returned to England after retiring from ranching in Argentina (see Fig. 27). Seated front right is his son (seen as a boy in an early snapshot - Fig. 4), an engineer visiting from Argentina with his family. The year of the photograph is judged from the ages of the children and from a record of their return to Buenos Aires in February 1915 on a ship's passenger list. The niece who returned with them is thought to have been the photographer on this occasion.

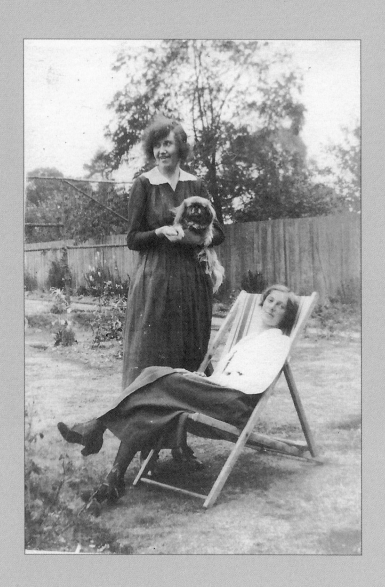

Fig. 10 Garden scene, 1918-20

This unidentified snapshot was one of many photographs displayed in a Kodak album inscribed 'Christmas 1917' inside the front cover (Fig.50). Although earlier photographs could be inserted into a new album, usually the pictures inside will be of later date. Dress clues date this scene closely to c.1918-20, especially the high-waisted 'barrel' shaped dress with a wide, flat collar worn by the standing woman, the blouse and skirt combination worn by her companion being another fashionable outfit of the era. Sun loungers and deck chairs occur often by now in casual photographs of families relaxing in their back gardens, as do household pets.

Fig. 11 Garden scene, c.1920-23

Another unmarked snapshot from the same 1917 family photograph album as Fig. 10, this is datable to c.1920-23 from the dress clues, particularly the woman's collared dress, long beads and deep-crowned hat. The little boy wears the belted tunic and shorts outfit fashionable for small boys in the 1910s/early 1920s, while his older brothers both wear knitted jerseys, the usual garment for school and play after the war. Privileged children had been riding tricycles since the 1860s/1870s but by the 1920s they were mass-produced and were becoming a familiar item in more ordinary households.

Fig. 12 Inside Hazeldene, Greywell, Hampshire, 1930s

This family snapshot offers a rare view of an inter-war domestic interior. The scene is full of interesting detail and allows a glimpse of an authentic room setting from the past, complete with furniture, ornaments and other household objects. It is thought to have been taken inside the family house depicted in Fig. 13, the relative (born 1893) who owned the property being seated on the right here with friends or neighbours, or it may have been taken inside a neighbouring Greywell house. Although the women are dressed plainly, their short waved hairstyles and the style of their cardigans, jackets and other clothing suggest a date in the 1930s.

Fig. 13 Outside Hazeldene, Greywell, Hampshire, 1940s
Family members posing on the front doorstep of their house are a common theme, this unmarked snapshot dateable to the 1940s from the appearance of the lady (also seen in Fig. 12). The house, named after her maiden name, was built in 1926, three years after she and her husband were married (see Ch 5 Fig. 27). It was their joint home until her death in 1966, he remaining there until 1984, when it passed to his younger brother. When he died in 2009, aged 91, the property was sold with a view to being redeveloped – a new chapter in the building's history after over 80 years as one family's home.

Fig. 14 In the garden of Beta Cottage, Barton-in-the-Clay, Beds, 1946

This snapshot of an elderly ancestor was taken by her grandson five years before she died, aged 96. The 'cottage' seen here - a fairly substantial detached house - had been built in the early 1890s on the front of some older cottages as a family home by her husband (the young plumber and decorator seen in Ch 2 Fig. 19). He also built two semi-detached houses called Alpha Cottages: these are still standing, although sadly Beta Cottage was demolished in the 1960s. Were the year of this photograph not known, the best dating clue would be the style of the lady's hat, which is typical of the headwear worn by older women in the mid-late 1940s.

Fig. 15 The 'Bath Arms', Minsterley, Shropshire, 1880s

This photograph depicts the front of the public house seen in Fig. 2, possibly being the work of an itinerant photographer. It shows the female proprietor and two of her daughters from the earlier photograph, her husband having died in 1878 (note the removal of his name on the board outside). This picture dates from the 1880s, as suggested by the ages of the grown-up daughters and supported by dress clues: the women wear plain work dresses without the bustle fashionable c.1883/4-1889, but some of the men in the scene - inn 'regulars' - wear the fashionable tall-crowned bowler hats of the decade. This public house, known as the 'Angel Inn' until its name was changed during the 1860s, was reputedly run by successive generations of the same family for around 300 years, although historical research has so far only established a continuing family connection from the mid-18th century until 1936, when the business was sold following a family dispute. The freehold of the building seems to have been owned by the Bath (Longleat) Estate for many years between the 18th and early 20th centuries, before its tenants - descendants of the ancestors seen in this photograph - finally purchased it in around 1930. Sadly the property, which had a long and interesting history, was demolished c.2005.

Fig. 16 Bishopstoke Fire Brigade, January 1887

An elderly relative remembers this photograph hanging above the fireplace at home when he was growing up - a treasured family possession. A version of the picture was also published in a local book, in which the 'Bishopstoke Fire Brigade' was equated with the 'first Carriage Works Brigade', suggesting that the Victorian fire crew captured here was linked with the local railway carriage works. This makes perfect sense as one of the volunteer firemen in the group (seen in the middle of the back row) was an ancestor who worked as a railway signal linesman in Eastleigh, Hampshire. The brass helmets and double-breasted tunics worn as uniforms here remained more or less unchanged until well into the 20th century.

March 6. 1896

Fig. 17 Boiler maker, Ruston's yard, Lincoln, 1896

This ancestor was employed at Ruston's manufacturers of industrial equipment in Lincoln from 1860 until his retirement c.1913, working his way up to Foreman Boiler Maker. Here he poses for the camera in his working lounge suit and bowler hat on the occasion of his 50th birthday in 1896, assessing damage to a boiler tube plate. In the background are a boiler and firebox for a locomotive (or possibly a traction engine). He was a busy man who served on around thirty or forty committees during his lifetime, at least six at any one time. He left behind valuable written details about his life and experiences in the form of a short autobiography, eighteen years of diaries and travel journals covering five trips throughout Europe which he undertook on company business between 1889 and 1900, these charmingly illustrated by a friend.

Fig. 18 Gardeners at Mystole Park, Chartham, Kent, c.1900-1903
This photograph, probably an amateur snapshot, depicts two gardeners in a greenhouse at Mystole Park, a former country estate in Kent. The relative connected with this picture held the position of Head Gardener there, in charge of 16 men, but was made redundant in around 1910 after the heir to the estate gambled away the family fortune. At the beginning of the 20th century manual work was often carried out in everyday clothing, although men's suit jackets were often removed and they worked in their shirt sleeves, as seen here. The two different styles of shirt collars - one standing, the other turned down - and neat cloth caps worn by these gardeners suggest a date of around 1900 or soon after.

292

Fig. 19 Nurses at Southampton Hospital, 1916

Some photographs of the 1910s depict scenes connected to the First World War and there is no mistaking these nurses photographed in 1916 in the grounds of Southampton Hospital - the occasion recorded in a handwritten note in the album. The nurses are neat and spotless in appearance: their hair is pinned back under starched white caps and their coloured dresses are protected by full-length bibbed aprons, detachable starched collars and separate sleeves, attached with safety pins. One wears a wrist watch, the 'modern' time piece that replaced the watch and chain.

Fig. 20 Off to work, Deefords Avenue, Chester, 1916 or 1918
This snapshot is one of two prints of the same photograph - one dated on the back 1916, the other, confusingly, 1918. Either year would be possible, judging from the young woman's smart, businesslike outfit: her wide, calf-length skirt confirms a date of at least 1915 and is worn with a matching belted jacket and white blouse with a fashionable wide collar. Photographed outside her home, she was about to cycle to work at Lloyds Bank in Chester.

Fig. 21 Outside the sweetshop in South Road, Waterloo, Liverpool, c.1919
This snapshot was taken outside a sweetshop and tobacconist in Liverpool, a business owned for many years by the female relative seen in Ch 4 Fig. 9 and run with help from her daughters. The photograph is undated but a date of around 1919 seems likely judging from the children in the shop doorway, identifiable as two of her grandchildren, born in 1915 and 1917. The boy wears the belted tunic and shorts suit popular for small boys at the time, while the little girl's short smock dress showing her voluminous knickers is also typical of the later 1910s.

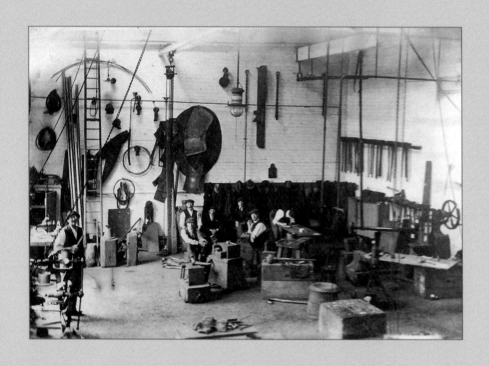

Fig. 22 Coppersmiths workshop, Bass Brewery, Burton-On-Trent, 1932
This snapshot, found amongst a large collection of family photographs, had the work location and date written by hand on the reverse. Two relatives worked as coppersmiths at this workshop, although they do not appear to be in this photograph which shows their colleagues working in their cloth caps and shirt sleeves. A few years later, early in the Second World War, the metalworking skills of one relative were to take him to Khartoum in the Sudan as a member of the Royal Army Ordnance Corps, where duties involved repairing tanks, other military vehicles and guns. Researching this picture further online led to a community website, Staffordshire Past-Track (www.staffspasttrack.org.uk), on whose pages an identical photograph appeared, giving the names of these men in the Bass Brewery workshop.

Fig. 23 Outside family butcher's shop, Harpenden, Herts, c.1930s
This undated snapshot is thought to date from the 1930s and there is nothing in the image to overturn that theory. The relative who owned this butcher's shop stands outside while his brother poses in the pony and trap. The butcher, who lived over and behind the shop, made his own highly-seasoned sausages using a sausage-making machine in the basement. When serving customers he would call out the bill to his wife to take the money at the back of the shop: she looked after the financial side of the business. On Sunday mornings singing was heard from the chapel next door, seen to the left of the photograph. A family visit to the area some years ago revealed that the premises had become a cycle shop.

Fig. 24 Grocer's shop, Dunfermline, c.1935-7
This snapshot, thought to date from c.1935-7, shows a Scottish relative (centre) who worked in a grocer's shop before her marriage. An image like this would usually be difficult to date closely, although the women's short, waved hairstyles confirm a 1930s date. By then it was usual for food shop assistants to wear protective white front-buttoning coats - a form of protective working dress still worn today in some situations. The shop interior displaying a wide variety of fresh, dry and tinned foods offers an interesting documentary record of an era which few can remember today.

298

HOLIDAYS AND OUTINGS

Fig. 25 Family gathering at Wimbledon Camp, July 1866

This picture is both a very early outdoor photograph from a family collection and a record of a significant social and sporting event from the past. The meeting of the National Rifle Association (established 1859) took place annually on Wimbledon Common from 1860 until 1889 - an occasion that attracted thousands of riflemen and their families and other spectators. In 1866, when these ancestors were photographed at the camp, the event ran for twelve days in July. This fascinating image shows 16 members of this upper-middle class family, aged ten to 63, relaxing in front of their tents. Rarely are mid-Victorian ladies seen sprawling on the ground in their crinolines, but here they are, one young lady (second left) even dressed in dull black clothing signifying deep mourning following the death of her husband. The seated man at the back, wearing a bowler hat, is thought to be the novelist, George Alfred Henty, who was related to the family.

Fig. 26 Family day out at Cannock Chase, Staffordshire, c.1870-72

This photograph depicts an ancestor (1815-86) who came from humble origins but built a successful shoemaking business employing 200 men in Stafford, where he eventually became Mayor. He married twice and is here depicted with one of his wives and four of his 22 children at Cannock Chase, a scenic area between Stafford and Birmingham which is now a designated Area of Outstanding Natural Beauty and would have been a popular 19th century 'beauty spot'. This family day out was probably photographed by one of the photographers who plied their trade at local places of interest. A date in the early 1870s is suggested by the birth date of one of the daughters in 1854 and this is supported by the evidence of dress, especially the ladies' fashionable layered and flounced outfits, elaborate hairstyles and tilted *postillion* hats.

Fig. 27 Picnic in the Argentine, 1899

This unusual picnic scene in the Argentine bush depicts some of the female ancestors (left) from Figs. 3 & 4 on a visit to their sister and brother-in-law, who had been cattle ranchers in Argentina since 1870. The men's broad-brimmed hats, jodhpurs and leather riding boots reflect their active, outdoor lifestyle, while the younger women wear the practical blouses and skirts that were usual for every day wear by the late 19th century, their full sleeves indicating a date of c.1895-1900. The family historian, consulting ships' passenger lists on Ancestry, found a record of the English guests landing in Argentina in March 1899. A bottle of wine or champagne is being opened, suggesting a special outing, or a comfortable existence, and the white china teacups are in use, as was customary for Victorian and Edwardian picnics.

Fig. 28 On holiday beside the River Wharfe, Grassington, Yorkshire, 1900
This is an unusually casual family photograph for its date, another early amateur snapshot taken by the ancestor who was a Lancashire cotton mill under-manager. He and his family and their relatives enjoyed annual summer holidays together in the north of England, staying in Grassington at least twice (see Fig. 5, taken on an earlier holiday there). The year of this visit is judged from the sleeping baby, born in October 1899. The photographer's wife (also a mill worker) and sister-in-law lounge in their long skirts beside the River Wharfe, shaded from the late-summer sun by their umbrellas, a white ladies' cloth cap removed and lying on the ground. In the foreground are boots and woollen stockings probably discarded by their sons to go paddling in the nearby river.

Fig. 29 On holiday beside the River Wharfe, Grassington, Yorkshire, 1900

Another annotated snapshot from the same summer holiday as Fig. 28, this shows the two families on the rocks by the river, a timeless setting and yet the Victorian date is clear from their clothing - comfortable for its time but formal and impractical to modern eyes. The man (the same ancestor seen in Fig. 7) wears a three-piece suit, his white tie and broad-brimmed hat only minor concessions to the season. The ladies wear their full-sleeved blouses again and plain cloth skirts which would no doubt have felt hot, being worn over black woollen stockings and leather boots. The boys, aged 13, 11 and 7, look slightly more comfortable, their shorts or trousers and shirt sleeves rolled up. Babies were generally well-protected from the sun, this little girl wearing a cotton smock dress and sun bonnet.

Fig. 30 On holiday at Arnside, Southern Westmoreland, 1902
Another holiday snapshot from the same collection as Figs. 28 & 29, this photograph shows the same
families and some unidentified companions on another family holiday, this time in Arnside, a seaside
town on the River Kent estuary north of Lancaster. The stifling heat of the late summer day is evident
as the group shelters in the shade of a tree. The ladies wear cotton print dresses or white blouses and
plain skirts, their narrow sleeves in vogue by the early 1900s. Their straw hats, several made in the boater
style, were the height of fashion for Edwardian summers. The women and girls hold bunches of daisies
picked on their walk and have decorated their hats and bodices with more flowers – a simple, pleasurable
and harmless act in the eyes of early-20th century forebears (see also Ch 2 Fig.33), but nowadays
considered destructive to nature.

Fig. 31 Ferry boat crossing, Morecambe Bay, Lancashire, c.1910-14

This photograph shows a relative (back row, centre left) with colleagues or friends on an outing on the water. Their boat journey has recently been identified following research into a similar (torn) photograph from the same collection - a postcard bearing the name 'Sankey, Photo Press, Barrow' on the reverse. Online research into the photographer unexpectedly led to a link to a very helpful passenger ship website, www.simplonpc.co.uk, which held the key to both of these images. Information on the site indicated that the photographs were taken on passenger ferry boats across Morecambe Bay, part of the Barrow-Fleetwood paddle steamer service which operated until 1914 when some of the boats were requisitioned for the war. This fitted in with the 1910-14 date range suggested by the passengers' appearance – especially their clothing and hat styles - and also with what is known of the family's location at that time.

Fig. 32 Car outing, Stamford, Connecticut, USA, c.1918-19
Snapshots survive in greater numbers from the late 1910s onwards and researchers with fairly affluent
forebears may discover pictures showing early family motor cars. This undated photograph, taken
shortly after a house move from New York City to Highfields Farm in Connecticut in 1918, depicts these
relatives' first automobile at a time when private car ownership was a luxury. The intrepid lady motorist
is driving a 1916 Overland 81 Touring, the vehicle identified by the Surrey Vintage Vehicle Society
(www.svvs.org). The estimated date of the photograph is based on this information, the likely age of the
daughter in the back (born in 1913), and dress details such as the mother's hat and broad collar.

Fig. 33 Family beach scene, c.1919-21

Walking and picnicking outdoors were popular in the early 20th century, whatever the weather, as demonstrated by this family snapshot taken at an unidentified beach location, apparently in the winter. The photograph is unlabelled but an early post-WW1 date is confirmed by the style of the women's outfits. Their fashionable, loose winter-weight coats all feature wide fur collars and their hats exemplify various styles in vogue at the turn of the 1910s and 1920s. The male relative at the back (also seen in Ch 2, Figs. 34, 38 & 41) wears a felt hat in the new trilby style, his un-starched shirt collar showing the characteristic crease often noticed in photographs of this era.

Fig. 34 Car journey with friends, c.1920-26

This unidentified snapshot was taken somewhere in Britain, or possibly Ireland, although its precise location may never be known. As a very close date was proving difficult to establish, the picture was sent to the Surrey Vintage Vehicle Society who identified the car as a Ford Model T Special dating from after 1919 and before 1927. Most early cars were open-topped, exposed to the elements and motorists at risk of becoming cold, wet and dusty often donned special weather-proof motoring gear. The loose coats worn by these companions are identical to the 'Gents Single-Breasted crash Motor Dust Coats' pictured in 1920s catalogues for motorists' Dust Clothing. Their cloth caps and casual Tam o' Shanter-style hats would also have afforded some protection.

Fig. 35 Bathing on Thurlston Beach, Devon, 1924
This snapshot from an album of family photographs was annotated on the back with the date and location
- an accurate documentary record of a holiday taken by earlier generations. British beach holidays were
usual before foreign travel became more convenient and affordable, Devon always a popular destination.
The modest bathing suits worn by all three relatives here are typical of the early-mid 1920s, the women's
costumes still made with short sleeves and legs and the man's traditional suit featuring a vest. By the end
of the decade and during the 1930s, female swimsuits were becoming more cut-away, in keeping with
the new vogue for sunbathing.

Fig. 36 Church group outing, c.1926-30

Membership of church groups and social clubs was high in the inter-war era, these organisations often
arranging day trips and events for their members. This family snapshot depicts what was probably a
church group outing for women and children. It is undated but the style of the women's outfits confirms
a date between 1926 and 1930. Fashionable features are the deep-crowned cloche hats, soft jersey-knit
dresses and suits and the short hemlines, worn to just below the knee by 1926, especially by younger
women. Short cotton sleeveless or short-sleeved dresses were popular for small girls in the summer,
while boys' outfits of shirt, shorts and tailored jackets or blazers made few distinctions between school
and home wear at this date.

Fig. 37 Great Southern Railways charabanc outing, Ireland, c.1927-30
Charabancs were often used for group outings in the inter-war era and this snapshot shows colleagues or friends riding in a charabanc bearing the crest of the Great Southern Railways. The Surrey Vintage Vehicle Society advised that the GSR was an Irish railway company formed in 1924 which also had an extensive bus fleet and took over a number of private bus operators in Ireland between 1926 and 1929. They identified the vehicle as a 1927 Lancia Charabanc, offering the earliest possible year for the photograph. The appearance of the relative centre right (also seen in Figs. 33 & 34, of slightly earlier date) and the styles of clothing worn by the men suggests a date no later than 1930.

Fig. 38 Dulwich College Officers' Training Corps, Aldershot, 1930

The school boys pictured here at military camp in Aldershot were members of Dulwich College Officer's Training Corps, an organisation which internet research shows was formed in 1908 from the earlier Rifle Volunteer Corps. The Dulwich Contingent still exists today as part of the Combined Cadet Force (CCF) supported by the Ministry of Defence, which aims to encourage leadership skills, endurance, resourcefulness, responsibility and a sense of public service, leading in some cases to recruitment of officers into the Regular Forces. The young relative in the foreground, like his fellow Corps members, wears school blazer and shorts, the boys' open-necked shirts typical of the 1930s when more casual styles became fashionable.

Fig. 39 On the beach in Yugoslavia (Croatia), 1932

This family snapshot depicts a relative (left) and a fellow sailor, both crew members of the Royal Navy C-class light cruiser *HMS Coventry*. A handwritten note on the back explains that the photograph was taken 'At 'Abbazia' Jugo-Slavia. August 1932'. Internet research showed Abbazia (Italian for Opatija) to be a popular resort on the Adriatic coast of western Croatia, formerly Yugoslavia. This was one of many ports that the ship docked at between April and October 1932. Here the young sailors, enjoying time off, pose in their naval caps and bathing costumes which, following 1920s lines, still incorporate a vest section. Unfortunately this family member died when he fell out of his hammock on the destroyer *HMS Faulknor* and broke his neck, on Christmas Day 1940.

Fig. 40 On holiday, possibly Selsey, East Sussex, 1946

A hand-written date on the back of this snapshot shows that the author's mother was photographed here in 1946 when she was aged 15. She lived in London but families quickly returned to Britain's beaches after the war and this may have been taken on the Sussex coast where the family had friends. Her short, halter-neck cotton-print sundress was a casual style of beachwear first worn in the 1930s but very popular by the 1940s. Initially it seemed odd that she would be carrying what appeared to be a small surfboard at that early date, but advice from the Museum of British Surfing (www.museumofbritishsurfing.org.uk) confirmed that this was indeed an early type of board, then sometimes called a 'surf rider board' and similar to today's bellyboards. 'Surf riding' had already begun to attract enthusiasts between the wars and was recommended as a 'health-giving, invigorating, exhilarating and relaxing' sport.

Fig. 41 Army families' outing, Bovington, Dorset 1946

The relative third man from the right in this photograph served with the Royal Armoured Corps (RAC) during the Second World War (See also Ch 2 Fig. 49), transferring to the Royal Electrical and Mechanical Engineers (REME) in 1946. The army often arranged events for military personnel and their families and this photograph on a postcard depicts an unknown outing from the Bovington base in 1946. The clothing worn is typical of the 1940s, the men wearing wide trousers, sports jackets and in some cases patterned ties and knitted waistcoats, while the women and girls wear knee-length skirts and jackets or coats with padded shoulders.

Fig. 42 Day out in the car, 1949

Motoring was a new activity for many ordinary people after the Second World War and enabled city-dwellers like these London-based relatives to enjoy days out in the country. This was the first car owned by the couple seen back and right in this snapshot, which bears the handwritten date 1949 on the back. The Surrey Vintage Vehicle Society have identified the vehicle as a Ford Prefect E93A Saloon, built either in 1940, or more likely 1945. The limited view of the number plate shows part of the letter 'M', signifying Middlesex County Council registration between 1920 and 1965: the letter before, were it visible, would have confirmed the year of manufacture. The snapshot was taken by the author's father, who was a keen amateur photographer, but the location here remains unidentified, highlighting the importance of consulting living relatives about family photographs before it is too late.

Fig. 43 Playing tennis in the garden of Beta Cottage, c.1916-20

This snapshot, taken with a Box Brownie camera, shows a relative playing tennis in the large garden of Beta Cottage, the family home also seen in Fig. 14. Undated, the photograph is dateable to c.1916-20 from the young woman's appearance, especially her loose, belted blouse and plain, wide-brimmed hat. Although white garments were, like today, usual for tennis, styles were based on fashionable ladies' day wear until the 1920s when shorter, more practical tennis outfits began to be worn.

Fig. 44 Francis Drake Bowls Club, Hilly Fields, Brockley, S E London, c.1920s

The setting of this photograph was identified and internet research has revealed that the Francis Drake Bowls Club, established in Hilly Fields in 1906, still thrives today as a venue for playing outdoor lawn bowls. A relative (seated third from right) poses here with other players from the men's team on the occasion of a match against visiting Ladywell. Nowadays club blazer, tie and white trousers are usual for official bowls matches, but in the early 20th century it seems that everyday clothing was worn, the styles of dress seen here aiding dating of the photograph. In particular the mens' three piece lounge suits feature the narrow trousers of the 1920s, while their hats demonstrate the wide variety of headwear then in fashion.

Fig. 45 Displaying the winner's cup following cycle race at Brooklands Race Course, 1939
Annotated on the back with the date and details of the occasion, this snapshot portrays a relative, born in 1918, who was a keen cyclist in his youth and, judging from family photographs, belonged to a cycling club as well as entering competitive races. He poses here wearing shorts, open-necked shirt and linen or cotton jacket - the usual clothing worn for cycling in the 1930s and 1940s. His cup was won at Brooklands in Surrey, the world's first purpose-built motor racing circuit. The History page of the Brooklands Museum website, www.brooklandsmuseum.com, explains that a 100-kilometre cycle race was held there in 1933 to select a team for the World Championships at Montlhéry and that the track continued as a regular venue for cycle races throughout the 1930s. Between April and August of 1939, the year of this photograph, 19 races were held at Brooklands.

319

Fig. 46 Swimming at the British military base, Khartoum, Egypt, 1940

This snapshot depicts the relative seen in Fig. 45 along with a group of fellow soldiers from the Royal Army Ordnance Corps swimming at the pool of their military base in North Africa early in the Second World War. Comparing this photograph with Fig. 39, taken only eight years earlier, reveals how significant developments had occurred in the design of men's swimwear during the 1930s, leading to the disappearance of the traditional costume with vest section. These companions are wearing an early form of men's swimming trunks or shorts (army issue) which fit the abdomen and thighs closely, being made of stretchy woollen fabric. During the 1940s swimming shorts were fashioned so as to cover the navel and incorporated webbing belts which impart a consciously 'dressed' look, although the relative on the right has turned down the waistband of his shorts.

Fig. 47 Cycle and tandem tour of the Isle of Wight, 1941

This snapshot was dated 1941 on the back but the location was not identified. An internet search for the name of the butcher's shop seen in the background, P.M. Colegate, provided a link to an independent website covering the history and culture of the Isle of Wight (www.invectis.co.uk/iow), on which this local business was listed as having operated as P.M.Colegate & Son, No.1 Regent Street in Shanklin in 1957. The friends from Kent pictured here with a bicycle and tandem were clearly enjoying a cycle tour of the Isle of Wight - unusual, perhaps, during the Second World War. They all wear the casual shorts, lightweight cotton or linen jackets and open-necked shirts usually seen in cycling photographs of the 1930s and 1940s.

Fig. 48 Shooting in the Interior Plateau, British Columbia, Canada, 1945
This snapshot shows the same relative who appeared on her wedding day in Ch 5 Fig. 36, now enjoying an outdoor lifestyle in Canada - one of several photographs enclosed in letters home to England that spoke volumes about her new life away from her family. In January 1945 she had arrived at her new husband's home in the Okanagan Valley and, accompanied by his faithful gun dog - a beloved household pet for many years - her husband taught her to shoot in the hills above the valley which form part of the Interior Plateau. Wearing cropped trousers and a close-fitting jersey, she is comfortably yet fashionably dressed in the type of casual separates that were popular with the younger generation on both sides of the Atlantic during and after the war.

Fig. 49 Cricket team, North London, c.1946-49

This undated snapshot was taken soon after the Second World War, judging from the appearance of the author's father, seated second right, front row. Born in 1917, he belonged to the generation that valued the benefits of sport and outdoor exercise and was a keen sportsman throughout the 1930s-1950s. During the war he played cricket for the Royal Engineers and at the time of this photograph belonged to a local cricket club in North London. He poses here with team mates after winning a cup, all wearing conventional cricket whites or 'flannels' - white flannel trousers, V-necked sweaters and open-necked sports shirts - another 'timeless' scene.

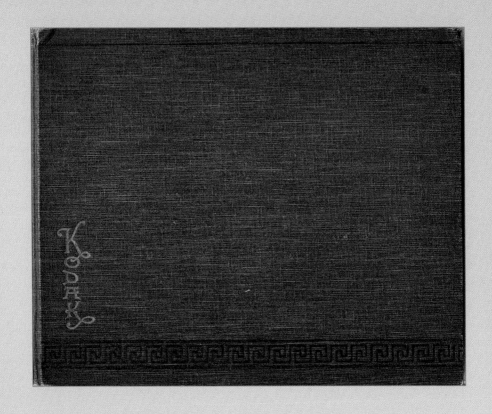

Fig. 50 Kodak snapshot album, dated Christmas 1917
One of several family albums from a large collection, this Kodak photograph album bears a handwritten inscription inside the cover which gives the date - Christmas 1917. At that time amateur photography was becoming very popular, Kodak having been largely responsible for bringing photography to the masses and very much a household name. Albums of this era were often slight in their dimensions but offered plenty of space for the small snapshots displayed inside. All the photographs found in this album were of post-1917 date.

SEVEN

CHAPTER SEVEN

Preserving, copying, sharing and publishing family pictures

T his final chapter of the book considers what to do next with pictures once they have been dated and investigated and assigned a meaningful place within the family archive. The vast majority of original artworks in private collections are over 160 years old - some being considerably older - while even family photographs may have been around for well over a century, the earliest examples almost 170 years old. Inevitably such fragile items deteriorate over time due to the nature of the materials used and because of environmental changes, so the continuing survival of these precious heirlooms throughout and beyond the 21st century depends upon protecting them from damaging external factors and on sensible handling, storage and display. In the following pages are recommendations for looking after different kinds of pictures and suggestions about where to go for expert guidance and specialist help.

Partly in order to save over-handling of the originals, creating digital copies of original artworks and photographs is advisable and some basic help with scanning images and ideas about digital image restoration are included later on in the chapter. Sharing pictures with others online can be a very rewarding experience but careful choices have to be made if treasured portraits of ancestors and relatives are to be uploaded safely onto the internet. Ultimately, researchers may wish to produce scrap books or photo books containing family pictures and some of the options currently available are discussed at the end of the chapter.

Looking after original artworks

Readers who are fortunate in owning original artworks - oil paintings, watercolours, pencil and ink sketches and chalk, crayon or pastel drawings - should be aware that they have inherited not only special personal possessions but also important historical artifacts which need careful looking after if they are to be enjoyed to the full and successfully preserved for future generations. Unfortunately the various original materials used in artworks are complex, vulnerable to accidental damage and also highly sensitive to their surroundings, often responding dramatically to unsuitable conditions. Damage to oil paintings typically ranges from split and punctured canvases through faded, cracked and flaking paint to mildew, dirt, dust and insect damage. Similarly works on paper may be subject to fading, brittleness of the paper, insect damage, mould, wrinkling, spotting or 'foxing' and other stains. Many of these and other problems are caused by unsatisfactory environmental conditions, especially extreme or fluctuating temperature and humidity, harsh light, pollution and dirt; they may well also be the result of poor handling, storage and mounting. In a museum or gallery the environment in which paintings, prints and drawings are displayed is carefully controlled with strictly regulated air conditioning and modified lighting but these are not usually an option in the average family home, where pictures can suffer quite easily from high and low humidity, too much exposure to the light and other adverse factors. Damage and deterioration spoil the physical appearance of pictures, greatly undermine their chances of long term survival and will certainly impact on their monetary value.

In the following sections are some basic tips for looking after original artworks in the home, but for a more detailed guide to understanding and effectively caring for different types of paintings and drawings it is recommended that readers visit the website of the Institute of Conservation - www.icon.org.uk - the leading organisation for the conservation and preservation of cultural heritage in the UK. This is an invaluable and trustworthy source of information about securing, displaying, storing and maintaining all types of historical objects. In the main website menu click on 'How to care for..' for a list of downloadable leaflets dealing with a wide range of items including oil paintings, prints and watercolours, as well as many other articles that may have been passed down through the family such as photographs, costume and textiles and jewellery. The points below derive from the official advice given by the Institute.

Caring for oil paintings

(1) Moving and handling

Always plan ahead when moving an oil portrait, checking that there is somewhere suitable to put it before it is moved from its original location. Hands should be clean and dry when touching the picture and it should be secure in its frame. Ideally when taken down from the wall, paintings should rest face outwards against a clear wall, on a padded surface, well away from doorways, furniture and passing people. When carrying a painting, always use both hands and have the picture facing the body: this operation may require two people if the portrait is large and heavy.

(2) Hanging a painting

Always consider the position of a painting in relation to other objects and people so that it cannot be easily knocked. For example avoid hanging it close to shelves, furniture, behind doors or in busy corridors. Think carefully also about the environmental conditions in the space in which the painting is to hang. In the summer in Britain a well-ventilated room should be suitable, but in winter conditions may become unsatisfactory, due to central heating, or damp. Try to avoid hanging over direct heat or moisture sources such over fires, radiators or other heaters, in bathrooms or kitchens, on damp walls, or next to outdoor vents. Be aware that picture lights attached to or near the top of a painting can get very hot and will heat that area of the picture. Paintings will also build up dirt quickly in rooms with an open fire, or in which people smoke.

(3) Housekeeping

Dust can be removed from paintings using a very soft, non-metal brush, but preferably not feather dusters or sheepskin dusters as these can catch. Do not attempt to dust if the picture surface seems unstable, for example if the paint is flaking. If the painting is covered by glass, this will need cleaning now and again. Always spray cleaner onto the cloth, not the glass, and spray well away from the picture. It is very unwise to attempt any direct cleaning of the canvas, or picture repairs, as home methods may cause irreparable damage: these are skilled processes that should only be carried out by a qualified and experienced conservator.
See also Icon leaflet: *Care and Conservation of Oil Paintings*

Caring for prints, drawings and watercolours

Works of art on paper are especially fragile as not only can the artistic material used, (watercolour paint, ink, crayon, chalk and so on) become faded, but the whole structure of the paper may become weak through over-exposure to light and changes in temperature and humidity. The way in which these items are mounted and framed is also very significant.

(1) Environment

Essentially, try to protect framed prints, drawings and watercolours from daylight. Avoid south facing light and consider using ultraviolet (UV) glass for framing. If possible do not hang these pictures on the inside of an outside house wall or near to a radiator or spotlight. Ideally works of art on paper should be stored in a cool, stable environment. Museums aim for a temperature of 16-19 degrees C and relative humidity of 45-60%. This may be difficult in the home but a low and stable relative humidity of below 60% will help to slow deterioration and reduce the potential for pest and mould damage.

(2) Handling

In general, handle all works of art as little as possible and do not touch the image itself. Pastel and charcoal drawings may need extra care as these materials are soft and may smudge easily. It is a good idea to keep these permanently in a rebated mount, to prevent any static or friction.

(3) Storage

If prints, drawings and watercolours are not on display, it is preferable to keep them horizontally in a plan chest or specially designed case such as a Solander box, where they will be protected from light and dirt. Inside they can be placed in conservation quality folders (not ordinary plastic sleeves) for convenient handling (see below for more about archival storage products). When deciding where to store artworks on paper, avoid damp basements and un-insulated lofts or attics. Items in storage should be checked regularly for signs of damage.

(4) Mounting and framing

Good quality mounting and framing is one of the most effective ways of preserving and conserving artworks on paper. Poor mounts and frames damage more works of art on paper than any other factors. It is recommended that readers consult the Icon leaflet downloadable from their website: *Guidelines for conservation mounting and framing of works of art on paper.* See also Icon leaflet: *Care and conservation of prints, drawings and watercolours.*

Seeking specialist advice

With luck, family artworks will have been well looked after in the past, although this is not always the case: earlier generations did not have the benefit of modern knowledge and specialist expertise and may not have respected historical artifacts to the extent that most of us do today. Even if inherited pictures appear in a reasonable state of preservation, it is never too soon to consider how their condition might be improved and maintained for the future. If they have already suffered accidental damage, are in poor physical shape, show early signs of deteriorating, need proper cleaning, or if there are any queries at all about how to look after them, it is *always* advisable to seek expert advice and help from a professional picture conservator-restorer. A reputable conservator who understands the composition of different objects and how to conserve them sympathetically so that their life can be extended as far as possible will be able to explain more about the condition of a family picture and suggest appropriate treatments and recommendations for ongoing care. As mentioned in Chapter 1, most local art galleries or museums will advise on the date and artistic merits of a privately owned picture: some institutions also have regular sessions where visitors can talk to both curators and conservators (though do check the situation and if necessary make an appointment before turning up with a valuable or fragile work of art). There are also many independent conservation specialists operating throughout the country, although finding a suitable person close to home can be a minefield as levels of expertise and fees vary enormously. The Institute of Conservation also operates a Conservation Register (see 'Find A Conservator' in the main website menu) which provides information on accredited conservator-restorers in the UK and Ireland. This useful facility enables inquirers to search online for an appropriate professional picture conservator in their local area.

Caring for photographs

Photographs may seem commonplace items but they may be complex objects and often consist of multiple layers, each containing different substances which react to outside influences in various ways. Unfortunately this can mean that some types of photograph deterioration are untreatable, so the most practical advice is to try to prevent common problems in the first place. The potential causes of damage and deterioration to photographs are as follows:

High temperatures, which speed up fading and tarnishing; exposure to light, especially sunlight, which causes fading; damp conditions, which can produce mould or discolouration; very dry conditions, which cause brittleness and cracking; poor quality or inappropriate storage, framing and mounting methods, which may emit pollutants, leading to fading, discolouration and tarnishing and can also cause physical damage such as tears and creases, and staining from sticky adhesive tapes and album pages; some photographs are at risk from insect attack such as silverfish, woodworm, booklice and carpet beetle; handling causes further deterioration as dirt can scratch vulnerable surfaces, while fingers may leave prints and damaging moisture from the skin. It is a fact that many old photographs are handled frequently, because they are so popular and portable, but there are many ways of preventing and reducing deterioration of precious photographs.

(1) Storage

Photographs should be stored in a cool place where conditions are neither very damp nor very dry: therefore they should not be kept in damp basements or garages or in stuffy, un-insulated lofts. Preferably there should be no significant fluctuations, a stable environment with a relative humidity within the range 30-40% being ideal. As with other pictures on paper and card, it is important to store and file photographs using boxes and envelopes of suitable archival quality (see below). Original daguerreotype and ambrotype frames and cases and old albums should be regarded as integral to the photographs they contain and in these instances it is important to keep the whole artefact intact. If any elements have a problem, for example if a case is broken, this should be dealt with by a professional conservator who will use processes geared towards maintaining the integrity of the photograph in its original context.

(2) Display

Although it is tempting to exhibit old family photographs where they can be seen, try to avoid displaying them at high light levels, or for long periods of time. Ultraviolet (UV) filtering glass helps to protect photographs during periods of light exposure. Framing materials should also be of high quality.

(3) Handling

Try to keep handling of original photographs to a minimum, but if it is necessary, make sure that hands are clean and dry or, ideally, wear lint-free cotton researchers' gloves. Hold photographs by their edges and use a supporting base such as stiff paper or card to move fragile photographs. Scanning photographs then storing them suitably, working instead from printed copies or digital images on the computer saves further regular handling of the fragile originals.

For more detailed information about looking after photographs, visit the website of the Institute of Conservation - www.icon.org.uk . The downloadable Icon leaflet *Care and Conservation of Photographic Materials* offers further information. As with original artworks, if in any doubt at all about care and repair of old photographs in any format, professional advice is always recommended: the aim of photograph conservation is to reverse damage, if this is possible, and to ensure that future deterioration is reduced to a minimum.

Conservation quality archival storage materials

Public museums, art galleries and archives always preserve their photographs and artworks on paper (as well as other items such as historical documents and old books) in specially designed conservation quality storage systems. Essentially these provide fragile and potentially vulnerable objects with physical support and protection against permanent damage and decay in an acid-free environment. The kinds of products used by professional institutions are also commercially available to the wider public and so there is no excuse not to take good care of precious family pictures and other important keepsakes. This applies not only to historical material but also to more recent photographs and papers that need to be preserved for future generations. The archival products available offer many different storage and display possibilities, including acid-free boxes of varying shapes and sizes, ring binder systems, album pages, folders, envelopes, pockets, sleeves and even CD cases (Fig. 1). Particularly useful for convenient handling and viewing of photographs of different sizes are transparent inert polyester pockets which contain no harmful chemicals and are safe for long-term storage. Other accessories include researchers' lint-free cotton gloves (Fig. 2), pH neutral pens and mounting products such as acid-free paper, mount strips and adhesive. These and other conservation products are readily available from specialist companies, who may also be able to offer advice about the best products for particular requirements, and from some general genealogical suppliers.

Creating digital images

Family picture researchers with computer skills will already be familiar with making digital copies of photographs and even artworks and storing these as compressed image files on the computer or other electronic media. It is always a good idea to create digital versions of old pictures as these can be used for basic research purposes to save handling the fragile originals; they are also easy to share with others on the internet, can easily be uploaded onto websites and are also suitable for publication. Framed paintings and framed or cased daguerreotypes and ambrotypes, being three-dimensional objects, are best photographed using a digital camera, with the images then downloaded onto a computer. Using flash when taking the photograph will inevitably produce a bright glare in the middle of the picture so avoid flash and wait for good natural daylight conditions. Flat, unframed portraits such as photographic prints can be easily copied using a scanner and saved as digital picture files: both JPEG (jpg) and GIF digital image formats are currently in widespread use, jpg being the more popular and considered by many users the most convenient format. Various kinds of scanner are available, many nowadays being built in to a desktop printer and these are usually suitable for scanning photographs, small unframed artworks, prints and documents.

When scanning photographs, it is advisable to copy each picture individually rather than several at a time, as they may need to be separated later anyway for research purposes and, additionally, the details will be larger and clearer if scanned separately. It is preferable to scan as colour pictures, rather than greyscale: scanning at normal size, at a resolution of 300 dpi (dots per inch) is a good choice for cartes, cabinets, postcards, and most other images. The resolution does not generally need to be any higher, unless the original picture is very small - for example a tiny snapshot, which may benefit from being scanned at 600 dpi so that it can be enlarged later, if necessary, without loss of image quality. Picture files of 300 dpi and higher resolutions naturally take up more computer or disc space than those scanned at a lower resolution or the scanner default setting, but these high quality pictures will be suitable for most purposes, including reproduction in most kinds of printed publications. For picture researchers uncertain about scanning or without suitable equipment, there are many commercial photo-scanning companies who will carry out this work at a cost. Some high street outlets provide this service although, depending on the number of pictures to be copied, it may be worth searching the internet for the most cost effective option. If having pictures scanned commercially involves sending original material through the post, be sure to use the most secure postal service available, such as registered post, or a reputable courier company offering parcel tracking facilities. Alternatively some of the popular genealogy websites offer a scanning service as part of the package.

Finally, if storing digital images and any other important data on discs and other electronic media, remember to protect them from environmental damage and accidents. Clean computer drives routinely to prevent damage to the media and only handle CDs by the very edges, storing them well away from liquids, dust, extreme heat and direct sunlight. Rigid purpose-designed storage containers are ideal, conservation quality CD cases affording the best protection.

Digital photo restoration

Family photographs are not always in perfect condition, especially if they have not been very well looked after in the past. They may be spotted, faded, scratched, creased or torn and unfortunately there is little that can be done to repair or undo damage already done to the originals, except to protect them from further deterioration, as outlined above. However it is possible to create new, improved versions of old photographs, using digital restoration and enhancement techniques - processes which can remove marks, repair tears and creases, restore or add colours and bring fresh clarity and brightness to washed out images. Digital technology can also be used, if required, to manipulate and modify pictures, for example by extending the scene, removing or adding figures, and creating collages and montages; however if photographs are being edited, it is important to keep a careful record of what visual changes have been made and to retain the original versions on which they are based, so that future generations of researchers do not have the additional problem of working out what is an authentic image and what is a 21st century fabrication.

It may be possible to carry out digital enhancement of photographs on the computer at home. Often software is supplied with a computer that enables simple adjustments to colour and sharpness and cropping of pictures, such as Windows Live Photo Gallery. Various basic image editing programs can also be freely downloaded from the internet, such as Google's Picasa. Some of these programs are also useful for organising and sharing images (see below for more on sharing pictures online). More complex image editing may require specialised graphics software such as Adobe Photoshop, GIMP (the GNU Image Manipulation Program) or Pixelmator, designed for Mac operating systems. A wide range of software is available to suit all levels of technical expertise, from beginners to advanced level. Alternatively there is always the option of using a professional photo restorer: a quick internet search or browse through the advertisement pages of any family history magazine will reveal many commercial companies carrying out this kind of work.

Sharing family pictures

Family photographs and portraits in other media are very personal heirlooms, more intimate than many other types of historical material. Some researchers feel strongly about privacy when it comes to their inherited pictures, while others are keen to publicise them as widely as possible. Making images available for others in the genealogical community to see can be a great way of finding out more about them and is also a good excuse to contact more remote relatives: distant family members may be delighted to see old photographs of common forebears and, if they have been researching the same ancestral lines, they might even have useful information to pass on about identical or similar pictures in their possession. There are various methods of displaying and circulating pictures more widely online and when making decisions about how to go about this, researchers should consider what best suits their purpose and may also take into account what will be acceptable to other family members.

Many of the genealogy software packages commonly used for storing family history research also provide the opportunity to upload photographs and further material to share with other researchers. Facilities offered by Ancestry, Findmypast, Genes Reunited and other online data providers can be very useful, but before submitting data take the time to consider questions of privacy and ownership. As an initial precaution, make sure that the terms and conditions of the site in question are fully understood, especially concerning what can happen to personal details and who can use them in the future: for example some genealogy sites retain members' information even after subscription or registration is cancelled, adding personal details to their own wider collection of data. Alternatively researchers may be considering uploading family photographs onto well-known social networking sites like Facebook and MySpace, or onto photo-sharing sites operated by well-known photographic companies such as Truprint or Kodak. There are also popular sites like Flickr and Photobucket which provide a convenient means of inviting online discussion about pictures. There are many possibilities of potential interest, but before making a decision it is important to be aware that security levels vary enormously between different sites: in addition, some sites may operate policies whereby they can effectively claim ownership over members' accounts and the data in them. Therefore when choosing a website for sharing pictures it is good practice to visit the security or privacy options page and, if going ahead, set the required options *before* uploading images and other material: there may, for example, be different options for keeping details private or making them accessible to all - or it may be possible to restrict the information available to the wider public. Some sites, such as Arcalife, are especially geared towards creating digital scrapbooks and personal archives for the benefit of family members. Choosing a reputable site offering adequate security at all levels of usage is a good way to maintain control over personal pictures, but if in doubt, or if certain images are sensitive for whatever reason, it may be advisable not to upload those images onto a public site.

Publishing family pictures

Researchers often go to great lengths to trace and compile their family history, but do little with the results. Producing a photo book or scrapbook is a good way to organise and publish family pictures, either as part of a larger project including other genealogical material, or that can stand alone as a pictorial album - a visual record of past generations. Picture books or scrapbooks can be produced as one-off personal keepsakes, but often researchers like to publish - or have published - several copies, to give to existing family members or to pass on to children. Nowadays there are many ways of publishing the fruits of family research, including pictures, and technology is evolving all the time, making it possible to use data stored on the computer in a variety of ways. Below are just a few ideas, although each individual's needs are different, so, as with sharing photographs, it is always advisable to investigate all the different options available - once again bearing in mind issues of privacy and security if uploading images onto a website or sending them to a commercial company.

Some of the main genealogy websites already mentioned provide the tools for organising family pictures into albums or scrapbooks on the computer, while sites such as Arcalife now even offer the means of publishing and printing personal scrapbooks. A number of the well-known photographic companies, including Truprint and Kodak, also offer various photo book options, although not all of these may be ideal for family history requirements. Researchers may like to publish their own books and there is a wide range of software available for the preparation of personal photo books, such as MyPublisher or BookMark Self Publishing, to name just two of many currently on the market. Microsoft Publisher is another possible option, this having been used to create the family scrapbook seen in Fig. 3. However, once again, for those who would rather hand this process over to a professional, there are various independent companies who specialise in preparing and printing books for genealogists and who can tailor the product according to the needs of the individual. Their details can usually be found through an online search or in advertisements in family history publications.

Family pictures are wonderful heirlooms, unique and irreplaceable. There are many ways of storing them safely, having them restored if necessary, making copies, sharing, organising, displaying and publishing them. Let us make sure that they are recorded and preserved effectively for the benefit of future generations.

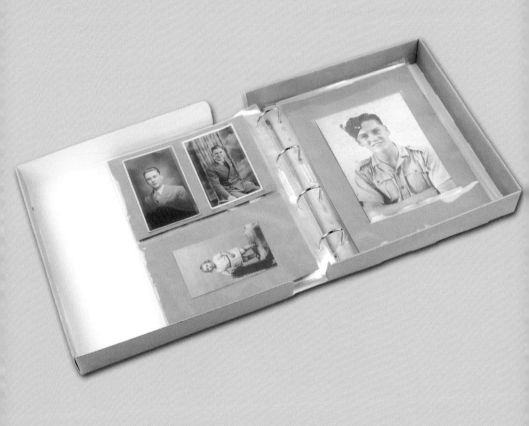

Fig. 1 Conservation quality archival storage products
Photographs, drawings and other original papers should ideally be protected from damage and deterioration in specially designed conservation quality archival storage containers. These products from the Timecare Collection (Conservation by Design) include an acid free box, mounting sheets, clear polyester pages and v-mounts for reversible mounting - perfect for storing and displaying precious family photographs.

Fig. 2 The author dating photographs for PFH magazine at 'Who Do You Think You Are? Live', Olympia, 2010

Family photographs are often passed around a great deal: using lint-free cotton researchers' gloves when handling original photographs prevents dust, dirt and grease from being transferred between the hands and the vulnerable surface of the picture. Inexpensive, comfortable to wear and easily washed, these accessories, used by museum and archive professionals, can be ordered from suppliers of conservation products. Photograph courtesy ABM Publishing.

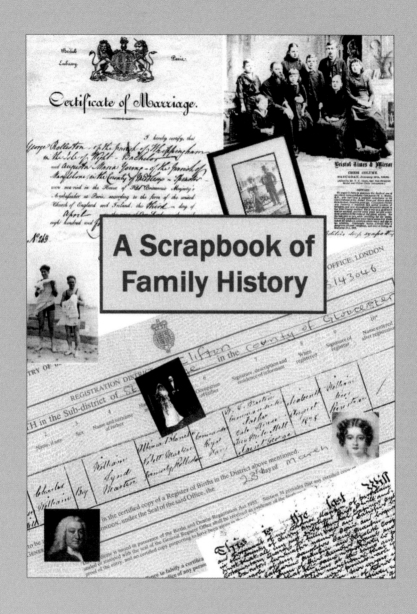

Fig. 3 Family scrapbook

This interesting family scrapbook contains numerous reproductions of family pictures, as well as supporting documents such as birth certificates and newspaper reports, which have been successfully combined to form a narrative covering several branches of the family. It was produced at home using Microsoft 'Publisher' and was printed using an ordinary computer printer, the binding and laminating also done 'in-house'.

PICTURE CREDITS

I am indebted to everyone who has generously allowed pictures from their personal collections to be reproduced in this book. Contributors' names are listed alphabetically below, along with numbered references to their pictures, although some have requested not to be identified in this way, in which cases only their names are mentioned.

Fiona Adams Chapter 2: 23, 24, 54; Chapter 4: 1, 5, 33; Chapter 6: 10, 11, 35
Margaret Appleton Chapter 5: 22, 29
Chris Bentley Chapter 5: 34
Pat Brady Chapter 6: 3, 4, 9, 25, 27
Robert Calkin Chapter 5: 2
Chris Cobb Chapter 1: 7, 11; Chapter 2: Title Picture, 1, 2, 5, 6
Anna Cook Chapter 5: 9
Joan Coulson Chapter 2: 43; Chapter 4: 9; Chapter 6: 21
Alex Davidson Chapter 2: 33; Chapter 5: 17
Patrick Davison Chapter 2: 11, 18, 32, 36; Chapter 4: 34, 36; Chapter 6: 16, 39
Judith Day Chapter 5: 5
Claire Dulanty Chapter 2: 34, 38, 41, 44, 47; Chapter 4: 3, 16, 35; Chapter 6: Title picture, 8, 32-34, 37
Jon Easter Chapter 2: 15, 16, 45, 46, 53; Chapter 4: 4, 10, 15, 21, 24, 26-28, 38; Chapter 5: 3; Chapter 6: 24
Kathleen Edmonds Chapter 6: 5, 20
Stuart Ellis Chapter 5: 30, 31
Robin Fairservice Chapter 2: 14, 20; Chapter 4: 23; Chapter 5: 1
Pat FitzSimmons Chapter 2: 21; Chapter 4: 8; Chapter 5: 24
Alan Fraser Chapter 2: 49; Chapter 4: Fig. 40; Chapter 6: 41
Martin Gough Chapter 5: 14
Philip Green Chapter 5: 28, 37

Note

If readers recognise anyone in these pictures or an unidentified scene and feel that they can add further details, please feel free to contact the author, who may be able to put them in touch with the owner of the work of art or photograph in question.

BIBLIOGRAPHY

BIBLIOGRAPHY

Portraiture and original artworks

Portraiture, Shearer West (Oxford University Press, 2004).
The Dictionary of Portrait Painters in Britain up to 1920, Brian Stewart and Mervyn Cutten (Antique Collectors' Club, 1997).
The British Portrait, 1660-1960 (Antique Collectors' Club, 1991).
Hanging the Head: Portraiture and Social Formation in Eighteenth-century England, Marcia Pointon (Yale University Press, 1993, paperback edition 1997).
Victorian Painters, Christopher Wood (antique Collectors' Club, 1995).
The Victorians: Photographic Portraits, Audrey Linkman (Tauris Parke Books, 1993). [Chapter One looks at the portrait tradition].
The English Face, David Piper (National Portrait Gallery, 1992).
Two Hundred Years of English Naïve Art, 1700-1900, James Ayres (Art Services International, Alexandria, 1996) [See chapter on portraiture].
India and British Portraiture 1770-1825, Mildred Archer (Sotheby Parke Bernet, 1979).
The Dictionary of Scottish Painters, 1600 to the Present, Julian Halsby and Paul Harris (2nd ed., Cannongate, 1998).
Miniatures: Dictionary and Guide, Daphne Foskett (Antique Collectors' Club, 1987)
The Portrait Miniature in England Katherine Coombs (V & A Publishing, 1998)
British Silhouette Artists and their Work 1760-1860, Sue McKechnie (Sotheby Parke Bernet, 1978).

Regional artist studies

This covers some useful published sources on artists working in specific geographical areas but is not a complete list. For further titles see Understanding

343

British Portraits website (www.portraits.specialistnetwork.org.uk) under
Resources: Toolkits: Researching Portraiture Collections: Resources.

Artists in Wales, c.1740-c.1851, Paul Joyner (The National Library of Wales, 1997).

The Artists of Northumbria, Marshall Hall (2nd ed., Art Dictionaries, 2005).

Manchester's Victorian Art Scene & its unrecognised artists, Susan W Thomson
(Manchester Art Press, 2007).

Artists of Yorkshire: a short dictionary, Harry Turnbull (Scolar Press, 1976).

The Norwich School of Artists, Andrew Moore (HMSO/Norwich Museums Service,
1985).

Chichester Artists, 1530-1900, Brian Stewart (Bladen Press, 1987).

Photographic history

This is not in any way a comprehensive list, but a selection of the most recent or
relevant publications.

The Birth of Photography, Brian Coe (Ash & Grant, 1976).

The History of Photography, Helmut & Alison Gernsheim (Thames & Hudson,
London, 1969).

Points of View: Capturing the 19th century in Photographs, John Falconer and
Louise Hide (The British Library, 2009).

The Victorians: Photographic Portraits, Audrey Linkman (Tauris Parke, 1993).

Victorian Photographers at Work, John Hannavy (Shire 1997).

Victorian Cartes-de-visite, Robin and Carold Wichard (Shire, 1999).

Real Photo Postcard Guide: The People's Photography, Robert Bogdan and Todd
Weseloh (Syracuse University Press, 2006).

The Snapshot Photograph: The Rise of Popular Photography, 1888-1939, Brian
Coe & Paul Gates (Ash & Grant, 1977).

Regional photographers

A Directory of London Photographers 1841-1908, Michael Pritchard
(PhotoResearch, 1994).

Professional photographers in Birmingham 1842-1914, C E John Aston et al (RPS
Historical Group, 1987).

Early Photography in Leeds, 1839-1870, Adrian Budge (Leeds Art Galleries, 1981)

Photographers in Victorian Doncaster 1842-1900, Keith I P Adamson (Doncaster
Museum Service, 1998).

Photographs and Photographers of York: The early years 1844-1879, Hugh Murray
(Yorkshire Architectural and York Archaeological Society, 1988).

Directory of Hampshire Photographers 1850-1969, Martin Norgate (Hampshire
County Council Museums Service, 1995).

Photographers in Wiltshire 1842-1939, Martin Norgate et al (Wiltshire Library & Museum Service, 1985).

Views and likenesses: early photographers and their work in Cornwall and the Isles of Scilly 1839-1870, Charles Thomas (Royal Institution of Cornwall, 1988).

Jersey Through the Lens, Richard Mayne and Joan Stevens (Phillimore, 1975).

Through the brass-lidded eye: photography in Ireland 1839-1900, E Chandler & P Walsh (Guinness Museum, 1989).

Scottish Photography: A Bibliography 1839-1939, Sara Stevenson & A D Morrison-Low (Salvia Books & Scottish Society for the History of Photography, 1990)

Paisley Photographers 1850-1900, Don McCoo (Foulis Archive Press, Paisley, 1986).

Photograph dating

The Expert Guide to Dating Family Photographs, Audrey Linkman (Greater Manchester County record Office, 2000).

Dating Nineteenth Century Photographs, Robert Pols (The Alden Press, 2005).

Dating Twentieth Century Photographs, Robert Pols (The Alden Press, 2005).

Family Photographs and How to Date Them, Jayne Shrimpton (Countryside Books, 2008).

Fashion in photographs

Fashion in Photographs series published by B.T. Batsford in conjunction with the National Portrait Gallery.

Fashion in Photographs, 1860-1880, Miles Lambert (1991).

Fashion in Photographs, 1880-1900, Sarah Levitt (1991).

Fashion in Photographs, 1900-1920, Katrina Rolley (1992).

Fashion in Photographs, 1920-1940, Elizabeth Owen (1993).

Victorian and Edwardian Fashion: A Photographic Survey, Alison Gernsheim (Dover Publications, 1963).

Everyday Fashions of the 20th Century, Avril Lansdell (Shire Publications, 1999).

Family Photographs and how to date Them, Jayne Shrimpton (Countryside Books, 2008) [This dating guide looks primarily at the fashions worn in photographs].

Dress History - general

These pictorial books are all written by recognised authorities and are still the best visual and historical guides to the chronology and development of fashion.

A Visual History of Costume: The Eighteenth Century, Aileen Ribeiro (B.T. Batsford, 1983).

Dress in Eighteenth Century Europe 1715-1789, Aileen Ribeiro (B.T. Batsford, 1984).

Jane Austen Fashion, Penelope Byrde (Excellent Press 1999, paperback edition 2008).

A Visual History of Costume: The Nineteenth Century, Vanda Foster (B.T. Batsford, 1984).

Nineteenth Century Fashion, Penelope Byrde (B.T. Batsford, 1992).

A Visual History of Costume: The Twentieth Century, Penelope Byrd (B T Batsford, 1986) [contains some photographs].

History of 20th Century Fashion, Elizabeth Ewing, (B T Batsford, 3rd ed. 1986).

Through the Looking Glass: A History of Dress from 1860 to the Present Day, Elizabeth Wilson and Lou Taylor (BBC Books, 1989) [contains some photographs].

Dress History- specialised

The Male Image: Men's Fashion in England, 1300-1970, Penelope Byrd ((B T Batsford, 1979).

Mourning Dress, Lou Taylor (George Allan & Unwin, 1983).

Occupational Costume and Working Clothes, 1776-1976, Avril Lansdell (Shire Publications, 1977).

Clothes & the Child: A handbook of children's dress in England 1500-1900, Anne Buck (Ruth Bean, 1996).

Children's Clothes, Clare Rose (B T Batsford, 1989).

History of Children's Costume, Elizabeth Ewing, (B T Batsford, 1977).

Wedding Dress

Marriage A la Mode: Three Centuries of Wedding Dress, Shelley Tobin et al (The National Trust, 2003).

Wedding Fashions, 1860-1940, Avril Lansdell (Shire Publications, 1983).

Wedding Customs and Folklore, Margaret Baker (David & Charles, 1977).

Military Uniforms

From Scarlet to Khaki, Jon Mills (Wardens Publishing, 1988).

Military Photographs and How to Date Them, Neil Storey (Countryside Books, 2009).

WEB RESOURCES

1. Original Artworks

Here are listed the websites of the main UK public art organisations and reputable portrait websites. A simple internet search will reveal other portrait websites and blogs, too numerous to list here, some hosted by private collectors, or commercial art dealers. They may well provide historical information about portraits and artists, or visual examples which can help with dating family pictures.

www.npg.org.uk
The National Portrait Gallery, London is the primary source for British portraiture, unrivalled anywhere in the UK. The website is a good starting point for discovering how the gallery and its facilities can help researchers.

In the main menu under Research there are many relevant sections.

For example 'Researching Portraits' provides a 'Publications' page listing useful published sources including the gallery's own and other portrait collection catalogues and additional titles covering portraiture.

'Family History at the National Portrait Gallery', explains about searching some of the NPG collections online, using the free public telephone and letter inquiry service and arranging to visit the Heinz Archive & Library. There is also a downloadable Family History leaflet.

Still under Research, 'Heinz Archive & Library' explains in more detail how to use this public research facility, while 'British portraits records' describes the extensive visual and written records that are on open access in the Public Study Room of the archive. 'Library' lists the types of published material that may also be consulted during a visit.

Also in Research, 'Research Programs', includes information on 'The Art of the Picture Frame' and 'Early history of mezzotint.'

www.vam.ac.uk

The Victoria & Albert Museum, London focuses on the decorative arts in general and its collection of miniatures and other small paintings is especially relevant to portrait research. The website itself is a good resource, and well worth a general browse but most helpful as regards family artworks are the visual examples and helpful background information about the history, techniques and functions of small portraits.

In the main menu under 'Collections': 'Paintings and Drawings' are links to sections covering portrait miniatures, other small portrait types such as silhouettes, as well as details of some of the artists responsible for them.

At the V & A Museum is also located the National Art Library, which is open to the public as a reference library only. In the main menu, click on Resources, then 'National Art Library' where different sections detail the library's holdings and visiting arrangements.

www.artguide.org

Art Guide is a comprehensive internet guide to the art collections of Great Britain and Ireland. The 'Museums Guide' link provides details of over 650 art galleries and museums so may help researchers to locate a local museum or art gallery for help with analysing their pictures. 'Artists on View' is an alphabetical listing of nearly 2000 named artists, with information about where some of their work may be seen.

www.portraits.specialistnetwork.org.uk

Understanding British Portraits website is a Museums, Archives and Libraries (MLA) specialist network aimed at enhancing knowledge and understanding of portraits in all media and facilitating debate and dialogue. Involving portrait professionals and independent enthusiasts and researchers, one of its objectives is to map private and public portrait collections throughout the UK and individuals are invited to register details of portraits in their care.

www.historicalportraits.com

This website offers an interesting image database, a picture library compiled by independent portrait expert and art dealer, Philip Mould. It is free for members of the public to browse and can be searched by artist, sitter, subject and century, or by using more advanced tools including date and medium. Although most images displayed here are accomplished works by well-known artists, it offers a good pictorial overview of portraiture which may be helpful for general comparison purposes and may aid researchers in recognising and dating the style of their pictures, or the clothing worn.

2. Photographs

(i) Websites with free searchable photographer databases

Database of 19th Century Photographers & Allied Trades in London, 1841-1901
www.photolondon.org.uk
This vast database, produced in collaboration with English Heritage's National Monument's Record, records around 9,000 London photographers, studios and photographic companies. The Highlights section profiles notable photographers and the A-Z Listing gives biographical details and operational dates for each entry.

History of Photography in Edinburgh
www.edinphoto.org.uk
This website covers the history of Edinburgh, including photography. Click on 'Professional Photographers' for A-Z listings spanning 1839-1939 and 1940 onwards.

Glasgow's Victorian Photographers
www.thelows.madasafish.com/main.htm
This interesting website which traces the development and practise of Victorian and Edwardian photography in Glasgow includes examples of photographs by named photographers (front and back views) and A-Z listing of photographers.

Victorian Professional Photographers in Wales, 1850-1925
www.genuki.org.uk/big/wal/VicPhoto1.html
A-Z databases of Welsh photographers, organised separately by county, offer operational dates based on specific trade directories (helpfully referenced here). However the Bibliography section does not include any recent publications.

Isle of Man Photographers
www.isle-of-man.com/manxnotebook/tourism/pgrphrs
This web page offers a brief history of photography on the island and an A-Z listing of 19th century resident and visiting photographers.

Photographers & Photographic Studios in Derbyshire
www.genealogy.rootsweb.ancestry.com/~brett/photos/dbyphotos.html
This well-organised website provides an extensive A-Z listing of Derbyshire studios, helpfully stating the sources used, and profiles many individual local photographers.

Victorian Photography Studios...in and around Birmingham and Warwickshire
www.hunimex.com/warwick/photogs.html
A-Z listings of photographers in Birmingham and the Midlands.

Early Photographic Studios
www.early-photographers.org.uk
A-Z directories of photographers in Norfolk, Suffolk and Cambridgeshire

Jersey Photographers and Studios
www.jerseyfamilyhistory.co.uk
An independent Jersey-related website hosted by a family historian who is also researching past photographers on the island.

Isle of Wight Photographers c.1840-1940
www.iowphotos.info/
A useful website introducing early photography on the Isle of Wight, with reading suggestions and a growing A-Z database of photographers who worked on the island.

Sussex Photo History
www.photohistory-sussex.co.uk/index.htm
A-Z photographer listings for East and West Sussex arranged by town.

Directory of Photographic Studios in Brighton & Hove 1841-1910
www.spartacus.schoolnet.co.uk/Brighton-Photographers.htm
This informative website charting the development of photography in Brighton and Hove includes biographies of several photographers and A-Z listing of local studios.

Photographers in Kent, 1855
www.kent-opc.org/photographers.html
A-Z listings, by town, and by photographer name, of photographic studios operating throughout Kent in the year 1855

Victorian and Edwardian Photographs - Roger Vaughan Personal Collection
www.cartes.freeuk.com
A good site for browsing, click on 'Date an Old Photograph' for various topics including a helpful visual survey of the designs on photograph backs and A-Z List of Dated Photographs and 1000 Photographs (although be aware that some of the photographs arranged by year have estimated, *not* firm dates).

This section also includes links to Roger Vaughan's alphabetical list of Bristol Photographers U.K. (1852-1972), names and addresses compiled from Bristol area trade directories, and Photographic Studios for some parts of England and Wales in the year 1868, a list extracted from Slater's Directory of 1868.

Also links to a useful site which can help with identifying and dating postcard stamp boxes: www.playle.com/realphoto/

(ii) Professional photograph websites and independent photo dating services

Index of UK portrait & studio photographers c.1840-1950
www.earlyphotographers.org.uk
This website offers tips on analysing old photographs and provides useful onward links to regional photographer/photography websites. Data can be supplied on individual photographers for a small fee.

Photographers of Great Britain and Ireland, 1840-1940
www.cartedevisite.co.uk
This significant resource covers 19th and early-20th century photographs, photographers, photographic studios and their customers. Special features for family historians include researching photographer ancestors and A-Z lists of sitters named on photographs in the collection - 'lost' ancestors who may link up with researchers' own family history. Data is available for over 62,000 photographers on payment of a small fee, or visitors can pay to use the photo Dating Wizard to date their photographic mounts. The site's operator also offers a custom dating service using photographer's operational dates and the physical characteristics of card-mounted photographs.

www.jayneshrimpton.co.uk
The author's website offers a unique picture dating and analysis service for researchers seeking a professional opinion from a qualified dress historian and experienced portrait specialist. Close, accurate date ranges for photographs or original artworks are provided for a small fee, based on clothing styles and other visual clues, supported by photographer/artist dates where relevant and physical features of the picture. More detailed reports on individual pictures are also available.

Watch the Birdie
http://qvictoriapress.com
This private photograph collector's blog displays some interesting photographic examples and offers selected photographer dates. The blog host also offers to undertake photograph research where possible.

(iii) Public Photographic Collections in the UK

Many local record offices and archives hold useful photographic material but here are some of the main British collections.

National Portrait Gallery
www.npg.org.uk

National Media Museum, Bradford
www.nationalmediamuseum.org.uk

Victoria & Albert Museum, London
www.vam.ac.uk

The British Library (Photographically Illustrated Books Collection)
www.bl.uk

Documentary Photography Archive, Manchester
www.gmcro.co.uk/Photography/DPA/collections.htm

Scottish Life Archive, Edinburgh
www.nms.ac.uk/our_collections/scottish_life_archive.aspx

Museum of English Rural Life, Reading
www.reading.ac.uk/merl

3. Further Resources and Research Tools

Historical image websites
www.english-heritage.org.uk
www.imagesofengland.org.uk
www.historypin.com
www.francisfrith.com

Family history research
www.sog.org.uk
www.nationalarchives.gov.uk

Birth, marriage and death indexes
www.ukbmd.org.uk
www.freebmd.org.uk

www.thegenealogist.co.uk
www.bmdregisters.co.uk

Census returns
www.nationalarchives.gov.uk
www.ancestry.co.uk
www.thegenealogist.co.uk
www.findmypast.co.uk
www.freecen.org.uk
www.scotlandspeople.gov.uk

Local and Trade Directories
www.historicaldirectories.org

House History
www.cassinimaps.com.uk
www.ordnancesurvey.co.uk
www.old.maps.co.uk

Ships' Passenger Lists
www.findmypast.co.uk
www.ancestorsonboard.com
www.ancestry.co.uk

Military Service Records
www.veterans-uk.info/service

INDEX

Selsey, East Sussex *314*
Shanklin, Isle of Wight *321*
sharing pictures online 327, 335-6
ships' passenger lists 274, *283, 301*
Shrewsbury, Shropshire *88*
Shropshire *33, 88, 276, 289*
silhouettes (profile shades) 1, 6-7, *24, 32,*
48
sketch *see* drawing.
sitter, sitting 1, 2, 6, 7, 9, 12, 15, *35,* 44,
49, 61
social status 2-4, 7, 11-12, 139, 153, *172,*
214, 217
   middle-class 3, 5, 8, 45, 55, 63, *64,*
   124, 164, *166, 196,* 214-5, 217-9,
   229, 235, 255, 299
   upper-class, prosperous, elite 7, 47, *71,*
   77, 120, 162, 207, 210-212, 215, 217-
   9, 221, *224, 245,* 264-5, *306*
   working-class, poor, humble 7, 47, 48,
   50, *74,* 120, 123-24, 126, 136, 140,
   162, *174, 179, 188,* 207, 210-11, 213-
   9, *227, 244, 255,* 265, *300*
Society of Genealogists 18
Somerset 3, 6, *32,* 44, *115, 238*
South Africa *241*
South America *245*
South Moor, Co. Durham *244*
South Wales Borderers *247*
Southampton, Hampshire 3
Southampton Hospital *293*
Southend-on-Sea, Essex 56
Southwark, Surrey (now S E London)
   235
Staffordshire *35, 237, 296, 300*
Stamford, Connecticut, USA *306*
stamp, stamp box 53
Stepney, E London *223*
Stevington, Bedfordshire *236*
Stoke Ash, Suffolk *280*
Stuart, Lady Arabella *21*
studio setting (photographer's) *66,*
   70, 72- 74, 78, 89, 91, 95, 97-99, 120-
   23, *183,* 210, *232,* 263-4, 270

Suffolk *36, 172, 275, 280*
Surrey *235, 238, 242, 247, 249, 254, 256*
Surrey Vintage Vehicle Society 272, *306,*
   308, 311, 316
Sussex *314*

T
Tasmania, Australia *75*
Teddington, Middlesex *283*
Temple, Shirley 144
Thurlston Beach, Devon *309*
Tividale, Staffordshire *237*
trade directories 18, 57, 58, *86*
Tring, Hertfordshire *94*
Truro, Cornwall 44
Tudor 2, 159

U
Utility clothing *112,* 134, *257*
Uttoxeter, Staffordshire *35*

V
valuation (artworks)
Vicky, Princess 212
Victoria, Queen 160, 210-12
Victoria & Albert Museum 18-19, 222

W
Wales 69, 125, *243, 247*
Walthamstow, N E London *246*
Warwickshire *82, 228*
Waterloo, Liverpool *295*
Waverley, Edinburgh *109*
weddings, marriage and wedding pictures
   1, 5, 7, 15, *30-34, 74, 81, 88,* 153-4,
   159-160, *184-8,* 207-222, *223-60,* 264-6
wedding anniversary 1, 7, *28, 39,* 153,
   160-1, *187-8*
wedding and bridal attire 140, 146, 154,
   160, *185, 186,* 207-222, *223-60* [and
   earlier]
Wellington, Herefordshire, *256*
Wellington, Salop (Shropshire) *33*
West Midlands *82*

About the SOCIETY
OF GENEALOGISTS

Founded in 1911 the Society of Genealogists (SoG) is Britain's premier family history organisation. The Society maintains a splendid genealogical library and education centre in Clerkenwell.

The Society's collections are particularly valuable for research before the start of civil registration of births marriages and deaths in 1837 but there is plenty for the beginner too. Anyone starting their family history can book free help sessions in the open community access area where assistance can be given in searching online census indexes or looking for entries in birth, death and marriage indexes.

The Library contains Britain's largest collection of parish register copies, indexes and transcripts and many nonconformist registers. Most cover the period from the sixteenth century to 1837. Along with registers, the library holds local histories, copies of churchyard gravestone inscriptions, poll books, trade directories, census indexes and a wealth of information about the parishes where our ancestors lived.

Unique indexes include Boyd's Marriage Index with more than 7 million names compiled from 4300 churches between 1538-1837 and the Bernau Index with references to 4.5 million names in Chancery and other court proceedings. Also available are indexes of wills and marriage licences, and of apprentices and masters (1710-1774). Over the years the Society has rescued and made available records discarded by government departments and institutions but of great interest to family historians. These include records from the Bank of England, Trinity House and information on Teachers and Civil Servants.

Boyd's and other unique databases are published on line on **www.origins.com**, on **www.findmypast.com** and on the Society's own website **www.sog.org.uk**. There is free access to these and many other genealogical sites within the Library's Internet suite.

The Society is the ideal place to discover if a family history has already been researched with its huge collection of unique manuscript notes, extensive collections of past research and printed and unpublished family histories. If you expect to be carrying out family history research in the British Isles then membership is very worthwhile although non-members can use the library for a small search fee.

The Society of Genealogists is an educational charity. It holds study days, lectures, tutorials and evening classes and speakers from the Society regularly speak to groups around the country. The SoG runs workshops demonstrating computer programs of use to family historians. A diary of events and booking forms are available from the Society on 020 7553 3290 or on the website **www.sog.org.uk** .

Members enjoy free access to the Library, certain borrowing rights, free copies of the quarterly *Genealogists Magazine* and various discounts of publications, courses, postal searches along with free access to data on the members' area of our website and each quarter to our data on **www.origins.com**.

More details about the Society can be found on its extensive website at **www.sog.org.uk**

For a free Membership Pack contact the Society at:

14 Charterhouse Buildings,
Goswell Road,
London EC1M 7BA
Telephone 020 7553 3291
Fax 020 7250 1800

The Society is always happy to help with enquiries and the following contacts may be of assistance.

Library & shop hours:

Monday	Closed
Tuesday	10am - 6pm
Wednesday	10am - 6pm
Thursday	10am - 8pm
Friday	Closed
Saturday	10am - 6pm
Sunday	Closed

Contacts:

Membership
Tel: 020 7553 3291
Email: membership@sog.org.uk

Lectures & courses
Tel: 020 7553 3290
Email: events@sog.org.uk

Family history advice line
Tel: 020 7490 8911
See website for availability

SOCIETY OF GENEALOGISTS
The National Library & Education Centre for Family History

Other SoG titles...

MY ANCESTORS WERE

GYPSIES
SHARON SILLERS FLOATE
A guide to Gypsy sources for family historians
Third edition

£8.99

MY ANCESTOR WAS...

IN SERVICE
PAMELA HORN
A guide to sources for family historians

£8.50

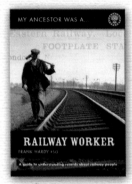

MY ANCESTOR WAS A...

RAILWAY WORKER
FRANK HARDY FSG
A guide to understanding records about railway people

£7.50

MY ANCESTOR WAS AN...

Agricultural Labourer
IAN H WALLER
A guide to agricultural labourer sources for family historians. Revised edition

£8.99

MY ANCESTOR WAS A...

COALMINER
DAVID TONKS
A guide to coalminer sources for family historians. Second edition

£9.50

MY ANCESTOR WAS IN...

The British Army
MICHAEL J WATTS & CHRISTOPHER T. WATTS
A guide to British Army sources for family historians

£9.99

Order online at: **www.sog.org.uk** or call: 020 7702 5483.
Also available from the Society's bookshop.

14 Charterhouse Buildings, Goswell Road, London EC1M 7BA
Tel: 020 7251 8799 | Fax: 020 7250 1800 | **www.sog.org.uk**

Registered Charity No. 233701. Company limited by guarantee. Registered No. 115703.
Registered office, 14 Charterhouse Buildings, London, EC1M 7BA. Registered in England & Wales